Proceedings of the Boston Area Colloquium in Ancient Philosophy

Proceedings of the Boston Area Colloquium in Ancient Philosophy

VOLUME XXXII

Edited by

Gary M. Gurtler, S.J.
William Wians

BRILL

LEIDEN | BOSTON

This paperback is also published in hardback under ISBN 978-90-04-34813-4.

Typeface for the Latin, Greek, and Cyrillic scripts: "Brill". See and download: brill.com/brill-typeface.

ISSN 1059-986X
ISBN 978-90-04-34810-3

Copyright 2017 by Koninklijke Brill NV, Leiden, The Netherlands.
Koninklijke Brill NV incorporates the imprints Brill, Brill Hes & De Graaf, Brill Nijhoff, Brill Rodopi and Hotei Publishing.
All rights reserved. No part of this publication may be reproduced, translated, stored in a retrieval system, or transmitted in any form or by any means, electronic, mechanical, photocopying, recording or otherwise, without prior written permission from the publisher.
Authorization to photocopy items for internal or personal use is granted by Koninklijke Brill NV provided that the appropriate fees are paid directly to The Copyright Clearance Center, 222 Rosewood Drive, Suite 910, Danvers, MA 01923, USA. Fees are subject to change.

This book is printed on acid-free paper and produced in a sustainable manner.

Contents

Preface   VII
Notes on Contributors   IX

COLLOQUIUM 1
Stoic Blends   1
    Anna Marmodoro
Commentary on Marmodoro   25
    Rose Cherubin
Marmodoro/Cherubin Bibliography   38

COLLOQUIUM 2
Telling Good Love from Bad in Plato's *Phaedrus*   41
    Nickolas Pappas
Commentary on Pappas   59
    Deborah De Chiara-Quenzer
Pappas/De Chiara-Quenzer Bibliography   66

COLLOQUIUM 3
The Place of Perception in Plato's Tripartite Soul   69
    Peter D. Larsen
Commentary on Larsen   100
    Jessica Moss
Larsen/Moss Bibliography   111

COLLOQUIUM 4
The Stoics on Identity, Identification, and Peculiar Qualities   113
    Tamer Nawar
Commentary on Nawar   160
    Sarah Byers
Nawar/Byers Bibliography   166

COLLOQUIUM 5
Plato's Philosophical Politics   169
    V. Bradley Lewis

Commentary on Lewis   191
   Joseph P. Lawrence
Lewis/Lawrence Bibliography   200

Index   203

Preface

Volume 32 contains papers and commentaries presented to the Boston Area Colloquium in Ancient Philosophy during the academic year 2015-16. The Colloquia for this year centered on Platonic and Stoic themes, but to be noted is the robust character of the comments, which challenged the presenters' theses in significant ways. The first encounter was about blending as the Stoic explanation for the constitution and causation of bodies. The comment confronts this Stoic theory with a discussion of their difference from the Aristotelian notion of form and matter as well as a discussion of the 'Eleatic Principle' attributed to the Stoic position in relation to the arguments of the historical Eleatics. The second colloquium discusses eros in the *Phaedrus* and the puzzle for the beloved in determining whether the lover is divinely inspired or merely crazed. The comment finds resources in the *Phaedrus* for discerning this difference in the Platonic text, with the different wings, left and right, torpedoing and elevating, complemented by the use of collection and division. The third looks to the tripartite soul in the *Republic*, with a tightly argued account of perception that brings it in close relation to the rational part of the soul for all but the most elemental aspects of perception. The comment defends a more independent account of perception, similar to Aristotle's account of imagination, that allows it to generate complex cognitions of its own, open to reason's higher level of criticism and correction. The fourth presentation returns to the Stoics and the issue of peculiar qualities and their relation to the identity of a particular individual. The comment counters that these peculiar qualities are simply traceable to each thing's particular spatial location. The final presentation revisits the relation of the *Republic* and the *Laws*, tracing their different approaches to the events of Plato's life, the death of Socrates and the failure of his visit to Sicily. The comment finds the Platonic center of gravity in philosophy rather than politics.

The papers and commentaries appear in the order they were given at the different meetings of the Boston Area Colloquium in Ancient Philosophy at one of the following participating institutions: Assumption College, Boston College, the College of the Holy Cross, and St. Anselm College. The dialogical character of the colloquia is partially preserved by publishing both paper and commentary from each of the meetings. In many cases these oral presentations have been extensively revised, not to mention expanded, by their authors in the light of subsequent discussions, and especially in response to critical comments from our external referees. For their generous assistance as referees

I would like to thank the following scholars: Scott Berman, Bernard Collette, M. Ross Romero, S.J., Christopher Shields, and Thomas Tuozzo. At the end of the volume, together with the section 'About our Contributors,' readers will find a general index of names which was collated by our editorial assistant, Sean Driscoll.

In conclusion, I wish to thank my colleagues on the BACAP committee, whose voluntary service structures the reality to which these Proceedings stand at one remove. Furthermore, I am much indebted to William Wians, who continues to serve as co-editor. I would also like to thank our editorial assistant, Sean Driscoll, for his outstanding work in preparing the copy for this volume in the Philosophy Department at Boston College, and for his countless other efforts in assisting the editors and the contributors in the process of bringing the papers to finished form. Finally, I want to acknowledge the continued financial assistance provided by the administration at Boston College, whose support for this project has remained most generous over the years.

Gary Gurtler, S.J.
Boston College

Notes on Contributors

Sarah Catherine Byers
is Associate Professor in the Philosophy Department at Boston College. She is the author of the monograph *Perception, Sensibility, and Moral Motivation in Augustine: A Stoic-Platonic Synthesis* (Cambridge University Press: 2013) and of articles in, for example, the *Journal of the History of Philosophy*, the *Cambridge History of Moral Philosophy*, the *Routledge Handbook of the Stoic Tradition*, *A Companion to Augustine* (Wiley-Blackwell), and *Augustine's City of God: A Critical Guide* (Cambridge Critical Guides).

Rose Cherubin
is Associate Professor of Philosophy at George Mason University. She was educated at the School of Visual Arts and at the Graduate School and University Center of the City University of New York. Her research has focused on the Eleatic philosophers, Plato, Aristotle, and Alain Locke.

Deborah De Chiara-Quenzer
is Professor of the Practice of Philosophy in the Philosophy Department at Boston College. She was an associate professor of philosophy for more than a decade at St. John's Seminary in Boston, and has since been at Boston College in the Honors Program in Arts & Sciences, and the Perspectives Program in Philosophy. Her lectures and writings have been on Plato and Aristotle.

Peter D. Larsen
is an Adjunct Lecturer in the Department of Philosophy at Trinity College Dublin. He was educated at American University in Washington, DC and Trinity College Dublin. He is currently engaged in a large research project on Plato's theory of sense perception.

Joseph P. Lawrence
is Professor of Philosophy at the College of the Holy Cross. He is the author of *Schellings Philosophie des ewigen Anfangs* (Königshausen, 1989) and *Socrates among Strangers* (Northwestern, 2015). He has published articles on Greek and German philosophy, on English and German literature, and on Christian, Islamic, and Buddhist religion. His translation of Schelling's 1811 *Weltalter* is scheduled for publication by SUNY Press in 2017.

V. Bradley Lewis

is Associate Professor of Philosophy at The Catholic University of America, where he has taught since 1997. He studied at the University of Maryland and the University of Notre Dame, and has published articles on the political thought of Plato and Aristotle, as well as on some contemporary problems of legal and political philosophy. He is currently working on a book on the idea of the common good and serves as associate editor of the *American Journal of Jurisprudence*.

Anna Marmodoro

is a Fellow of Corpus Christi College, at the University of Oxford. She was educated at the University of Edinburgh and the University of Pisa. She has published on both ancient philosophy and contemporary metaphysics, including her *Everything in Everything. Anaxagoras' Metaphysics* (Oxford 2017), *Aristotle on Perceiving Objects* (Oxford, 2014), and *The Metaphysics of Relations* (Oxford, 2015), co-edited with David Yates.

Jessica Moss

is Professor of Philosophy at NYU. She was educated at Yale and Princeton, and has taught at the University of Pittsburgh and Balliol College, Oxford. She is the author of *Aristotle on the Apparent Good* (2012), and of various articles on moral psychology, ethics, and epistemology in Plato and Aristotle.

Tamer Nawar

is Assistant Professor of Philosophy at the University of Groningen. Before that he was a postdoctoral research fellow at the University of Oxford and before that he received his Ph.D. from the University of Cambridge. In addition to publishing on ancient and medieval philosophy, he has interests in metaphysics and epistemology.

Nickolas Pappas

is Professor of Philosophy at City College and the Graduate Center, the City University of New York. He has published on topics in ancient philosophy and aesthetics. His books include the *Guidebook to Plato's* Republic, now in its third edition (Routledge, 2013); *Politics and Philosophy in Plato's Menexenus*, co-authored with Mark Zelcer (Routledge, 2014); and most recently *The Philosopher's New Clothes: The Theaetetus, the Academy, and Philosophy's Turn against Fashion* (Routledge, 2015).

COLLOQUIUM 1

Stoic Blends

Anna Marmodoro
Corpus Christi College, Oxford

Abstract

The Stoics' guiding principle in ontology is the Eleatic principle. Their existents are bodies that have the power to act and be acted upon. They account both for the constitution of material objects and the causal interactions among them in terms of such dynamic bodies. Blending is the physical mechanism that explains both constitution and causation; and is facilitated by the fact that for the Stoics all bodies exist as unlimited divided. In this paper I offer a novel analysis of this Stoic stance, and of the role it plays in their metaphysics. I argue that when blended, the substances involved become *sharing subjects* of qualities and structural features.

Keywords

Stoics – compenetration – mixture – unlimited division – gunk

I   Introduction

Ancient Greek and Roman philosophy comprises a variety of ontologies that have each marked a conceptual milestone in Western thought, ranging from Heraclitus's process metaphysics, to Plato's transcendental metaphysics, to Aristotle's empiricist metaphysics. Surprisingly, Stoic metaphysics, which is

---

*   The work leading to this publication was part of my research program *Power Structuralism in Ancient Ontologies*, supported by a starting investigator award from the European Research Council (award number 263484). Its completion was done during my research stay at the Fondation Maison des sciences de l'homme (Paris). Earlier versions of the paper were presented at the University of Oxford, Columbia, Penn, Princeton, and Harvard, and at the Boston Area Colloquium in Ancient Philosophy. I am grateful for the feedback received on such occasions from the audience, and also in personal correspondence afterwards, in particular from my BACAP commentator Rose M Cherubin, and from Katja Vogt and Vanessa de Harven.

also a highly original system, has not yet been given its due place on the map. This paper is a contribution towards rectifying this omission.[1] The most distinctive Stoic stance is their *extreme physicalism*: for them, everything that exists is body. To be closer to their way of speaking, we can call their view *corporealism*. Their motivation for this stance, I submit, is the Eleatic Principle (expressed by Plato in the *Sophist*, at 247d–e), according to which only what is causally powerful exists; for Stoics, only bodies can be causally powerful. Coming after Aristotle, the Stoics are enriched with the whole range of metaphysical principles and distinctions he (and Plato) had introduced, and tailor fit them to their own physicalist assumptions, thereby innovating in metaphysics. In this paper I will argue that the Stoics innovate in the way their corporealism accounts for the constitution of ordinary material objects; for their possession of properties;[2] and for causality. The key to understanding the very original Stoic physicalist account of these metaphysical core issues is their belief that reality is *atomless*: for the Stoics all bodies (the simple elements and their composites) have parts 'all the way down,' that is, they exist as unlimitedly divided.

---

[1] I take my approach to be aligned with Katja Vogt's, in that we both argue that the Stoics have a distinctive take in their philosophical explanations of reality, very different from Plato's and Aristotle's, on account of their corporealism. Where Vogt and I differ, to my mind, is in how we see the Stoics putting their corporealism to work. In this paper I argue that the Stoics use *physical operations*, such as division and mixture of the basic elements in their ontology (which are bodies), to do *metaphysical work* in their system. Vogt on the other hand has argued that for the Stoics there is no separation between physics and metaphysics and that it is physics rather than metaphysics that delivers for them the most basic account of reality. In this, she identifies the Stoic philosophical distinctiveness. Vogt writes that "Their focus on corporeals … explains why the Stoics do not have the kind of theory that, with respect to Plato and Aristotle, we call metaphysics…." (Vogt 2009, 137). "Talk about 'Stoic ontology' is clearly more directly rooted in the texts [than talk of 'Stoic metaphysics']. But even here, it seems important to keep in mind that we are not referring to a theory that is separate from particular investigations in physics, logic, and ethics, or that would offer a deeper understanding of reality than these disciplines do…." (Vogt 2009, 145). "[T]he Stoics are Sons of the Earth in the metaphorical sense that they look at the earth and think that the most basic account that philosophy can offer is an account that explains the physical universe (Vogt 2009, 149)." Also arguing that the Stoics have a worked out metaphysics is, among others, Vanessa de Harven ("Stoic incorporeals: a grounded account," unpublished manuscript), who concludes that, "Thus there is good reason to extend Brunschwig's suggestion that the Stoics were masters of their theoretical domain, leading with their ontology and going beyond physics to metaphysics."

[2] Although the Stoics do not believe universals exist, they hold that ordinary material objects can each be classified under various concepts (which they reify, in line with their physicalism). This generates for them the explanatory need to account for why they fall under such concepts.

I will argue that the unlimited division of bodies allows for their *colocation* in the same spatio-temporal region; and colocation does crucial explanatory work in the Stoic account of some fundamental physical and metaphysical relations in their system.[3]

II Unlimited Division

There is explicit textual evidence that the Stoics believe in unlimited division of body, for example in the following texts:

T1: Stobaeus (I. 142, 2–6; LS 50A)

> Chrysippus said that bodies are divided to infinity, and likewise things comparable to bodies, such as surface, line, place, void and time....
>
> Χρύσιππος ἔφασκε τὰ σώματα εἰς ἄπειρον τέμνεσθαι καὶ τὰ τοῖς σώμασι προσεοικότα, οἷον ἐπιφάνειαν γραμμὴν τόπον κενὸν χρόνον·....

T2: Sextus *Against the professors* (10.121–126, 139–142; LS 50F)

> Let us start our argument with the first school of thought, according to which all are divided to infinity. [... Such school of thought comprises] those who say that bodies, places and times are divided to infinity, namely the Stoics.
>
> τάξει δὲ ἀπὸ τῆς πρώτης στάσεως ποιώμεθα τὴν ἐπιχείρησιν, καθ' ἣν πάντα εἰς ἄπειρον τέμνεται.... τοὺς εἰς ἄπειρον τέμνεσθαι λέγοντας τά τε σώματα καὶ τοὺς τόπους καὶ τοὺς χρόνους (οὗτοι δέ εἰσιν οἱ ἀπὸ τῆς Στοᾶς) ταῦθ' ἥρμοζε λέγειν.

The language used in these texts is neutral as to whether the division of bodies under discussion is an infinite division into *points*, or an infinite division into *parts*. There is however additional textual evidence that shows that for the Stoics the division of body generates parts (μέρη, see **T3** here below). What

---

[3] As other interpreters have done, I will develop my arguments on the assumption that it is legitimate to speak of the Stoics as a whole, at least in relation to some core views that unify the school, such as the ones this paper is about. A defense of this assumption is beyond the scope of the paper.

makes the metaphysical picture far from straightforward is that in the very same report where Stobaeus talks about infinite division (which is the text from which T1 is taken), he surprises us with a *prima facie* puzzling claim attributed to Chrysippus, concerning the parts resulting from the unlimited division of body:

T3: Plutarch *On common conceptions* (1081C–1082A; LS 50 C)

> ... With respect to the ultimate parts, it must be said neither of which parts we consist, nor, likewise, of how many, either infinite or finite. I believe I have quoted his [Chrysippus'] actual words.... (Translation modified)[4]

> ... τὰ ἔσχατα μέρη ... ῥητέον οὔτ᾽ ἔκ τινων συνεστάναι, καὶ ὁμοίως οὔτ᾽ ἐξ ὁποσωνοῦν, οὔτ᾽ ἐξ ἀπείρων οὔτ᾽ ἐκ πεπερασμένων. καί μοι δοκῶ ταῖς ἐκείνου κεχρῆσθαι λέξεσιν αὐταῖς....

We know that Chrysippus also holds that what a three dimensional body is divided into are *not* infinitely many three dimensional bodies. (Similarly, surfaces are not divided into infinitely many surfaces, or lines into infinitely many lines.)

T4: Stobaeus (I. 142, 2–6; LS 50A)

> ... But although these [bodies] are divided to infinity, a body does not consist of infinitely many bodies [resulting from the division], and the same applies to surface, line and place.

> ... εἰς ἄπειρόν τε τούτων τεμνομένων οὔτε σῶμα ἐξ ἀπείρων σωμάτων συνέστηκεν οὔτ᾽ ἐπιφάνεια οὔτε γραμμὴ οὔτε τόπος.

So, what does Chrysippus think of the parts? Why does infinite division of a body not deliver infinitely many bodily parts? T3 tells us that for Chrysippus

---

4 I prefer to translate the expression ἔκ τινων as 'which parts'; and not as 'what parts' like L&S do. The English expression 'what parts' is ambiguous, and could be understood either as 'what sort of parts' or as 'which parts.' But Chrysippus's concern here, I argue, is the *lack of distinctness* of the parts resulting from unlimited division of body; this concern is more accurately captured by the translation I offer. I also note that the text from T3 as extracted is presented as a word-by-word report of Chrysippus's views.

bodies have no ultimate parts; and also that a body's ultimate components are neither infinitely many items, nor finitely many. T4 says that a body is not made up of infinitely many (bodily) parts. At the same time, nothing in the text indicates that Chrysippus thought that unlimited division destroys body, so that there are no parts left. My interpretation of T3 and T4 taken together is that for the Stoics it is not the case that there are no parts, but rather that there is *no set of items that are the ultimate parts* of body, because there is *no end* to the division.[5] The division is unceasing, as reported for instance here:

T5: Diogenes Laertius (7.150–1; LS 50B)

> Division is to infinity, or 'infinite' according to Chrysippus (for there is not some infinity which the division reaches; it is just unceasing)....
>
> ἥ τε τομὴ εἰς ἄπειρόν ἐστιν (ἣν ἄπειρον, <οὐκ εἰς ἄπειρόν> φησιν ὁ Χρύσιππος· οὐ γάρ ἐστί τι ἄπειρον, εἰς ὃ γίνεται ἡ τομή. ἀλλ' ἀκατάληκτός ἐστι)....

I reconstruct Chrysippus's thought as follows: if we look for the ultimate parts, we are looking for the end of the division of the body. Let us suppose that at each step, we divide each part of the body into half. What do we get at the end of all divisions? Every step is a multiplication by 2 of the items in the previous step. So this way to proceed will never get us to infinity, since starting with finitely many parts and doubling them will always give us a finite number. This means that any row of division Chrysippus counted, would have finitely many items. This is true of all rows—ultimate, or not—and gives reason to say the parts are finitely many. But the rows towards the ultimate one are infinitely many, that is, the 'ultimate' row is at infinity. Hence, Chrysippus says, the ultimate parts are neither finite nor infinite. This means that there is a reason to call them finite, and there is reason to call them infinite. So, Chrysippus concludes, they are neither.

The textual evidence is clear that the Stoics held that the division of body is unlimited. What we need to explore now is the metaphysical significance of this stance. If unlimited, the division does not stop at any kind of atoms. I derive this conclusion from the claim that the ultimate parts are neither infinite nor finite (T3) and that the division is unceasing (T5); therefore the

---

5 The division has no *physical* end, rather than no temporal end.

division does not stop either at extended atoms, or extension-less points.[6] So what are the parts of unceasing division like? I submit that the unlimited division of a body generates *parts whose size converges on zero extension*. The constituent parts of unlimitedly divided bodies are infinite series of parts converging on zero extension or point-size, without ever reaching this limit. To use a modern way of talking to explicate the Stoic stance, at the foundations of their system there is atomless *gunk*. What is gunk? In the words of the contemporary philosopher Ted Sider:

> Borrowing a term from David Lewis (see for example Lewis (1991, 20)), let us say that an object is made of 'atomless gunk' if it has no (mereological) atoms as parts. If something is made of atomless gunk then it divides forever into smaller and smaller parts—it is infinitely divisible. However, a line segment is infinitely divisible, and yet has atomic parts: the points. A hunk of gunk does not even have atomic parts 'at infinity'; all parts of such an object have proper parts. (Sider 1993, 286)[7]

Importantly, for the Stoics bodies exist as unlimitedly *divided*, and not merely divisible (in contrast with Sider's description here above of gunk as *divisible*), because for them the division is ongoing.[8] We can capture this by saying that the Stoics believe in *actual* gunk. In order to assess the philosophical soundness of the view I thus attribute to the Stoics, we need to consider whether there are special difficulties about *conceptualising* actual gunk that do not arise with potential gunk. To address this question, let us look at another modern description of gunk, which interestingly is formulated in a way that can be

---

[6] We do talk of lines as being infinitely divided into points, but the Stoics would not allow bodies to consist of extension-less points, since points, as mathematical limits, are, according to the Stoics, neither corporeal nor incorporeal. Infinite division is always division into extended (and so divisible) parts. Similarly division of lines and time, etc., because these are incorporeals (namely, physical and dependent on bodies) while points are neither physical incorporeals nor corporeals.

[7] In the case of a line segment, the points into which it is infinitely divisible are extension-less; points have no extension in any dimension. It is usually taken to follow, and is here assumed, that points are simple, and do not have parts. Under this conception, points are the atoms of the line segment, and the line segment is not gunky. One might on the other hand think of a line segment as not being divisible into extension-less points, but only into smaller and smaller segments ad infinitum. In that case, the line segment is gunky. Similarly, if a surface has line or point atoms, it is divisible into lines or points, which are its atoms. If a surface is gunky, it is divisible into smaller and smaller surfaces, all of which have surfaces as proper parts.

[8] In the sense that there is no physical end to the division.

read as referring to either potential or actual unlimited division. Achille Varzi explicates "the hypothesis that the universe might consist of 'atomless gunk'" (Lewis 1991, 20) as follows: "either space and time or matter, or both, divide forever into smaller and smaller parts."[9] It is the expression 'divide forever' that may refer to potential or actual unlimited division. My thought is that conceiving of unlimitedly divided matter or of continuous matter with unlimitedly many parts has the same conceptual complexity. So my conclusion is that there aren't special conceptual difficulties with the structure of actual gunk, if one is willing to allow for potential gunk.[10]

While modern metaphysicians have explored the *conceptual possibility* that the universe may be an atomless continuum, I will argue in this paper that actual gunk is the 'tool,' as it were, that the Stoics need to build their own physical universe. A stance such that the building blocks of reality are actually unlimitedly divided may come across to us as surprising; so it must have been to the Stoics' contemporaries too. Yet, I will argue that the Stoics need to take this stance, specifically to allow for colocation of bodies. Colocation is, as I will argue, the *physical* relation the Stoics use to account for key *metaphysical* issues such as constitution and property possession, in ways that fit in with their corporealism. Colocation is also a precondition for causation for the Stoics, whom I take to endorse the general principle of no action at a distance. The following sections of the paper will investigate these issues. Before concluding the present section, I want to make a further point, to corroborate the historical plausibility of my interpretation that the Stoics held that the building blocks of reality are actually gunky. Surprising as their stance may be, the Stoics were not the only ones in antiquity to hold it, and not the first. Anaxagoras of Clazomenae (5th century BC) held a view in important respects similar to the Stoics. He too believes the building blocks of reality are actually gunky, and makes use of gunk to do metaphysical work in his system.[11]

III   Colocation

Colocation is a Stoic thesis that has exercised the commentators since antiquity. Alexander of Aphrodisias reports:

---

9   Varzi (2015) <http://plato.stanford.edu/entries/mereology/>, downloaded on 01/12/2015.
10 Of course there are on the other hand known conceptual difficulties on account of the infinity, for both versions of gunk.
11 An exposition of Anaxagoras's view and a detailed comparison between Anaxagoras and the Stoics are outside the scope of this paper. See my *Everything in Everything*.

T6: Alexander, *On Mixture* (216,14 217,12; LS 48C)

> Chrysippus has the following theory of blending: ... when certain substances and their qualities are mutually co-extended through and through, with the original substances and their qualities being preserved in such a mixture; this kind of mixture he calls specifically 'blending' ... he believes that such a coextension of blended bodies occurs when they pass through one another, so that no part among them fails to participate in everything contained in such a blend....

> ἔστι δὲ ἡ Χρυσίππου δόξα περὶ κράσεως ἥδε· ... δι' ὅλων τινῶν οὐσιῶν τε καὶ τῶν τούτων ποιοτήτων ἀντιπαρεκτεινομένων ἀλλήλαις μετὰ τοῦ τὰς ἐξ ἀρχῆς οὐσίας τε καὶ ποιότητας σώζειν ἐν τῇ μίξει τῇ τοιᾷδε, ἥντινα τῶν μίξεων κρᾶσιν ἰδίως εἶναι λέγει.... τὴν δὲ τοιαύτην ἀντιπαρέκτασιν τῶν κιρναμένων ὑπολαμβάνει γίνεσθαι χωρούντων δι' ἀλλήλων τῶν κιρναμένων σωμάτων, ὡς μηδὲν μόριον ἐν αὐτοῖς εἶναι μὴ μετέχον πάντων τῶν ἐν τῷ τοιούτῳ κεκραμένῳ μίγματι....

The substances in question are corporeal (σώματα); as we will see from other texts, they may be simple bodies (such as the basic elements in the Stoic system, πνεῦμα and ὕλη) or composite bodies, such as for instance water and wine (which result ultimately from the combination of πνεῦμα and ὕλη). The view the Stoics hold is that some substances can be thoroughly blended with each other, that is, collocated in a given spatiotemporal region over which they co-extend.[12] By this the Stoics mean that when collocated such substances come to occupy the same region of space, as each would on its own. This claim is as counterintuitive to us as it might have been to the Stoics' contemporaries. One could uncharitably say that it is nonsensical. How is colocation of bodies such as water and wine possible, so that there is some water wherever there is some wine? No Stoic account has survived, if any was given. I argue that the Stoics posit unlimited division of body to provide an account for the coextension of bodies that would not defy any laws of physics. Recall that gunk has parts converging to zero extension; this, I argue, allows the Stoics to explain blending in

---

12   One may wonder: given that all things exist as divided, why do only some of them come to be collocated by blending? The Stoics do not address this question in the texts that have survived. The answer could be simply based on experience: we find out empirically what does and what does not blend. One can only conjecture whether the Stoics would have given this answer, or a metaphysical reason.

terms of the collocation of the parts of the blended substances, each of which *approaches zero extension* and thus can be located where another is located.[13]

It will be helpful to contrast my interpretation to that of Daniel Nolan (2006). Nolan too argues the Stoics believe in gunk; but he does not use what I take to be the most relevant feature of gunk (namely, the convergence of the parts to zero extension) to explain how the Stoics can account for colocation. Nolan offers for colocation an alternative interpretation my own. He thinks the solution to the question of how blended substances can occupy the same spatiotemporal location lies in drawing a distinction between 'loose' and 'exact' or 'strict' location. Briefly, the distinction can thus be illustrated: I am loosely located in the room, but exactly or strictly located where I stand. Nolan argues that for the Stoics, the mixants can be collocated in a blend, not because their parts approach zero extension, but because, he thinks, the mixants do not retain an exact location when mixed. Nolan writes:

> Q and Q' [the blended substances] will not be located anywhere at all (though we may still say that they are in a loose sense, since they will retain an important connection to the place where O [the blend] is). If we do this, then we are not forced to say the mixed substances are in the same place—the mixture is in a specific location, true enough, but while they remain mixed the components are not in a place at all (at least in the strict sense). (Nolan 2006, 174)

There are a number of difficulties with Nolan's interpretation, with which I disagree; while a full discussion would be outside the scope of this paper, there are three main issues that can be briefly mentioned.[14] Nolan treats divided gunk as if the parts 'lost' their location—as if by having only loose location, the components of the blend were not in a place at all. There is no evidence in the surviving texts that the Stoics took this view; additionally, this is, philosophically, a view that would need more explication and defence, for it is a puzzling one: how can division of body 'dislocate' its parts?[15] Secondly, and as already discussed in the modern philosophical literature, loose and strict locations are not definable independently from one another, contrary to what Nolan

---

13   Even if there is no explicit evidence that the Stoics thought this way, in order to allow com-presence of material objects such as water and wine they must be committed to giving up continuity of matter.

14   For a fuller discussion, see my *Everything in Everything*.

15   Nolan's account of non-located gunk fits more those who believe that actual division into gunk destroys matter—but Nolan does not commit himself either way.

implicitly assumes.[16] Finally, Nolan holds that as long as the mixants are loosely located in the mixture, there is no obstacle as it were to their being thoroughly blended with each other. But the 'purity' of the mixants, which Nolan assumes, entails that they are still metaphorically 'rubbing shoulders' in the blend, like wheat and lentils or pepper and salt.[17] I conclude that Nolan does not offer a sound solution for how the Stoics could have accounted for colocation of bodies.

The next question I want to address is: what does colocation explain in Stoic metaphysics? I will argue that it accounts for constitution of material bodies, property possession and causation. I start with constitution.

IV   The Constitution of Material Bodies; the Active-Passive Distinction

The Stoics inherit from Aristotle his metaphysical analysis of material objects in terms of matter and form, or in short, what is known as his hylomorphism. They posit two cosmological principles (ἀρχαί) out of which everything is made. These first principles are, in Stoic terminology: that which acts (πνεῦμα or breath or god), and that which is acted upon (ὕλη or matter).[18] Both are everlasting, un-generated and indestructible. Ὕλη, the passive principle, is entirely unqualified in itself, but is at all times inseparably connected to, and qualified by (in the sense I will explain below) πνεῦμα. πνεῦμα also exists always as combined with ὕλη.[19] Together πνεῦμα and ὕλη make up the four elements

---

16   See e.g., Parsons 2007, and Leonard 2014.
17   This issue has also been raised by ancient commentators such as Alexander of Aphrodisias, and is also discussed in modern philosophical literature; see e.g., Parsons 2007.
18   Some scholars (e.g., Cooper 2009) have made the point that the two fundamental entities the Stoics posit in their system, πνεῦμα and ἄποιος ὕλη, are both first principles but only πνεῦμα is a cause, because it is that which acts. This interpretation identifies being a cause with being a causal agent. I disagree with it and take both to be causally powerful, for reasons that I explain in this section of the paper.
19   I will not discuss here the phenomenon or ontology of conflagration, about which I remain skeptical, like other scholars, including, e.g., Vogt. I cannot enter here into a discussion of the relevant issues.

(fire, air, earth, and water)[20] and from them, ordinary material objects.[21] The two principles are thus described:

T8: Diogenes Laertius (7.134; SVF 2.300, part 2.299; LS 44B)

> They [the Stoics] think that there are two principles of the universe, that which acts and that which is acted upon. That which is acted upon is unqualified [ἄποιος] substance, i.e. matter;[22] that which acts is the reason [*logos*] in it, i.e. god. For this ... constructs every single thing [composite] throughout all matter.[23]
>
> Δοκεῖ δ' αὐτοῖς ἀρχὰς εἶναι τῶν ὅλων δύο, τὸ ποιοῦν καὶ τὸ πάσχον. τὸ μὲν οὖν πάσχον εἶναι τὴν ἄποιον οὐσίαν τὴν ὕλην, τὸ δὲ ποιοῦν τὸν ἐν αὐτῇ λόγον τὸν θεόν· τοῦτον γὰρ ... διὰ πάσης αὐτῆς δημιουργεῖν ἕκαστα.

There are a number of issues to investigate in relation to this characterization of the two principles. Two are of particular interest to us here (and have not yet received due attention in the secondary literature). We know that for the Stoics both πνεῦμα and ὕλη are bodies (σώματα), because all that exist is body. (They are not abstract entities like Aristotle's matter and form.) On the other hand, the way πνεῦμα and ὕλη are characterized in T8 requires us to examine the

---

20 The division between πνεῦμα and ὕλη is (in the doxography) to some degree contextual (just as the division of matter and form in Aristotle is to the same degree contextual). So for instance: "T7: Galen, *Of Plethora* (7.525,9–14; SVF 2.439; LS 47F)" / "The breathy substance is what sustains, and the material substance what is sustained. And so they say that air and fire [=breath] sustain, and earth and water are sustained." / "τὴν μὲν γὰρ πνευματικὴν οὐσίαν τὸ συνέχον, τὴν δὲ ὑλικὴν τὸ συνεχόμενον, ὅθεν ἀέρα μὲν καὶ πῦρ συνέχειν φασί, γῆν δὲ καὶ ὕδωρ συνέχεσθαι." For present purposes I will use πνεῦμα to refer as it were collectively to what the Stoics call in different contexts reason, god, the active principle, sustaining power, breath, the mixture of fire and air; they are all *one type* of fundamental body. I will use ὕλη to refer to the property-less substratum, the passive principle, water and earth, matter, etc.; i.e., to *the other type* of fundamental body.

21 I take it that for the Stoics, qualitative difference and structure are primitives in their ontology. Both qualitative difference and structure are found primitively in god. That god is the active principle and matter is the passive one is also a primitive in the Stoic system.

22 This is the equivalent metaphysical principle to the substratum that Aristotle introduces it in *Metaphysics* Z.3. Both Aristotle and the Stoics take abstraction to the lowest level of abstract entity—the property-less.

23 Property-less matter is not space or generally the individuating principle of substances, according to the Stoics. Particulars are individuated by their respective individual forms, and are, in Stoic terminology, *peculiarly qualified* (see e.g., LS 28 I).

question of what body is, for the Stoics. Πνεῦμα is corporeal (it is body, σῶμα); but has no matter (ὕλη) in its constitution. So in the Stoic conception, 'body' cannot be what has matter. At the same time, ὕλη is property-less (ἄποιος), and yet, body (σῶμα), too. Hence being a body cannot depend on having any type of property. What does 'body' mean for the Stoics, then? We know that body is three-dimensional (see, for example, LS 45 E), and causally powerful (see, for example, LS 45 A). I submit that the Stoics are operating on a conception of body that is pre-Aristotelian and pre-Platonic. On my understanding, 'body' for the Stoics means *extended causal powerfulness*. (I argued elsewhere that Anaxagoras too thought of being physical in this way, as being a causal power extended in three dimensions.[24] As already mentioned above, Anaxagoras's ontology has many common features with Stoic ontology.) A second issue of special interest for the present argument is the question of why the Stoics posited ὕλη in their system. Could the Stoics have done without it? It seems *prima facie* that πνεῦμα has/is everything the Stoics need to build the universe. My thought is that the Stoics *could* have done without ὕλη, save for their theological assumptions. On my interpretation of the Stoic metaphysical system, their main motivation for positing matter (ὕλη) as the passive principle in the constitution of the universe is what we could call 'division of causal labour.' For the Stoics πνεῦμα is not only what is qualified and gives qualities to everything there is (thereby playing the metaphysical role of Aristotle's forms); it is also divine. As Aristotle wanted god to be pure actuality with no matter, I submit the Stoics want god to be purely active. Assuming that to account for change there needs to be in a system something that is active and something that is passive, if in the Stoic system there were no matter for god to act on, god itself would have needed to play both an active and a passive role. But it is not apt for the divine to be passive. So ὕλη, I submit, is posited to serve as the passive principle in the Stoic account of the constitution and changes of material objects.[25] I take ὕλη to be for the Stoics the ultimate principle of passivity, in itself ἄποιος. I conjecture that passivity and property-less-ness are conceptually connected

---

24 It is intuitive to think of such properties as heat as extended causal powers; but it is less intuitive to think of a property-less something (i.e., ὕλη) as an extended causal power. Nevertheless, Plato did think this about the receptacle (in the *Timaeus*, which influenced the Stoics); the receptacle can be thought of as causally powerful empty space. The relevant arguments cannot be developed in this context because they are outside the scope of this paper.

25 There is some doxographic evidence (e.g., Calcidius 293, LS 44 C) that suggests that the Stoics might have thought that matter is needed in their system, for the same reasons as Aristotle's, to address Parmenidean concerns. To my mind this evidence misrepresents the Stoics view.

and that the Stoics must have thought along these lines: property, form, structure (that is, god) are ways of being active; they *shape, form,* and *qualify* property-less being, hence, they have an active *constitutive* causal role on being. So the ultimate principle of passivity cannot be qualified.[26]

We know that for the Stoics all πνεῦμα is collocated or blended with ὕλη throughout nature, and interacts with it. For example we read:

T9: Alexander, *On Mixture* (216–217; LS 48 C1, 4)

> Chrysippus has the following theory of blending: he first assumes that the whole of substance is unified by a breath which pervades it all, and by which the universe is sustained and stabilized and made interactive with itself.
>
> ἔστι δὲ ἡ Χρυσίππου δόξα περὶ κράσεως ἥδε· ἡνῶσθαι μὲν ὑποτίθεται τὴν σύμπασαν οὐσίαν, πνεύματός τινος διὰ πάσης αὐτῆς διήκοντος, ὑφ' οὗ συνέχεταί τε καὶ συμμένει καὶ συμπαθές ἐστιν αὐτῷ τὸ πᾶν.

The question for us to address is this: how do ὕλη and the πνεῦμα interact with each other, and make up things, according to the Stoics? Their interaction cannot be efficient causation of the Aristotelian kind (which presupposes causal powers in both agent and patient, see for example *Physics* III 3), because the property-less matter has no powers or dispositions for causal interaction.[27] Additionally, from T9 we learn that the relation of ὕλη and πνεῦμα is presupposed for the universe to become causally interactive. So their relation could not be an instance of the same type of interaction as the one they are posited to explain, on pain of regress.

To make progress in understanding the Stoics' views regarding the interaction between ὕλη and the πνεῦμα, we need to investigate further in what the difference between active and passive bodies lies for the Stoics. I will argue that the active-passive distinction, despite its Aristotelian 'pedigree,' is very different from how Aristotle understands it. Consider for instance the blend of a

---

26 See the following section of the paper for an account of the constitutive causal role πνεῦμα has on ὕλη.

27 The notion of ὕλη as bare potentiality is Aristotle's, but such an entity, if there is one, is not capable of efficient causal interaction. Even if the Stoics made it a body, they still think of it as *dependent* on πνεῦμα—e.g., it is not separate and discrete in virtue of itself; it is always found in composition with πνεῦμα. So its status of being a body does not *ipso facto* endow it with causal efficacy *qua body*.

pair of composite bodies (each of them made of πνεῦμα and ὕλη) like water and wine. When blended, neither is passive or active on the other, notwithstanding that they are causally interactive. In their interaction, neither operates on the other, bringing about changes *in* the other (by contrast to Aristotle's conception of causal powers). Causal interaction for the Stoics doesn't require that the active 'compromise' the passive.[28] Rather, I see the terms active and passive as used by the Stoics as expressing an *ontological asymmetry* between πνεῦμα-ὕλη. Their asymmetry must be grounded in the Stoic view that πνεῦμα comprises qualities, while ὕλη is quality-less. Furthermore, recall that according to Stoics, ὕλη and πνεῦμα can never separate. Although ὕλη and πνεῦμα are physically blended the way that ordinary material objects are, for example wine and water, ὕλη and πνεῦμα can never be found separately, while ordinary material objects can be separated even after having been blended, as the Stoics mention in the sponge experiment (Stobaeus 1.155; LS 48 D).[29] So, there is an ontological difference between the two types of blend; both are blends, but in addition, there must be a relation of ontological dependence holding between ὕλη and πνεῦμα, which does not hold between ordinary material objects that blend, such as water and wine. Ὕλη and πνεῦμα do not depend on each other to be or become bodies; the Stoics presuppose that they are both bodies. Still, πνεῦμα and ὕλη are different with respect to one being a qualified body and the other a quality-less body. Although each of them as such is everlasting, they need to combine to generate our world of qualified individual material objects. I submit the Stoics' description of πνεῦμα as active and ὕλη as passive is the Stoic way to express the *interdependence* of the two for the existence of the universe, which is all there exists. This is in line with what Alexander of Aphrodisias reports, when saying (in T10, immediately below; see also T9 above) that for the Stoics, the relation of πνεῦμα to ὕλη is what sustains and stabilises the universe, and makes it interactive (σύμπαθες) with itself. This shows their interrelation to be necessary for the existence of the universe and for the existence of causal interaction in the universe.

T10: Alexander *On mixture* (225,1–2; LS 45 H)

... They [the Stoics] say that god is mixed with matter, pervading all of it and so shaping it, structuring it, and making it into the world.

---

28 The ἄποιος ὕλη can be passive only in a *receptive* sense (à la Plato's receptacle), rather than by *suffering* compromise (à la Aristotle's patient of change).

29 An oiled sponge dropped into a container of water and wine would be able to separate these totally.

... μεμῖχθαι τῇ ὕλῃ λέγειν τὸν θεόν, διὰ πάσης αὐτῆς διήκοντα καὶ σχηματίζοντα αὐτήν, καὶ μορφοῦντα καὶ κοσμοποιοῦντα τούτῳ τῷ τρόπῳ.

So ὕλη and πνεῦμα are (the only) active and passive bodies in the universe, and are always *interlocked* together everywhere in the universe. The interlocking is over and above their blending, since natural bodies that blend can separate, but ὕλη and πνεῦμα cannot separate. In conclusion, on my reading (the tensile tenor of) πνεῦμα has a *constitutive* causal role, rather than efficient causal one, on ὕλη; and it fulfils it by means of its colocation with ὕλη.[30] This constitutive causal role results in the *necessary colocation* of ὕλη and πνεῦμα. (By contrast, ordinary material substances, each of which is a blend of ὕλη and πνεῦμα, are only contingently and not necessarily collocated.)

V Sharing Subjects

The next question for us to address is: what results from the blending of two bodies? As we saw, there are two types of blending for the Stoics: between ὕλη and πνεῦμα (see Alexander, *On Mixture* 216,14–217,12; LS 48C 1) and between blends of ὕλη and πνεῦμα, which are the ordinary material objects in nature, such as water and wine (see Alexander, *On Mixture* 216,14–217,12; LS 48C 4–12). Our sources have preserved a more detailed description of the latter type of blend; but we can reasonably assume that the two types of blends are underpinned by the same (physical) mechanism: πνεῦμα pervades ὕλη the same way as composites pervade each other when thoroughly mixed. Let us examine first the case of the πνεῦμα-ὕλη blend. In general terms, we can say, with the Stoics, that in the blend πνεῦμα endows ὕλη with properties and causal powers; but it does so in a very specific way. The blending of property-less ὕλη and πνεῦμα results in the *qualification of the composite*, not the qualification of ὕλη

---

30 My interpretation differs from an existing one that many share, represented, e.g., by A.A. Long and D. Sedley, who argue: "In order to do justice to Stoic intuitions, we should regard the *two things that occupy the same space* not as two determinate and independently existing bodies, but as the two bodily *functions* (breadth and matter) which *jointly constitute* every determinate and independently existing body" (Sedley 1987, 294, my emphasis). This line of interpretation rightly points out that the Stoics use colocation, of matter (ὕλη) and breath (πνεῦμα), to account for the composition of composite things. It is true that two functions of a body, like, e.g., elasticity and its malleability, can be co-instantiated in the same matter. This is unproblematic because functions are not material bodies, but qualifications of matter. But ὕλη and πνεῦμα are not qualities: the Stoics claim they are coextended not as functions, but as bodies.

itself. Ὕλη is by definition property-less; it is also everlasting. So it cannot survive acquiring properties. So how can properties be bestowed on property-less matter? The Stoics solve this problem with blending: the property-less can be collocated with the qualified, and this suffices for it to be empowered with properties and causal powers. The mechanism the Stoics posit is *sui generis*. For Aristotle, matter instantiates a universal form; for Plato, objects participate in the Forms. For the Stoics, matter is collocated with, and interlocked with (independently) embodied-form(s), namely πνεῦμα. Alexander describes in some detail the Stoic account of blended composite substances; we can lean on it to understand their account of the blend of simples (ὕλη-πνεῦμα) too:

T11: Alexander, *On Mixture* (216–217; LS 48 C4–C9)

> ... Other mixtures occur, he argues, when certain substances and their qualities are mutually coextended through and through, with the original substances and their qualities being preserved in such a mixture; this kind of mixture he calls specifically 'blending'; ... for the capacity to be separated again from one another is a peculiarity of blended substances, and this only occurs if they preserve their own natures in the mixture.
>
> Since all this is so, they say there is nothing remarkable in the fact that certain bodies, when assisted by one another, are so *mutually unified* through and through that while being preserved together with their own qualities, they are *mutually coextended* as whole through and through, even if some of them are small in bulk and incapable by themselves of spreading so far and preserving their own qualities. (My emphasis)

> ... τὰς δέ τινας γίνεσθαι μίξεις λέγει δι' ὅλων τινῶν οὐσιῶν τε καὶ τῶν τούτων ποιοτήτων ἀντιπαρεκτεινομένων ἀλλήλαις μετὰ τοῦ τὰς ἐξ ἀρχῆς οὐσίας τε καὶ ποιότητας σώζειν ἐν τῇ μίξει τῇ τοιᾷδε, ἥντινα τῶν μίξεων κρᾶσιν ἰδίως εἶναι λέγει .... εἶναι γὰρ ἴδιον τῶν κεκραμένων τὸ δύνασθαι χωρίζεσθαι πάλιν ἀπ' ἀλλήλων, ὃ μόνως γίνεται τῷ σώζειν ἐν τῇ μίξει τὰ κεκραμένα τὰς αὐτῶν φύσεις .... ὧν οὕτως ἐχόντων οὐδέν φασι θαυμαστὸν τὸ καὶ σώματά τινα βοηθούμενα ὑπ' ἀλλήλων οὕτως ἀλλήλοις ἑνοῦσθαι δι' ὅλων, ὡς αὐτὰ σωζόμενα μετὰ τῶν οἰκείων ποιοτήτων ἀντιπαρεκτείνεσθαι ἀλλήλοις δι' ὅλων ὅλα, κἂν ᾖ τινα ἐλάττω τὸν ὄγκον καὶ μὴ δυνάμενα καθ' αὑτὰ ἐπὶ τοσοῦτον χεῖσθαί τε καὶ σώζειν τὰς οἰκείας ποιότητας. οὕτω γὰρ καὶ τὸν κύαθον τοῦ οἴνου κιρνᾶσθαι τῷ ὕδατι τῷ πολλῷ βοηθούμενον ὑπ' αὐτοῦ εἰς τὴν ἐπὶ τοσοῦτον ἔκτασιν.

I take the coextension and the mutual unification or interlocking of bodies mentioned in T11 to coincide temporally, rather than to happen sequentially;[31] yet they are different events. The interlocking is the ontological dependence discussed above. As a result of collocation and interlocking, the blend itself comes to manifest the properties of one of the mixants. Whenever the mixants are ὕλη and πνεῦμα, the ὕλη-πνεῦμα composite becomes causally efficacious in virtue of the com-presence of πνεῦμα's causal properties. I call this the *empowerment* of ὕλη with πνεῦμα's qualities. Although ὕλη does not come to possess the properties of πνεῦμα, ὕλη can 'use' them. So, for example, the heat of the composite of ὕλη and πνεῦμα is the *totality* of the heat present at the location of their blend, in this case, the heat of πνεῦμα. In this way the composite of ὕλη and πνεῦμα comes to be hot, and thereby the ὕλη too can be thought of as if coming to be hot.[32] The Stoics talk as if ὕλη is qualified by the properties of its com-present πνεῦμα. But, as I argued, in the blend, one of the entities is qualified,[33] and the other is in the presence of the property, so long as the property continues to be present.

The Stoics thus appear to distinguish between what we could call 'owning a property' and 'sharing its presence.' In what do these relations differ metaphysically? I explain blends, whether between simple or composite substances, as *a type of plural subject* in relation to their property possession. An example of plural subject-hood, already discussed by Plato, is that you and I are two (but each of us is one and neither is two).[34] Other instances of plural subjects are William and Mary reigning over England, or the Romans defeating the Gauls, or you and me playing a duet, etc. Stoic blends are a special kind of plural subjects. Typically, in case of plural subject-hood, the two or more subjects involved share *equally* one property-instance. By contrast, blends comprise *unequal partners* with respect to the ownership of the properties; one mixant owns it and the other shares in its presence. The Stoics are thereby introducing

---

31 While in T11 mutual unification is mentioned first and co-extension second, in other passages from Alexander their order is reversed, and there is first co-extension and then unification.

32 This way of thinking of how properties belong to a composite and to its matter is non-Aristotelian. On the other hand, it is like the way Platonic Forms come to be present in the receptacle. The receptacle does not become hot (in an Aristotelian sense), but somehow 'houses' heat in it. (For the Stoics, for ὕλη-πνεῦμα blends, πνεῦμα is permanently housed in ὕλη; for causal blends, they are temporarily housed in each other.)

33 Πνεῦμα strictly does not possess properties but *is* properties. Otherwise the Stoics would need a further account of how πνεῦμα comes to possess properties.

34 Plural subjects were known to the ancients, at least since Plato's *Hippias Major*; see Scaltsas 2006.

a different model of property possession, which I call *sharing subjects*, to distinguish them from plural subjects, allowing for inequality between partners.[35]

VI Causation

In the Stoic system, I submit, there are two different types of empowerment resulting from colocation of bodies.[36] I call them *property empowerment*, and *structural empowerment* respectively; they are both instances of causation. As we saw, there are two types of blend: blends of simple and of composite substances. Each of the two types of blend exhibits both types of empowerment. We have already discussed the ὕλη-πνεῦμα blends. Since πνεῦμα is both qualified and structured, its collocation with property-less ὕλη empowers ὕλη with properties and structure. The same model also accounts for the blend of composite substances that are themselves blends of ὕλη and πνεῦμα, and on these I will focus in what follows.

A. Property Empowerment. The example that follows is one that we would readily identify as one of efficient causation, where one composite substance makes another 'acquire' a new property, in this case being hot. The mechanism is blending:

T12: Alexander, *On Mixture* (218; LS 48 C11)

> They [the Stoics] say that fire as a whole passes through iron as a whole, while each of them preserves its own substance.
>
> ἀλλὰ καὶ τὸ πῦρ ὅλον δι' ὅλου χωρεῖν τοῦ σιδήρου λέγουσι, σώζοντος αὐτῶν ἑκατέρου τὴν οἰκείαν οὐσίαν.

---

35   Exploring the potential applicability of the Stoics' sharing subjects model beyond their metaphysics of blends, is outside the scope of this paper. Briefly, the sharing subjects model might offer to contemporary philosophy an ontology of complex activities where the involvement of the subjects in the activities have a variety of roles and contribution, such cases as: birth, punishment, etc.

36   One advantage that the Stoic account of blending has, both for instantiation of properties and causal efficacy, is that it brings the active and the passive in contact *everywhere*, not only surface contact. This pays justice to our intuitions that the agent must be present where the effect occurs. This is an Aristotelian intuition (placing the effect of the action of the mover in the moved), but to which (Aristotle's) surface contact in causal interaction does not pay justice.

The interaction between fire and iron does not involve any transfer of a property trope from fire to iron; there is only colocation of two bodies: it is the fire that is hot, and iron is in the presence of fire. Iron is a sharing subject with fire, sharing heat through colocation with fire and thereby becoming empowered with heat without possessing it.[37] When iron and fire (which stands in for heat)[38] are blended, iron is vicariously hot, through the presence of fire in it; when the fire moves out of the iron, heat moves out of the iron, too. The Stoics see the hot iron as an amalgam.[39] When we say it becomes cool, they say fire departed. For the Stoics a causal effect 'stays with' its cause, in contrast to the Aristotelian, neo-Aristotelian, and generally modern conception of the effect coming to belong to the passive agent by changing it. Relevant to this point is the following text:

T13: Clement, *Stromata* (8.9.33, 2; LS 55I)

> ... A 'sustaining' cause[40] is one during whose presence the effect remains and on whose removal the effect is removed ....
>
> ... συνεκτικὸν δέ ἐστιν αἴτιον, οὗ παρόντος μένει τὸ ἀποτέλεσμα καὶ αἰρομένου αἴρεται ....

This is the way sharing subjects work, metaphysically. The effect (being hot) remains until the cause (fire) is removed.

B. Structural Empowerment. To appreciate fully the philosophical significance of structural empowerment, it will be helpful to preface the discussion of this Stoics' position with a very brief (and necessarily 'gappy,' for reasons of space) excursus on how structure came into play in the history of metaphysics preceding the Stoics. The Milesians tried to account for everything in nature using (instances of) opposite powers, such as the hot and cold, wet and dry. On the other hand, the identification and reification of structure in ontology can be traced as far back as the first generation of thinkers after the Milesians. Most

---

37 Fire and iron relate to heat in very different ways, even if at the phenomenal level they both seem hot and we think of both as hot.
38 The Stoics do not distinguish, ontologically, fire from heat. For them there are no universals. Concepts are just descriptions of objects.
39 In physical terms, the heat of the two bodies, iron and fire, adds up while they are collocated, so that at the empirical level we find in that location hot iron.
40 The sustaining cause is typically for the Stoics πνεῦμα.

notably, Parmenides and Heraclitus built practically the whole of the universe out of structural features of being—a sphere that is simple, in the case of Parmenides; process, in the case of Heraclitus. The generation right after them distinguishes between opposite-properties and structure, and reifies structure as equally primitively present in the universe as the opposite forces. For instance, Philolaus distinguishes between the limiters and the unlimiteds. Anaxagoras posits primitive seeds in the ontology, from which asymmetrical individuals grow. Empedocles believes that parts of asymmetrical bodies exist primitively in the universe. Plato was the first to introduce structural universals, such as the Form of Bed. He also introduced a criterion to distinguish structures from opposites, which was a breakthrough in the history of metaphysics: structural universals are not comparatives, while opposites are; the hot can be hotter, but a human being cannot be more of a human being. Nevertheless, Plato was reluctant to introduce structural properties in his theory of Forms. After Plato, Aristotle championed structural universals in his substantial forms, which are metaphysically even richer than has hitherto been appreciated.[41]

The Stoics too distinguish structural from opposite properties, and develop a different account of the causation for each. They associate structural features and powers with πνεῦμα. Alexander for instance says that when πνεῦμα and ὕλη interact, 'the whole of substance is unified by a breath which pervades it all, and by which the universe is *sustained* and *stabilized*, and made *interactive* with itself' (T9, my emphasis).[42] All these causal effects, which result from blending of πνεῦμα and ὕλη, concern structural properties of objects in nature. Πνεῦμα has primitively these powers, with which ὕλη is endowed when πνεῦμα and ὕλη blend. What is more difficult to understand is the structural empowerment between composites of ὕλη and πνεῦμα, such as the blend of wine and water. Alexander gives three such examples: frankincense being burned; gold being mixed with drugs; and wine being mixed with water.[43]

---

41 For a fuller and argued account of the development of the distinction between opposite properties, structural properties and sortals in the history of Western thought before the Stoics, see my *Everything in Everything*.

42 The universe becomes interactive, *not* by acquiring new first order opposite properties, which the πνεῦμα already has, but by the *active* and the *passive* coming together.

43 The first is a case empowering via an event (burning) involving the other mixant (fire), while the second two cases are of empowerment by the other mixant's structure.

STOIC BLENDS

T14: Alexander, *On Mixture* (217; LS 48 C 8)

> The supporters of this theory [blending] advance as grounds for their belief in its truth the fact that many bodies preserve their own qualities whether they are present in evidently larger or smaller volume (as can be seen in the case of frankincense; when burnt it becomes rarefied, but it preserves its own quality over a very large extent), and the further fact that many bodies, which by themselves cannot advance to a certain size, do so with the assistance of others. Gold certainly, through being mixed with certain drugs, can be spread and rarefied to an extent which is not possible when it is simply beaten .... In this way too a measure of wine is blended with a large amount of water and *assisted* by it to attain an extension of that size.

> Τοῦ δὲ τοῦτο οἴεσθαι γίνεσθαι πίστεις φέρουσιν οἱ προϊστάμενοι τῆσδε τῆς δόξης τό τε πολλὰ τῶν σωμάτων σώζειν τὰς ἑαυτῶν ποιότητας ἐπί τ' ἐλαττόνων ἐναργῶν ὄγκων καὶ ἐπὶ μειζόνων ὄντα (ὡς ὁρᾶν ἔστιν ἐπὶ τοῦ λιβανωτοῦ, ὃς ἐν τῷ θυμιᾶσθαι λεπτυνόμενος ἐπὶ πλεῖστον τὴν αὑτοῦ φυλάσσει ποιότητα), ἔτι τε τὸ πολλὰ εἶναι, ἃ καθ' ἑαυτὰ μὴ οἷά τε ὄντα ἐπί τι ἐλθεῖν μέγεθος ὑπ' ἄλλων βοηθούμενα ἐπ' αὐτὸ πρόεισι. τὸν γοῦν χρυσὸν ὑπό τινων μιγνυμένων φαρμάκων ἐπὶ πλεῖστον χεῖσθαί τε καὶ λεπτύνεσθαι, ἐφ' ὅσον καθ' αὐτὸν ἐλαυνόμενος οὐκ ἐδύνατο.... οὕτω γὰρ καὶ τὸν κύαθον τοῦ οἴνου κιρνᾶσθαι τῷ ὕδατι τῷ πολλῷ βοηθούμενον ὑπ' αὐτοῦ εἰς τὴν ἐπὶ τοσοῦτον ἔκτασιν.

In the above passage we read that for the Stoics the blended substances 'preserve their own qualities, whether they are present in evidently larger or smaller masses.' For instance, when a drop of wine comes to be present in the whole ocean, the wine survives and preserves its own properties; but it expands—where expansion is a *structural* alteration. How are the blended substances able to achieve what they do, in terms of structural modifications? The Stoics tell us something surprising, but in keeping with their theory. Such blended substances are *assisted* in different ways by their co-mixants to achieve what they could not achieve on the strength of their own natures. Presumably in the case under discussion the Stoics thought that the *bulk* of the water enables the drop of wine to spread to an extent to which it could not spread on its own powers. What is important about this model is that it shows that the Stoics distinguish causation that results in *property empowerment* and causation that results in *structural empowerment*; in the case of water and wine what the one mixant 'gives' the other is not opposite properties, such as being hotter or softer, etc.; it is that the structure of the one enables the other to alter structurally.

In the case of frankincense, two things happen: blending (and through structural empowerment, spreading) and burning. Burning destroys the body that has the frankincense, but the scent survives and blends with fire/smoke, which spreads. What this case shows is that structural empowerment has its limits; frankincense is enabled to spread over a very large extent, *only*. Beyond that extent, its nature *cannot* sustain it and it dissipates. In that sense, structure is being treated by the Stoics dynamically, as a power; it is effective over a range and then gives way.

Finally, the example of gold, as described by Alexander in **T14**, is of particular interest to us, because it shows that the Stoics contrast the impact of efficient causation to blending: 'Gold certainly, through being mixed with certain drugs, can be spread and rarefied to an extent which is not possible when it is simply beaten' (LS 48 C8). The drugs blend with gold, thereby uniting with it and assisting it to spread while retaining its cohesiveness. Gold is thus structurally empowered to spread to an extent far beyond what it could achieve on its own powers, even when beaten flat.

VII Types of Ontological Unity

Bringing together the interpretative results achieved so far, I argue that the Stoics introduce the following types of ontological unity, all resulting from the colocation and blending of bodies that exist as unlimitedly divided:

i. Ὕλη-πνεῦμα unity. This is the type of unity that the universe as a whole enjoys qua composite of ὕλη and πνεῦμα, which have always been and will always be inseparably blended and interlocked together.
ii. Object unity. This is the type of unity that lumps of ὕλη and πνεῦμα enjoy when they are physically unified and made into discrete material objects in the universe, through (the physical movements of) πνεῦμα's sustaining powers.
iii. Causal unity. This is the unity that causally interacting material objects in the world enjoy, which may result in property empowerment or structural empowerment (or both).

These three types of unity are all cases of blending, and are to be contrasted to a fourth one, *fusion* (σύγχυσις), which is described for instance by Alexander thus:

T15: Alexander *On mixture* (216; LS 48 C 3)

> Other mixtures occur by through-and-through fusion of the substances themselves and their intrinsic qualities, which are destroyed together, as he [Chrysippus] says happens in the case of medical drugs when the things mixed together undergo mutual destruction and another body is generated out of them.

> τὰς δέ τινας συγχύσει δι' ὅλων τῶν τε οὐσιῶν αὐτῶν καὶ τῶν ἐν αὐταῖς ποιοτήτων συμφθειρομένων ἀλλήλαις, ὡς γίνεσθαί φησιν ἐπὶ τῶν ἰατρικῶν φαρμάκων κατὰ σύμφθαρσιν τῶν μιγνυμένων, ἄλλου τινὸς ἐξ αὐτῶν γεννωμένου σώματος.

Usually interpreters understand fusion as involving destruction of πνεῦμα, on account of Alexander's saying that the substances that are fused and their qualities are destroyed, as in the mixture of medical drugs. I argue for an alternative interpretation of fusion as a special type of causal interaction and mixing; I consider an advantage of my interpretation that it does *not* attribute to the Stoics the belief that πνεῦμα, which is god, gets destroyed when fusion occurs. I take the Stoics to distinguish two types of causal interaction between material objects, one resulting in blending (which can bring about property and structural empowerment), and the other resulting in fusion. The criterion that differentiates these two types is this: the unity of the objects involved in causal interaction is put under stress, as it were, by the novel causal unity that the causal interaction brings about. Object unity and causal unity compete with each other for different outcomes. If the object unity of the entities involved in causation is stronger than their causal unity, the objects and their qualities are preserved, in a blend. By contrast, if the object unity is weaker than the causal unity, the object and their qualities dissipate, in a fusion. So on my interpretation the destruction of the objects and their qualities in fusion is the loss of physical unity and continuity by each of the objects (rather than literal destruction), and hence their dispersal and disorganization. It is literally, as the Stoics call it, 'confusion.'

VIII Conclusions

The Stoics' guiding principle in ontology is the Eleatic principle. Their existents are bodies that have the power to act and be acted upon. They account both for the constitution of material objects and the causal interactions among them in terms of such dynamic bodies. Blending is the physical mechanism that explains both constitution and causation and is facilitated by the fact that for the Stoics all bodies exist as unlimited divided. When blended, the substances involved become sharing subjects of qualities and structural features. The model of sharing subjects explains how collocation has both physical and metaphysical impact on the collocated bodies. It presupposes ontological dependence (the 'mutual unification' in a blend), which is primitive in their system. By means of collocation and ontological dependence, the Stoics produced an account of the mutual empowerment of blended bodies, which explains in their system the constitution of material objects (ὕλη and πνεῦμα), their composition (such as water and wine), and causal interaction (iron and fire). It is a distinctive feature of the Stoics that they account for such core metaphysical issues without reifying abstract properties and universals, as their towering predecessors Plato and Aristotle had done.

COLLOQUIUM 1

Commentary on Marmodoro

Rose Cherubin
George Mason University

Abstract

This paper comments on Anna Marmodoro's "Stoic Blends." That essay argues that the "Eleatic Principle" is central to Stoic conceptions of what is. It also investigates a key difference between Stoic and Aristotelian conceptions of the roles of form and matter in constituting what is: the Stoics' insistence that form and matter are bodies, and their concomitant assertion that more than one independent body can occupy the exact same place. The present comment explores the relationships between the "Eleatic Principle," the arguments of the historical Eleatics, and Aristotle's hylomorphism.

Keywords

being – change – Aristotle – Stoics – Eleatics

Dr. Marmodoro's essay "Stoic Blends" is an important contribution to our understanding of the range of ancient responses to the questions of what is, why it is as it is, and what it means for things to change. The essay explores the ontological concerns reflected in Stoic accounts, and illuminates how these compare to the concerns that Aristotle addressed using similar terms.

As Dr. Marmodoro shows, Aristotle's form (τὸ τί ἦν εἶναι, λόγος) and matter (ὕλη) on the one hand, and the Stoics' active stuff (πνεῦμα, λόγος, θεός) and acted-upon stuff or matter (ὕλη) on the other, are both intended to account for why things that are are the way they are, and why some of them come to be and perish as they do. But the two accounts of form-matter pairs work in very different ways, and suggest very different conceptions of what it is for a thing to be. "Stoic Blends" begins by noting that the Stoic account is motivated by what is known in contemporary analytic metaphysics as the "Eleatic Principle,"[1] articulated by the Eleatic Visitor at *Sophist* 247d–e: the principle that what

---

[1] Within analytic philosophical study of ontology, Armstrong 1978 seems to have initiated serious exploration of the implications of the position articulated in the *Sophist* passage. In the

really is, is whatever has the power to affect something or to be affected by something.[2] By contrast, Aristotle's discussions of why what is is as it is, in the *Metaphysics* and the physical works, are in part a response to the work of the historical Eleatics.

This is why Dr. Marmodoro's insight into the role of the Eleatic Principle in Stoic metaphysics is so illuminating. There are sharp differences, even oppositions, between the Eleatic Principle and the positions presented by Parmenides, Zeno, and Melissus. There are also, I will propose, some genetic connections. In this comment, I will briefly explore those divergences and connections. I will then attempt to show how they are reflected in some of the differences between Aristotle's account of form and matter as causes on the one hand, and the Stoics' account of the interactions between πνεῦμα and ὕλη on the other.

I   The Eleatic Principle and the Eleatics

A   *Divergences*

The Eleatic Principle of *Sophist* 247d–e does not match anything articulated by Parmenides, Zeno, or Melissus. The Eleatic Principle holds that that which really is, is that which has the power to affect something or to be affected by something. In other words, the Eleatic Principle lays down that

> If something is, then that thing has the power to affect and/or to be affected, AND

> If something has the power to affect and/or to be affected, then that thing is.[3]

---

consequent discussion of Armstrong's work, the Visitor's position was referred to as the "Eleatic Principle" at least as early as Oddie 1982.

2   "All that has any power (δύναμις) of any kind, either to make (ποιεῖν) something other in nature/ make another of any nature [be], or to be affected (παθεῖν) even in the smallest [degree] by the most minor [thing], though it be only once; that really is (ὄντως εἶναι). For I lay down as a definition (τίθεμαι γὰρ ὅρον) to delineate (ὁρίζειν) the things that are, that it is nothing more than δύναμις."

3   From the context, 'is' appears to be meant existentially. I take ὄντως at 247e to mean 'really' in the sense of 'truly,' 'not only apparently,' or 'not only incidentally or in a certain respect.' That is, I do not assume that the presence of ὄντως is what makes εἶναι mean something like 'exists' here; it may simply draw attention to the assumptions underlying the Eleatic Visitor's proposal. I also do not suggest that either ὄντως or εἶναι here connotes bodily existence in particular, only that in context, the terms are supposed to allow for existence of bodies.

COMMENTARY ON MARMODORO   27

As Dr. Marmodoro notes (page 11), Diogenes Laertius reports at 7.134 that the Stoics espoused something extensionally equivalent to this. It seemed to them, he says, that there are two principles of the whole of what-is, namely that which acts or does something, and that which is acted upon.[4]

One obvious difference between the Eleatic Principle of the *Sophist* and the work of the Eleatics is that all three of the Eleatics were concerned to show that insupportable contradictions result from the claim that there are multiple things; and also from the claim that anything moves, changes, comes to be, or perishes. Some causal relationships are supposed to hold between distinct things; others may be said to hold between different aspects or states of the same entity. Thus one way or another, to say that something affects or that it is affected is to invoke multiplicity.[5] Some causal relationships also involve passage of time, change, coming to be, or destruction. Yet the Eleatic Principle, unlike the work of the historical Eleatic philosophers, presents causal relationships as unproblematic.

In the present section, I will begin with Melissus, whose work I think presents the starkest contrasts and the least compatibility or connection to the Eleatic Principle. Zeno offers some resources that address and could have informed the Eleatic Principle, so I consider him second. Parmenides offers a bit more, so the discussion of his work appears third.

1   Melissus[6]

Melissus argues that if anything is, it cannot come to be (Simplicius *in phys.* 103.13 and following and 162.24 and following, DK 30B1). This seems to mean first of all that what-is[7] (τὸ ὄν) cannot come into existence. But Melissus also argues that what-is cannot come to be other than it is, cannot change in quality

---

4 Δοκεῖ δ' αὐτοῖς ἀρχὰς εἶναι τῶν ὅλων δύο, τὸ ποιοῦν καὶ τὸ πάσχων.
5 Cf. Aristotle, *Physics* 185a4ff. and 186a28ff.
6 An obvious point of difference between Melissus and the Stoics is that whereas the Stoics claim that whatever is must be body, Melissus argues that what-is must not have body, and that body cannot be what is (B9). But this difference regarding body is independent of their respective positions on the Eleatic Principle. Nothing about the Eleatic Principle implies that what-is must be body or have body, and nothing about its denial implies that what-is must not involve body. The *Sophist* discussion that leads to the articulation of the Eleatic Principle explicitly allows for incorporeal beings (247c–d). As Dr. Marmodoro shows, the Stoics themselves saw the corporeality claim and the Eleatic Principle as axioms independent of one another. Therefore I will leave aside consideration of this difference between Melissus and the Stoics.
7 To avoid awkward phrases such as 'what is is,' I will use 'what-is' to translate Melissus's τὸ ὄν and Melissus's and Parmenides' τὸ ἐόν.

or state, because that would make it multiple in the sense of having more than one quality or feature or state. If it could change quality or state, it would be a different thing at different times (*in phys.* 103.13 and following, 111.18 and following, B7) and might be in a contradictory condition ("rarer and denser than itself," *in phys.* 104.6 and following). If there were more than one state, each would be limited in time, and would come to be and/or perish. Nothing could come from what-is-not, Melissus asserts, and what-is could neither come to be from nothing nor perish into nothing, nor come to be from or perish into what is (that is, into another thing or state). To introduce limits of any kind (temporal, spatial, qualitative, or other) would apparently be to suggest that being, or what-is, is not all that is, or is not self-sufficient (B2, B7, B8).[8] Thus multiplicity, Melissus argues, is incompatible with being what-is.

The connection between self-sufficiency, completeness, imperishability, and unity is especially clear in B7. There Melissus argues that what-is is not such as to feel pain (ἀλγεῖ), and that it must be healthy (ὑγιές). It is evident why Melissus would think that what-is could not undergo pain: Melissus considers pain to be the result of having something added, προσγινόμενον, or removed, ἀπογινόμενον. He has already argued that what-is is not accompanied (so nothing can be added),[9] and is not limited (if something were removed, each thing would be limited by the other); and that it does not change.

Today we generally understand health as a condition or state, hence as potentially transitory; and as an aspect that exists among others and is noticed mainly through contrast with its opposite. Therefore at first glance, it might seem incongruous or even inappropriate for Melissus to say that the unchanging, unaccompanied, homogeneous τὸ ὄν is ὑγιές. However, ὑγιές means something like 'appropriate, sufficient' at *Iliad* 8.524, 'sound, undamaged, unharmed' at Herodotus 4.76. Slightly later, in Plato, it often means 'whole, unbroken, undamaged,' as in the analogy of the jars at *Gorgias* 493e. A sense like this would be quite consistent with Melissus's description of what-is, and would not entail any transitions or differences of condition.

For Melissus, then, the Eleatic Principle is untenable because there cannot be multiple things that affect or are affected by one another. Nor, he argues, can there be multiple states or aspects of the one being that is. Where the

---

[8] Melissus does say that what-is ἦν and ἔσται, 'was' and 'will be,' e.g., in B1 and B2. The intent appears to be to emphasize permanence, not to suggest the reality of different states or times. See Palmer 2009, 210–211.

[9] Without claiming to know the order in which the fragments initially appeared, I believe it is safe to infer that B7 followed after the arguments mentioned previously. It begins, "In this way (οὕτως) it is everlasting, unlimited, and all alike. And neither (καὶ οὔτ᾽) would it perish…"

Eleatic Principle holds that whatever is has the capability of affecting or being affected, and that whatever can affect or be affected is something that is, Melissus asserts that whatever is must *not* be able to affect or to be affected, and that whatever affects or is affected (or, whatever is said to do so, B8) *cannot* be.

2   Zeno of Elea

The reports of Zeno's Millet Seed argument indicate that it engaged with the claim that anything can affect or be affected. Zeno reportedly argued that if a small portion of one millet seed does not make a sound when it falls to the ground, then a whole millet seed, or even a bushel of seeds, should not make a sound on hitting the ground; and if a whole seed or bushel of seeds makes a sound on hitting the ground, then so too must a tiny portion of a seed.[10]

Concerns about causality could be one reason why Zeno would advance such an argument. That is, at first glance, it might seem that the paradoxes of magnitude and the paradoxes of motion would make another argument about mobile material objects unnecessary. But suppose that someone were to say to Zeno: "We have empirical evidence of the existence of distinct material objects: they make distinct sounds." The magnitude and motion paradoxes would not address this challenge. First of all, they do not refer to auditory phenomena; and second, they do not say anything about causality. The view that something that makes a sound must be real, and that only real things have effects such as sounds, relies on something like the Eleatic Principle of the *Sophist*. Zeno's Millet Seed example seems to respond to this sort of view. In their reports on this argument of Zeno's, both Aristotle and Simplicius use ψοφεῖ, "sounds/makes a noise," that is, affects the ears; and Simplicius also uses ψόφον ποιεῖ, "produces a sound." If these reports accurately present Zeno's language, then, he was concerned to discuss situations in which something is said to affect or to be affected.

Aristotle does not offer details of Zeno's argument, but Simplicius does, or claims to do so. Simplicius holds that Zeno relied on the idea that the volume of the sound made varies with the number (including fractional numbers) of seeds that fall.[11] Thus on Simplicius's report, Zeno would have been arguing that if we agree that some quantity of millet seeds produces an auditory effect when it hits the ground, then so too must any smaller quantity of seeds, and

---

10 Aristotle, *Physics* 250a19ff., DK 29A29; Simplicius *in phys.* 1108.18–28.
11 This seems to mean only that greater portions of a seed make more noise than smaller ones, and that greater numbers make more noise than smaller numbers; not that there is some exact arithmetic or geometric proportion in effect.

any part of a seed. Otherwise we would be saying that a lack of auditory effect results from dividing or disaggregating auditory effects. Similarly, Zeno would have been arguing, if we agree that one seed, or a sufficiently small part of a seed, produces no auditory effect when it hits the ground, then we must agree that any larger quantity of seeds or parts produces no auditory effect. Otherwise, we would be saying that an auditory effect is an aggregate, or a multiple, of non-existent auditory effects (or absences of auditory effects). Agreeing to either premise would lead to problems; and to make matters worse, we tend to agree to both.

Expressed this way, the Millet Seed argument can be understood as challenging the Eleatic Principle. Zeno does not claim that something that is fails to affect anything or to be affected. Nor does he suggest that what has or undergoes an effect fails to be. Rather, he argues that our description and analysis of auditory effects is incoherent and self-contradictory. It is incoherent in that it implies that auditory effects are aggregates or multiplications of absences of auditory effect, and that an auditory effect can be divided or disassembled into non-existent components. It is self-contradictory in that it implies that any number or fraction of millet seeds both makes and does not make a sound upon hitting the same ground.

Aristotle criticizes Zeno's argument by challenging the assumption that an auditory effect involving a larger number or size of things must be an aggregate or multiple of auditory effects of smaller components. Sounds, Aristotle holds, are associated with movements of air. He argues that the fall of a small part of a seed will not move as much air as the fall of a bushel (*Physics* 250a19 and following, DK 29A29). Aristotle's observation, if true, would certainly explain why a small part of a seed would move a smaller amount of air than a larger volume of seed(s) and thus why the small part would make a softer sound than a larger volume. It would also explain, given Aristotle's understanding of physics and physiology, why no sound would be detectable by us when the small piece hit the ground: between the low intensity of the movements (we would say vibrations) of air, and the limitations of our hearing, we do not detect any sound when a seed or small piece of a seed hits the ground. With respect to the physical knowledge he has, Aristotle offers a reasonable explanation as to how the impact of a tiny object could produce no sound (in the sense of no effect on our hearing or on anything's hearing) while the impact of an aggregation of those same objects could produce a sound.

Yet Aristotle has not thereby entirely disarmed Zeno's challenge to the Eleatic Principle. If we accept Aristotle's explanation of sound production, we accept that all impacts move air, but also that there is a certain threshold of air movement below which no sound is produced.¹² Let us also accept, for the sake of argument, that something counts as a sound if it can be heard by some animal (not necessarily by a human). Then either all falling objects affect the air by moving it and a sensitive enough ear could perceive a sound in any arbitrarily small motion of air; or there is a threshold below which air movement is produced but is insufficient to be heard by the most sensitive possible ear. In either case, there will be some movements of air that do not affect the ears (do not result in sounds audible) for some animal; yet aggregates of those movements will affect the ears. There will be some movements of objects that do not affect the ears enough to be heard, while movements of aggregates of those objects will be audible. In other words, there will be things that affect other things while being composed of components that do not affect others in the same way.

3 Parmenides

In DK 28B2–B8.49, Parmenides' goddess presents arguments to the effect that if anything is, it must be unique, not lacking, and without motion or change. If what-is (τὸ ἐόν) is as the goddess says it must be on the road of inquiry she recommends in B8.1–49, then what is can neither affect nor be affected. The Eleatic Principle is therefore inconsistent with the recommended road of inquiry.

There is also no evidence for any embrace of the Eleatic Principle in the fragments of the goddess's discussion of mortals' untrustworthy opinions about what is.¹³ Mortals, she announces, believe that all is Light, Night, and composites of these. In the surviving fragments, however, the goddess says nothing in particular regarding mortals' beliefs about any relationship between being on the one hand, and affecting or being affected on the other.¹⁴

---

12   Thus some types of things such as wool or sponges, Aristotle thinks, will not produce sound when they move through air or water, or collide in air or water (*On the Soul* 419b4ff). He holds that their shape and texture are not conducive to reverberation. This is not to deny that it would be possible to configure these materials to produce sound, e.g., by felting the wool or packing the sponges into dense bales.

13   Although the extant fragments that discuss the opinions of mortals do not express support for the Eleatic Principle, Aristotle's and Theophrastus's interpretation of that part of Parmenides' work does imply some relationship to that principle. I discuss this below.

14   Another major divergence between Parmenides and the Stoics is that like Melissus, Parmenides does not insist that what is must have, or be, body. In fact, much of what is said about what-is in the goddess's discussion of the recommended road of inquiry seems to be incompatible with body. Parmenides does offer an account of body in terms of mortals' opinions. But he demonstrates the flaws in these opinions, such that mortals' notions

B *Convergences: Parmenides, Melissus, and the Eleatic Principle*

Like Melissus, Parmenides' goddess holds that nothing can come from what-is-not (or from nothing). While no arguments in support of this position survive in the fragments of Melissus, there are some in the fragments of Parmenides. The goddess argues that nothing can come from what-is-not or from nothing because in what-is-not there could be no reason why something would come to be at one time rather than another, and nothing from which to spring (B8.6–13). She also argues that nothing can come to be in addition to what-is (8.19–21, 31–33, 36–37), and that what-is cannot perish.

These arguments suggest that if something is not, it has no power or effect; and that what-is does not result in what-is-not. What-is-not is not the effect or result of something that what-is does, nor is it an effect or result of the perishing of what-is. Someone who accepts the Eleatic Principle must accept that what-is-not has no power and is not the result of some application of a power. In this respect, the Eleatic Principle fits with some arguments by Eleatic philosophers.

Significantly, though, Parmenides' goddess argues for a point that is essentially the *inverse* of the first conjunct of the Eleatic Principle. Whereas the first conjunct is that

> If something is, then that thing has the power to affect and/or to be affected,

Parmenides' goddess argues that

> If something is not, then it does not have the power to affect or to be affected.

The Stoics would certainly have accepted this inverse. However, the truth of the inverse of a proposition does not imply the truth of the original proposition: the truth of "If the streets are dry, it is not raining" does not imply the truth of "If the streets are not dry, it is raining." Still, the fact that Parmenides articulated this inverse of part of the Eleatic Principle could be part of the reason why the Eleatic Visitor articulates the principle. That is, the Visitor might

---

about what it is to have a body are not compatible with the implications of the claim that something is. As was the case with Melissus, the arguments in Parmenides that oppose the Eleatic Principle do not depend on the claim that what-is does not have body. As noted above, the Eleatic Principle neither depends on nor implies a claim that what-is has or is body.

be proposing a sort of variant or further development of what the historical Parmenides discussed.

As for the second conjunct,

> If something has the power to affect and/or to be affected, then that thing is,

we have seen that Melissus argues against this conjunct, and Parmenides' goddess argues that on a viable road of inquiry, we must say and conceive of what-is in a way that makes this conjunct impossible.

However, the section of Parmenides' goddess's speech that concerns the opinions of mortals offers two other possible roots for the Eleatic Principle. First, according to the goddess mortals claim that everything is Light, Night, or some blending of these.[15] Light, says the goddess, is lightweight, mild, fiery, and probably motile (αἰθέριον in 8.56 may mean that it rises); Night is heavy, dense, obscure, and in every way opposite to Light (B8.56–59). Therefore the goddess's Light and Night are not simply light and night, but rather, as Curd has termed them, "enantiomorphic" forms, that together incorporate or produce all observable characteristics of things.[16]

In the view the goddess attributes to mortals, Light and Night evidently do not affect themselves or one another in the sense of causing alteration of qualities or quantities.[17] However, Light and Night alone are responsible for the characteristics, motions, and changes that observable things seem to mortals to have. Thus in the goddess's characterization, Light and Night are for mortals that which is, and are the sole sources of all motions, changes, and characteristics of things. They are that which affects anything in so far as that thing can be affected; nothing else has any effects. The things that are have the characteristics and possibilities they do because of Light and Night, and only because of the Light and Night in them. Although nothing in the extant fragments indicates that mortals articulated the Eleatic Principle—we have no indication that the goddess claimed that mortals thought that *only* what can affect or be

---

15   B8.51–61, B9, and probably B16.1. This blending is not of matter and form, and nothing suggests that it would allow Light and Night to occupy exactly the same location at the same time.

16   Enantiomorphs: Curd 2004, 107ff.; supporting all observable characteristics of things: Cherubin 2005, 4–9.

17   If χωρὶς ἀλλήλων in B8.56 means that Light and Night must be spatially separate, so that any blending is a matter of arranging bits of each without changing the characteristics of these bits, then Light and Night do affect one another in the limited sense that they can push one another out of a space, or prevent one another from occupying the space.

affected *can* be, or that that which is *must* be able to affect or to be affected—it appears that the Light-Night conception is consistent with the Eleatic Principle.

If Aristotle and Theophrastus are accurate in their understanding of Parmenides B16, there is a second possible root of the Eleatic Principle to be found in Parmenides' account of the opinions of mortals. Aristotle and Theophrastus take the passage to be part of an account of sensation whereby being affected by Light and/or Night is the cause of sensation. According to this account, Light in a human body is affected only by Light in the environment, and Night in the body is affected only by Night. Theophrastus reports that Parmenides held that a dead person perceives cold and silence, but cannot perceive light, heat, or sound; for fire has left him/her (*De sensibus* 1.4, DK 28A46). The connection to the Eleatic Principle, then, would be that only Light and Night have the capacity to affect anything or to be affected. Sensation is a matter of being affected; and only Light and Night in the body have the capacity to be affected (and only such that Light in the body is affected by Light and Night in the body is affected by Night).

II   Aristotle's Hylomorphism, Stoic Blends, and Eleatic Arguments

Dr. Marmodoro illustrates several ways in which Stoic conceptions of matter and form differ from Aristotle's. First, she proposes a striking account of Stoic assertions that bodies can be colocated, that two bodies can occupy exactly the same place at the same time. She finds in the Stoics two kinds of colocation: that of the blending of ὕλη and πνεῦμα, and that which is at work in the blending of everyday things such as water and wine (pages 8 and 13-14). In both types, according to Dr. Marmodoro's proposals, the Stoics held in effect that any arbitrarily small portion (or area) of such a mixture would contain some of each ingredient. That is, any arbitrarily small droplet of sea water, or any arbitrarily small region of a sea, would contain both salt and water. This, Dr. Marmodoro proposes, is a conception that the Stoics supported with a notion that "the parts of the blended substances ... each [approach] zero extension" (7).[18]

Though "Stoic Blends" does not explore the point, it is worth noting that Aristotle would not have accepted the claim that two distinct and independent

---

18   Her term 'zero extension' is modern; but nothing in Dr. Marmodoro's essay attributes a notion of zero to the Stoics. The phrase 'no magnitude,' according to Simplicius found as early as Zeno of Elea, seems to me to express the notion in question, without loss of meaning.

bodies can occupy exactly the same primary place at the same time (*Physics* 209a6 and following).[19] For Aristotle, in contrast to the Stoics, the form or formula of a thing (τὸ τί ἦν εἶναι, λόγος) is not itself a body. Nor is matter by itself a body. Therefore Aristotle's account of bodies as having matter and form does not require that multiple mutually independent bodies occupy the same primary place. That is, he allows that two things may occupy the same primary place if one thing is a part or attribute of the other: If my body is in a primary place, then my blood, my knowledge of music, and my eye color are in that place (210a25–b8). But none of these are (currently) separate and independent of my body.

Nor would Aristotle have accepted the claim that there are extensionless parts of anything of magnitude (231a21–232a17). This is not exactly the same as rejecting the claims that Dr. Marmodoro attributes to the Stoics, namely, that the parts of things *approach* no-magnitude, and that this means that more than one such part can occupy a primary place at the same time. However, it does not seem that Aristotle would accept that there are bodies or parts of bodies that approach no-magnitude. First, Aristotle's response to Zeno's Millet Seed argument suggests that individual objects of very small magnitude may be expected to behave differently from aggregates of those tiny objects, but not that this would permit one to treat the tiny objects as entirely without magnitude or weight. Second, Aristotle argues in *Physics* A4 that no body or part of a body can be indefinitely or unlimitedly small, and that removing or dividing off pieces of definite size will eventually destroy a body (187b14 and following).[20]

The colocation thesis Dr. Marmodoro finds in Stoic thought is then all the more remarkable in light of Aristotle's detailed arguments in effective opposition, arguments the Stoics and their critics would have had available. Although Dr. Marmodoro characterizes the Stoic proposal of unlimited division of bodies as a way to "account for the coextension of bodies that would not defy any laws of physics" (page 8), Aristotle would not agree that the account defied no laws (or axioms or definitions) of physics. Therefore the question arises as to what if any the contemporary criticism was regarding this colocation thesis of the Stoics; and how if at all the Stoics responded.

As a further contrast between Aristotle's hylomorphism and that of the Stoics, Dr. Marmodoro notes that Aristotle's hylomorphism arises in large part

---

19 By axiom, the "primary place" is neither smaller nor larger than that of which it is the place, 211a2.

20 Aristotle allows for indefinitely small *magnitudes* with no minimum (207b3–16); but the fact that an object's magnitude can be divided indefinitely does not mean that the object can.

as a response to concerns raised by the Eleatics and asserts that the Stoic account does not (page 12n25). While I do not agree that Eleatic concerns could not have worked alongside theological concerns in the development of the Stoic notion of matter, this is a minor issue. More important, I think, is the nature of the response to Eleatic concerns in Aristotle's hylomorphism. I suggest this as a way of developing a hint that Dr. Marmodoro offers concerning the role of context.

Specifically, Aristotle introduces form and matter in his discussion of the ἐπιστήμη concerning φύσις, demonstrable knowledge of that which has in itself a principle of motion and of staying still.[21] An ἐπιστήμη must not include contradictions. In fact, all ἐπιστῆμαι have in common an axiom of non-contradiction (*Metaphysics* 1005b18–34). Form and matter are two of the four ways in which causes, αἰτίαι, are said. We invoke them, Aristotle says, in order to account for distinctions between things, and for motions and changes—which are precisely what the Eleatics argue that we cannot do without producing contradictions and incoherencies.

Aristotle's response to this is neither to argue that there really are multiple things, some of which move; nor to insist that it is simply unconditionally the case that there are multiple things, some of which move. Rather, he says that in the investigation of the ἐπιστήμη concerning φύσις, we assume (ὑποκείσθω) that there are things that move, and that this is clear from induction (ἐπαγωγή; *Physics* 185a12–14). And he notes that someone who, with the Eleatics, investigates whether what-is is one and unmoving are simply not inquiring about φύσις, just as someone who does away with the principles of geometry cannot inquire into geometry. In other words, Aristotle does not claim that it is either proven or axiomatic that there are things that move or change or stay still.

This adds a dimension to Dr. Marmodoro's observation that Aristotle's form and matter are "contextual," as are what the Stoics designate by those terms (page 11n20). That is, Aristotle's form and matter are contextual in an additional way that the Stoics' versions are not. This way is informed by his engagement with the Eleatics, the first philosophers known to have used deductive arguments, to have applied principles of non-contradiction, and to have investigated what-is *qua* what-is (if not in a way Aristotle could embrace).

For Aristotle, matter is necessary "by hypothesis" (ἐξ ὑποθέσεως ... ἀναγκαῖον, *Physics* 200a13–15 with 30–32). That is, there is no specific entity or kind of thing that must be matter, or that is matter unconditionally, or that is the

---

21   *Physics* 192b13–15 with 194b23ff. Form and matter appear of course in the *Metaphysics* as well, also as ways in which the "why" of things' identity, distinction, and motion or change are said (983a24–33).

matter of all things considered from the point of view of all sciences. Letters are the matter of syllables, and hypotheses the matter of conclusions, as much as bronze or stone is the matter of a statue (195a16 and following). Similarly, the form of a thing could be a number, a ratio, a shape, or whatever is defining or functions as a formula within a particular ἐπιστήμη. What functions as a formula in one ἐπιστήμη may not function that way in another. The defining characteristics of a human in, say, psychology, would not be the same as those in biology; and these are what Aristotle would identify as form.

If a bronze disk becomes dented and loses its circular shape, Melissus's or Parmenides' goddess would say that its circularity has been destroyed. They would infer that this requires us to say that the circularity is not, or that it has perished into nothing; and they would say that this involves a contradiction. Aristotle's physics provides a way to avoid this conclusion: the formula of a circle has not been destroyed when the disk changed shape, nor has the formula of the new shape come to be from nothing. They are eternal geometrical formulae.[22] A science of physics can be developed to the extent that any change (μεταβολή) one wants to explicate can also be represented as a motion (κίνησις, *Physics* 190b5–191a10, 191b10–30). That is, changes include coming-to-be and perishing, as well as motions; motions include locomotion, increase, decrease, and alteration (*Physics* 224b35–225b9). Any change that had to be described as an absolute generation or destruction would have no causal explanation, and thus could not be accounted for within the ἐπιστήμη of physics. We can explain the generation and destruction of the bronze disk within that science, for example, in so far as we do so in terms of the locomotions, increases, decreases, and alterations of the bronze.

In this way Aristotle's attention to Eleatic scruples informs his hylomorphism. This point is not new. But what Dr. Marmodoro's paper has now enabled us to see is the intimate connection between that attention, the radically contextualized aspect of Aristotelian hylomorphism, and the fundamental incompatibility of Aristotle's hylomorphism with the Stoic account. Dr. Marmodoro's work sheds very valuable and much-needed light on what is gained and what lost in the Stoics' move away from Aristotelian physics, metaphysics, and consequently epistemology.

---

22   It is quite possible that this would not satisfy Melissus's or Parmenides' goddess. "Yes, the geometrical formula was not destroyed when the disk was dented," they might say. "But the circular shape *of that disk*: what happened to that? It was before, you said; and now?"

COLLOQUIUM 1

Marmodoro/Cherubin Bibliography

Armstrong, D.M. 1978. *Universals and Scientific Realism.* Vol. 1: *Nominalism and Realism.* Cambridge: Cambridge University Press.

Apostle, H.G., tr. 1980. *Aristotle, Physics.* Grinnell: The Peripatetic Press.

Bailey, D.T.J. 2014. The Structure of Stoic Metaphysics. *Oxford Studies in Ancient Philosophy* XLVI:253–309.

Cherubin, R. 2005. Light, Night, and the Opinions of Mortals: Parmenides B8.51–61 and B9. *Ancient Philosophy* 25:1–23.

Cooper, J. 2014. Chrysippus on Physical Elements. In *God and Cosmos in Stoicism*, ed. R. Salles, 93–117. Oxford: Oxford University Press.

Curd, P. 2004. *The Legacy of Parmenides: Eleatic Monism and Later Presocratic Thought.* 2d ed. Las Vegas, NV: Parmenides Publishing.

De Harven, V. Stoic incorporeals: a grounded account (unpublished manuscript).

Diels, H., with W. Kranz. 1951. *Die Fragmente der Vorsokratiker.* 6th ed. Berlin: Weidmann.

Fine, K. 1998. Mixing Matters. *Ratio* XI:278–88.

Fowler, H.N., tr. 1921. *Plato VII: Theaetetus, Sophist.* The Loeb Classical Library. Cambridge: Harvard University Press.

Graham, D.W. 2010. *The Texts of Early Greek Philosophy: The Complete Fragments and Selected Testimonies of the Major Presocratics.* Vol. 1. Cambridge, UK: Cambridge University Press.

Jaeger, W., ed. 1957. *Aristotle, Metaphysica.* Oxford: Clarendon Press.

Judson, L., and V. Karasmanes, eds. 2006. *Remembering Socrates: philosophical essays.* Oxford: Clarendon Press.

Lamb, W.R.M., tr. 1925. *Plato III: Lysis, Symposium, Gorgias.* The Loeb Classical Library. Cambridge: Harvard University Press.

Leonard, M. 2014. Locating Gunky Water and Wine. *Ratio* 27.3:306–315.

Long, A.A., and D. Sedley, eds. 1987. *The Hellenistic Philosophers.* Cambridge: Cambridge University Press.

Marmodoro, A. (Forthcoming). *Everything in Everything. An essay on Anaxagoras' Metaphysics.* Oxford: Oxford University Press.

Nolan, D. 2006. Stoic gunk. *Phronesis* 51.2:162–183.

Oddie, G. 1982. Armstrong on the Eleatic Principle and Abstract Entities. *Philosophical Studies: An International Journal for Philosophy in the Analytic Tradition* 41:285–95.

Palmer, J.A. 2009. *Parmenides and Presocratic Philosophy.* Oxford: Oxford University Press.

Parson, J. 2007. Theories of Location. *Oxford Studies in Metaphysics* 3:201–232.

Ross, W.D., ed. 1950. *Aristotle, Physica.* Oxford: Clarendon Press.
Salles, R., ed. 2009. *God and Cosmos in Stoicism.* Oxford: Oxford University Press.
Scaltsas, T. 2006. Sharing a Property. In *Remembering Socrates: philosophical essays.* Ed, L. Judson and V. Karasmanes, eds. Oxford: Clarendon Press.
Sider, D., and H.W. Johnstone, eds. 1986. *The Fragments of Parmenides.* Bryn Mawr Greek Commentaries. Bryn Mawr: Thomas Library, Bryn Mawr College.
Sider T. 1993. Van Inwagen and the Possibility of Gunk. *Analysis* 53:285–9.
Stratton, G.M., tr. 1917. *Theophrastus and the Greek Physiological Psychology before Aristotle.* London: G. Allen & Unwin.
Varzi, A. 2015. Mereology. In *The Stanford Encyclopedia of Philosophy (Winter 2015 Edition)*, ed. E.N. Zalta, <http://plato.stanford.edu/archives/win2015/entries/mereology/>.
Vogt, K. 2009. Sons of the Earth: Are the Stoics Metaphysical Brutes? *Phronesis* 54:36–154.

COLLOQUIUM 2

Telling Good Love from Bad in Plato's *Phaedrus*

Nickolas Pappas
City College and the Graduate Center, City University of New York

Abstract

When the *Phaedrus* produces an account of *eros* that goes beyond earlier oversimplifying terms, it rests its analysis on a distinction between human and divine. The dialogue's attempts to articulate this distinction repeatedly fail. In part they rest on the difference between right and left, but in ways that problematize that difference as well. In the end this difficulty in definition casts a shadow over the prospect of the effective reciprocation of love, because the loved one will not be able to tell the difference between a lover in pursuit crazed by divine *eros* and the lover who is crazed in the ordinary and destructive fashion.

Keywords

Plato – *Phaedrus* – *eros* – divine – lefthandedness

I

Socrates has a feel for the holy.[1] Would you say a nose for it? That would be a species of misstatement or misunderstanding, although what exactly is being misstated in reference to the sacred is not always easy to articulate.

Regarding the feeling: Consider a moment when Socrates and Phaedrus have settled themselves to talk about *eros*, after a walk in the Athenian exterior. (Not quite the exterior, this being still part of Athens; but they are outside the city walls. They are in the part of Athens that has been designated something

---

[1] I am grateful to the audience that heard this paper and replied to it so thoughtfully at Boston College in November 2015; above all to Deborah De Chiara-Quenzer for her comment; but also very much to C. Wesley DeMarco, Gary Gurtler, Robert Kubala, Marina McCoy, and May Sim. Among other things, their remarks helped me keep my discussion focused not only on the good and bad in love but specifically on the line between divine and mundane.

© KONINKLIJKE BRILL NV, LEIDEN, 2017 | DOI 10.1163/22134417-00321P05

beyond Athens.) After embarking on his first speech, Socrates interrupts himself. Doesn't it seem that he is experiencing a θεῖον, "divine," passion? This place they have come to is really θεῖος (*Phaedrus* 238c).

After all, *eros* is a god, and if you want to produce a theory about love you will need an eye or ear for godly things. Phaedrus holds back from attending to divinities. So we find Socrates sensitizing him to the otherworldly. It will be the only way to get the young man past the erotic analyses he has been hearing from Lysias. Take the attitude that Phaedrus expresses early in their walk through the countryside, when they pass the spot where Boreas the north wind is said to have seized the Athenian girl Oreithuia. "Tell me Socrates," Phaedrus says, "do you believe this story is true?" (*Phdr.* 229c).[2]

Not believing the story is true means translating it into a rationalized alternative. A gust of wind might have blown the young woman off a cliff. But Socrates has more important things to do than go through every myth replacing godly acts with natural happenstances. His question turns inward. Is he wild as the earthborn monster Typho was said to be, or some other kind of creature, tame and simple (*Phdr.* 230a)?

His reply indicates the kind of enterprise that Socrates will undertake in the *Phaedrus*. First of all, he keeps his distance from scientific theories that his contemporaries found engaging, as he also does in that interlude in the *Phaedo* in which he recounts his disappointment with the materialism of Anaxagoras (*Phaedo* 97b–99d). And second, as also in that other passage, he wants to know himself and the actions he may expect to perform.

There is a third similarity between the passages that creates difficulties. In the *Phaedo* Socrates does not content himself with rejecting cosmologies, but tries to enlarge the theory of forms so that it can generate causal explanations rivaling those proffered by Anaxagoras (*Phd.* 105b–c). He seeks to replace the Anaxagorean theory, not merely to refute it. And in the *Phaedrus*, as the mention of Typho shows, Socrates will not content himself with rejecting naturalistic theories in favor of the old myths. By itself such religious conservatism will only preserve the mythic as it has been known thus far, and *that* mythic is not the same as the divine. Typho is mythic, but not the divinity that Socrates wants to discover within himself. Typho belongs to the earth and Socrates has turned his attention to heaven. It is in this respect, and not in any stuffy traditionalism, that Socrates wants to bring Phaedrus to detect the divine.

---

2 All translations from the *Phaedrus* are my own, although they have been considerably guided by the Nehamas/Woodruff translation (Nehamas and Woodruff 1995) and informed by Harvey Yunis's text and commentary (Yunis 2011).

The enterprise sounds more formidable when you describe it like that. How does Socrates turn Phaedrus's attention toward a divine realm unlike the one that Greek myths had already spoken of?

Boreas himself, however erotic his behavior may be, and despite his being a god, will not show the way to godly *eros*. Boreas seized Oreithuia by force, and the Athenians who built the altar in his honor that Socrates refers to (*Phdr.* 229c) and who re-tell the story of Oreithuia, do not merely accept this aggressiveness in his *eros* but celebrate it. Plato would have known from reading Herodotus, even if it were no longer common knowledge, that the Athenians took themselves to have been rescued by Boreas in 480, when a storm near Thessaly destroyed hundreds of ships of the Persian fleet.[3] As Karim Arafat proposes, the rape of Oreithuia would have been seen not as an embarrassing further act by an otherwise admirable deity but as a further manifestation of the same behavior the Athenians admired and thanked that deity for (Arafat 1997). Not to put too fine a point on it, Boreas fucked those Persians. It is in character for him to have abducted Oreithuia.

Even this splendid spot that Socrates and Phaedrus come to and sit in reminds those familiar with divine matters—familiar, I should say, with what the Greeks took divinity to be—of the dangers in *eros*. Socrates takes pious note of the shrines and calls his fluency in speech the work of nymphs (*Phdr.* 238c–d), and later hears the chirp of cicadas as a tribute to benevolent Muses (258e–259d). But as Bruce Thornton reminds us, the great erotic abductions of Greek mythology took place in just such bucolic settings. Hades burst out of the ground to seize Persephone from a beautiful floral meadow. While Creusa picked crocuses, Apollo came to rape her. Socrates speaks of the πλάτανος "plane tree" under which he and Phaedrus are sitting, and we might smile at the echo of Plato's name in the tree's. But if we can trust the testimony of later authors, it was under a plane tree that Zeus raped Europa.[4]

II

How do you keep the divine in view and still maintain a distance from the compromised divinity found in the mythological tradition? After they have

---

3 *Histories* 7.189.1–3. Oreithuia is part of the reason that the Athenians believe themselves to be protected by Boreas, now their γαμβρός "son-in-law" (*Hist.* 7.189.2).

4 The threat of rape and abuse (Thornton 1997, 4). Persephone picking flowers, *Homeric Hymn to Demeter* 5–14; Creusa picking crocuses, Euripides *Ion* 889 ff.; Socrates under plane tree, *Phaedrus* 229a; Zeus and Europa under plane tree, Theophrastus *History of Plants* 1.9.3, Pliny *Natural History* 12.5.

settled themselves to talk, Socrates will confront this challenge as he seeks out what he can call rightly divine in *eros*, and in the soul that experiences divine *eros*.

The soul and its desiring are both treated at length in what is known as the great speech of Socrates (*Phdr.* 244a–257b). Socrates introduces this speech as the work of the recanting poet Stesichorus, whom he calls the son of Euphemus (εὔφημος), in other words the son of the good thing to say, the good omen (244a). Stesichorus will be the father of this speech; and in accord with the Greek practice of naming a first son after his father's father, this *logos* itself may be called a euphemism, in the sense of being the propitious thing to say about love.

For Socrates the first announcement to make when speaking propitiously of divinities is that μανία, "madness," is not always bad. Madness brings the greatest goods for human beings when it has been divinely bestowed upon us (*Phdr.* 244a). Later in the dialogue, looking back on the speech to identify its merits, Socrates clarifies that they found two εἴδη, "species, kinds" of madness, the one caused by human illness and the other one θεία (265a, b). They chanced upon this distinction, he says in retrospect (265c). It would be nice if they could have made this point by means of a *techne*, "skill, professional knowledge" (265d).

Nice indeed. For if you did have a *techne*, I take it, then you could tell the unfortunate madness that makes someone a Typho from the divinely granted μανία that goes with being a better creature. For that matter you could distinguish the poet possessed by Muses (*Phdr.* 245a), whom I believe we can equate with the μουσικός (248d), from the other poet mentioned in the great speech, the mimetic poet who ranks sixth among the nine grades of embodied souls (248e).

And whether or not all nine ranks of embodied souls identified in the speech align with the presence or absence of divine madness in them, I think the two extreme ranks of the nine do correspond to the two kinds of *eros* that Socrates sets apart. Surely that "erotic" soul in the top rank experiences the god-given love (*Phdr.* 248d). Just as surely, the lowest-ranking type, the tyrant (248e), will feel and act upon bad and unbridled desire. Book IX of the *Republic* associates the tyrant with uncontrolled deviant sexuality, as do ancient traditions independent of Plato: the tales about Oedipus but also about Periander of Corinth, said to have committed incest with his mother.[5] So the skill or art of distin-

---

5 Tyrant in Plato, *Republic* IX, 571c–d; Periander, Diogenes Laertius *Lives of Eminent Philosophers* 1.96. Laius, who as father of Oedipus may be said to have introduced the essence of tyranny to Athenians, was also said to have brought about the horrors associated with his dynasty when he raped young Chrysippus.

guishing divinely mad souls from those that are mad in a bad sense should apply directly to telling a tyrant from a philosopher on one hand, from a legitimate king on the other (*Phdr.* 248d).

I also note that the act of dividing a genus into species (particularly when there are two species per genus) is illustrated at length in Plato's *Sophist* and *Statesman*. The *Statesman* puts the method to work distinguishing constitutional forms from one another. Telling the difference is a standard task for the one who studies constitutions. In language that evokes the *Phaedrus,* for example, the Stranger in Plato's *Statesman* separates monarchy from tyranny and aristocracy from oligarchy. In the latter case, "We call the one with a good name [εὐώνυμος] aristocracy; and there is oligarchy."[6] This is literally true about aristocracy, given that there is no better word than ἄριστος, "best," and ἀριστοκρατία, "the sovereignty of the best," is as good a name as a constitutional form could have. The dialectical act called division thus finds the difference between two political forms that superficially resemble each other.

But the word εὐώνυμος also has a religious sense, suggesting "good omen" as εὔφημος does, and we are back at the task of detecting the divine. And if the divine is not marked by its appearance in received stories of divinity, where will we find it?

The *Phaedrus* applies a steady pressure to this question, whether with the familiar Platonic appeal to vision or in its surprising extended imagery of wings. Regarding vision, Socrates calls beauty the form that humans perceive, a fact that makes the eye both part of the body and a point of contact with divine realities that outshine the body. In the same spirit we find the *Timaeus* calling the human head the θειότατον "most divine" part of the body (*Timaeus* 44d). Timaeus says that the neck shields the soul that is in the head from the mortal parts that have been housed further down (69e). The *Timaeus* pictures a soul distributed among the regions of the body, the most troublesome part in the most bodily "women's quarters" below the diaphragm (68e–70a), so that the head looks like a portico into the body. As the repository of the sense organs—the eyes especially, again (47e)—the head is also the threshold that leads out toward the divine.

The *Phaedrus* places analogous emphasis on the wing. One passage introduces the idea that the soul is winged, justifying this claim with the remark that the wing "communes with the divine more than anything else having to do with the body does" (*Phdr.* 246d–e). Bodies are things that fall, but wings draw them upward. Because ἔρως is divine, it's no wonder that Socrates makes the

---

6 Plato *Statesman*: separating constitutional forms, e.g., 291e; the εὐώνυμος one aristocracy, 302d.

wing its essence, etymologizing a connection between ἔρωτα and πτέρωτα, "winged, feathered" (252c).

If the reasoning appears to be paradoxical, consider it the inversion of a familiar habit of thinking that sets one body part aside as *least* divine. The wing of the soul, for all the unforgettable attributes that commentators have pointed out—rigidity, sensitivity, moistness (*Phdr.* 251b–d)—is meant to work not as phallic but as the opposite of a phallus, for it succeeds at the task at which the phallus failed. In Plato's time the flaps of an armored man's cuirass that covered his groin were known as πτέρυγες "wings."[7] As those winglets do, the wing of the soul covers the groin's organ, even if as a result the two things end up conceptually close together. The wing covers the penis as a euphemism covers the true nature of an object. Like a word for "worse" that appears to be saying "better," it signifies in two directions at once.

III

The wing as erotic soul-organ exemplifies the struggle that is enacted in all these examples—eye, head, location—what you may call the paradox of demarcating the otherworldly within the world. The struggle to perform that demarcation resembles the skeptic's predicament, as Stanley Cavell diagnoses it, of sometimes reasoning as though you could point to the occluded part of an object—flip side of an envelope; far side of the tomato—saying "This is the part you don't see" (Cavell 1979, 201). Special energies are enlisted in the task of identifying the *other* to experience by means of one more experience. For example: being as they are both in and beyond the body, the eyes belong metonymically among the unreliable senses but metaphorically alongside faculties of abstract thinking. Thus, the eye is a bodily thing that belongs among better things. The head in the *Timaeus* possesses the solidity of bone while also serving as the furthest reach of the body into divine realms.

I do not take myself to be showing that intermediary stages exist between the bodily and the heavenly, the head higher than the abdomen though beneath the disembodied soul. On the contrary, the *Phaedrus*'s divisions do not permit shades or grades. Socrates never allows for degrees of divinity in madness, only for the presence or absence in it of divinity. The *Phaedrus* presents a conceptual gulf between this realm and the other being marked within the area known as mundane; as if the body's world were more than itself,

---

7 Thus see Xenophon *On Horsemanship* 12.4; *Anabasis* 4.7.15.

somewhat as (I offer this only by way of analogy) the skeptic's experience includes that unseen far side of fruit that has been set outside experience.

Diotima in the *Symposium* does propose a continuous ascent, which you may call an ascent to heaven, from vulgar love to the best variety (*Symposium* 210a–211d). But in this regard the *Phaedrus* shares its goals rather with the myth that Aristophanes tells, for it makes *eros* a recuperative return to one's original state, which reads as a prenatal state.[8] The soul really belongs in the bodiless realm, and divine love takes it there, while love that is ordinary craziness fails to. There may be many stages along one's progress toward a new goal like the *Symposium*'s Form of Beauty. When you are returning home, you've either arrived or you haven't.

Even as an absolute distinction, the difference between divine and not-divine is easier to articulate at some times than at others. The eye does differ from the tongue. The wing's oppositeness to the phallus can be put into words. But Socrates' language about division gives another version of this struggle with thoughts, maybe its utmost formulation. He equates the drawing of distinctions with "being able to cut at the joints."[9] A species divides, as bodies do, into pairs of things that go by the same name: left and right thigh, left and right shank, and so on. In his own discussion of madness and love, Socrates says (looking back at that discussion later in their conversation), he cut away the madness ἐπ'ἀριστερὰ, "on the left," and divided that further till he found σκαιόν τινα ἔρωτα, "a gauche kind of love." The other speech searched through the right-hand μανία and discovered within it an *eros* that went by the same name, which is to say "love," but was θεῖον (*Phdr.* 266a).

We should resist the temptation to nod (in the sense of nodding at the familiar) at the valuation of right over left, or at the customary association of

---

8   There is no space here for the argument (only for a promise to make the argument elsewhere) that the myth told by Aristophanes is an allegory of childbirth. The pregnant mother with her baby inside is indeed a round creature possessing a total of four arms, four legs, and two similar faces; the navel we can look down upon is indeed, as in the myth, a reminder showing where we used to be connected to someone else. This means that true *eros* must be love for one's mother; an implication that heightens the irrationality, unsociability, and general impermissibility of the *eros* Aristophanes is describing. Plato's answer in the *Phaedrus* is that Aristophanes has misinterpreted birth, which is not about leaving the mother's body but about leaving the land of souls for one's own body.

9   *Phdr.* 265e. The metaphor makes a second and less specific appearance in Plato's *Statesman*, during a discussion of the *technai* that compete with the expertise of the legitimate king. Regarding those *technai* the Stranger says, "Let's distinguish them [διαιρώμεθα] into members [κατὰ μέλη] as we would with an animal for sacrifice [ἱερεῖον]" (*Stat.* 287c).

that valuation, in Greek thought, with Pythagorean principles.[10] Aristotle does tell us that the Pythagoreans set right favorably against left, as they set male against female and odd against even, and so on.[11] Nevertheless, Plato is not reflexively repeating after Pythagoras here: first because he does not always do so; second because of this passage's stress on same-named items; and because the *Phaedrus* harps on this talk of left and right; and for other reasons.

First of all the appeal to left and right is sufficiently meaningful as a reference to religious practice not to need Pythagorean explanation. Here and in the *Statesman*, cutting at the joints is what an officiant does with an animal being sacrificed. In that context, parts of the animal's right side not only could be distinguished from the left but had to be, as when the right thighbone was dedicated to the gods, or was the share assigned to the priest (Forstenpointner 2003, Gill 1974).[12]

Second, Plato does not always follow the Pythagoreans in opposing left to right. Although Aristotle shares the Pythagoreans' valuation of right over left, he considers them to be strangely fixated on those two directions to the exclusion of other dimensional oppositions.[13] Plato more often speaks as Aristotle does, treating left and right on a par with up and down or front and back.[14] This is not to mention the *Laws*'s advocacy of ambidextrous training. Pythagorean the idea may well be, but Plato did not take it over unthinkingly.

The repeated word ὁμώνυμος in this passage, "homonymous, having the same name," heightens the significance of left and right as something more than words for bad and good. The process that Socrates calls division here is

---

10 In saying this I specifically take issue with David Sider, who made this reply to me in his seminar (spring 2015) on *Symposium* and *Phaedrus*. My small disagreement is not meant to detract from the many ways in which we agreed or from the countless points at which I learned from Professor Sider.

11 Aristotle: *Metaphysics* A 5, 986a24; *De Caelo* II 2, 284b6; 285b23.

12 A parallel is sometimes proposed between Greek animal sacrifice and the Semitic rituals described in Leviticus 8. See the emphasis on the right hand at Leviticus 8.22–29, and especially the right thighbone at 8.26.

13 Aristotle agreeing with Pythagoreans: *Parts of Animals* III 3 665a26, which calls up superior to down, front to back, and right to left in animal bodies. Aristotle on their fixation on left and right, *Cael.* II.2, 285a10.

14 Thus at *Parmenides* 129c, Socrates repeats an argument that "divides" a body into six; and the Myth of Er (*Rep.* X, 614c) visualizes souls labeled either just (on their fronts) and marched upward to the right for reward, or (on their backs) unjust, heading down and left for punishment, so that the three positively valued directions coincide in one case and the negatively valued directions in the other.

binary, as Platonic subdivisions of genera often are not.[15] There are dialogues that draw two-way divisions wherever possible, but that process yields distinct subcategories. Here Socrates has his eye on a mode of distinction in which the items distinguished are also seen as indiscernible. Madness divides into madness and madness. Where people once spoke loosely of love, *we* philosophizing *now* will speak of both love and its homonym love.

The nearest parallels to such a subdividing act appear in Plato's *Statesman*. When the Stranger divides number into odd and even, the resulting species will resemble each other considerably, although no one would mistake odd numbers for even. And in politics, the Stranger says, rule by the majority is called democracy in all cases, although one has to divide it into two forms, both called the same thing, but one governing according to law and the other lawlessly. This example is close to the distinction between madnesses and loves, but nowhere near as consequential. In an orderly world democracy is a shabby system even when it's lawful, having value only as the best constitution for a lawless world.[16] The homonymous subdivision does not give us two classes of opposite status, and surely not in the way divine and mundane are opposite.

In the *Phaedrus* the homonymy of subspecies calls for the words left and right, evoking the challenge that children face in telling their hands apart. Children don't go through a process of learning to tell up from down. But left things and right things are indistinguishable. That is their nature, or rather it is the nature of left and right. For this reason Kant (1768) will famously call a right and left glove "incongruent counterparts," which define different spaces despite the identity of all internal relations within the objects.

Finally I said that the *Phaedrus* harps on the left-right difference, to an extent that makes it implausible to explain this passage as knee-jerk Pythagoreanism. Very early in the conversation, Socrates tells Phaedrus that he sees the speech Lysias wrote hidden under Phaedrus's left arm (*Phdr.* 228d). It may

---

15 See *Euthyphro* 11e–12e on finding piety in the larger category of justice, without the expectation that justice splits in two; or *Rep.* III, 392d dividing poetic narration into narration, imitation, and the combination of the two. Let me qualify the former of these examples, for as a reader for this paper pointed out, the *Euthyphro* passage might end up leading us to a two-way division within justice. But I do not see that a two-way division is written into that passage's methodology, as it is written into the dialectical practice of the *Phaedrus*.

16 *Stat.*: number into odd and even, 262e; general methodology of equal subdivisions, 262c–d; kinds of democracy have the same name, 292a, 302d; democracy best in bad world, worst in orderly, 303a–b. I am grateful to Burt Hopkins for discussing this peculiar turn of the dialectic with me.

be obvious that an object being carried surreptitiously would go under the left arm of a man in a ἱμάτιον. But then Plato is still making Socrates state the obvious to prepare for the later classification of ordinary love as the left-handed type, that being (from what we can tell) the only type Lysias understands.[17]

The distinction reaches up into the heavens. Aristotle says the Pythagoreans taught that the heavens have left and right sides (*De Caelo* II 2, 284b6). The *Phaedrus* assumes something similar. When Socrates describes the two horses that represent the soul's non-rational parts, as those parts are observable in heavenly life before embodiment, he mainly gives the two horses contrasting features that have self-evident moral meanings (*Phdr.* 253d–e). One stands straight while the other is crooked. Socrates also puts the noble horse "ἐν τῇ καλλίονι στάσει [on the better side]" (235d), which is to say on the right. The detail adds nothing, but it does yield a difference in motion for noble and ignoble love, another preparation for the talk of butchering that will locate divinely sanctioned *eros* on the right and moving rightward. Even when separated from your body you can draw that same gulfing divide between the bodily and the heavenly.

IV

These appearances of left and right are all nothing, in a way: nothing that needs explaining. But that is just what I find worth contemplating, that left and right are the most ordinary features of experience—ordinary, that is, for creatures whose experience is only bodily; for souls at home in bodies and comfortably inhabiting the space through which the bodies navigate. The kinds of things that we have become treat left and right as "second nature" in the exact sense of that phrase. We once had natures that did not orient themselves along these directions, but once translated into the embodied world, since our nativity, we acquired this new nature. The soul in pre-existence, and souls fresh from the Mysteries, have no idea how left and right would differ and no nose for the difference.[18]

---

17   A man wrapped his ἱμάτιον, "cloak," around himself so that the left side was the place to conceal an object. But that fact only explains what side you would hide an object, not why Socrates would call that side by name. Why not just have him say "You're hiding something"? Then this same fact about wrapping a ἱμάτιον would tell the reader where the speech is hidden.

18   I should acknowledge that a cognitive condition exists known as right-left confusion. I am not commenting on that condition or its neurological causes, although I imagine that Plato would find it significant. In one group of 364 university faculty members, 19%

Nevertheless, this is the model for telling your mundane from your divine. As with the wing or eye or head, features of embodiment by means of which animals imagine disembodied divinity, Plato is pressing for new indicators of divinity, as if inventing sign language to indicate a difference that myths in their degraded form no longer do.

This mention of language brings me to the greatest difficulty with this image of discovering the divine. If telling the difference between left and right in the sense of perceiving it is hard for a bodily neophyte, telling what the difference is, telling it *to* someone, can hardly be imagined.

The Greeks had three words for "left" (Lloyd 1962). When describing dialectical division Socrates speaks of the σκαιός love, and the word sounds forced there. It is unaccustomed as a directional term, which is why I used "gauche" in translating it. In the prose and verse of Plato's time, and in generations before his, σκαιός had only metaphorical applications: crass, unlucky, clumsy, anything that was not sophisticated (Halliwell 2012, 20–21; Dover 1974, 122).[19] Despite its original reference to the spatial direction, in this passage the word provides a derivative judgment for worldly love, following some other separation into left and right.

The other two words for "left," εὐώνυμος and ἀριστερός, are euphemisms. Many classical authors use them interchangeably.[20] Plato almost never says εὐώνυμος in a directional sense, maybe because he uses that word in its literal sense of "good name" or "good omen." In the dialectical division cited above from the *Statesman*, the Eleatic Stranger calls aristocracy εὐώνυμος, but he means that as a favorable contrast with oligarchy, surely not because he would put it on the left. The issue again may come down to the body's two sides having the same names. Where two items in a distinction are called the same thing, it would scarcely make sense to set one of them aside as well named.

But we are no better off in dialectical practice with ἀριστερός, the other word that appears in this passage from the *Phaedrus*, and elsewhere in the dialogue, and generally in Plato, as the word for "left." The adjective ἀριστερός is one more euphemism. It appears to have been constructed out of ἄριστος "best," the

---

reported some difficulty, if only occasionally, in telling the difference between left and right (Harris and Gitterman 1978). In a later study involving 1,182 college students, 26 percent reported the same difficulty (Hannay *et al.* 1990). Incidentally while one of these studies shows that women are more prone to the difficulty, the other says that men are.

19 See Aristophanes *Wasps* 1013, *Frogs* 1036, *Wealth* 60; Demosthenes 6.19. In Herodotus the word appears in two passages, metaphorically in both (*Hist.* 1.129.3, 3.53.4).

20 By my count, Herodotus, to name only one, uses εὐώνυμος six times to mean "left," ἀριστερός sixteen.

superlative of ἀγαθός, together with the comparative ending—ερος, as if to say "best-er" or "very much the best."

The result is the variety of euphemism in which one does not merely play down the badness of a thing but insists on its goodness. It would be inattentive to overlook the fact that the *Phaedrus* (and not, to my knowledge, any other dialogue) draws attention to precisely this trick of language. Phaedrus tells Socrates that someone called Lysias a λογόγραφος "speechwriter." Wasn't that said to insult him (*Phdr.* 257c–d)? Socrates guides Phaedrus to the contrary thought that words can carry valences opposite to their apparent ones. Sailors on the Nile call one of its difficult turns the sweet bend in the river (257e). You would not want to say "The deadly turn is coming" and be blamed for having let out those unlucky words if the boat went on to capsize. So the Greeks might call a malicious spirit the ἀγαθός δαίμων "good spirit" to propitiate it (Burkert 1977, 181).[21] Actors today speak of the Scottish play. Without the superstitious logic, but still mindful of the harm in insulting or negative names, the father fish in Disney's *Finding Nemo* (2003) calls his son's injured fin the "lucky fin."

The ambivalence of the word for "left" is present again, or almost present, when Socrates revisits the putative term of abuse "speechwriter." How do we assess the writing of a *logos*? Socrates goes back to Egypt to ask what writing is and tells Phaedrus the memorable story of its invention (*Phdr.* 274c–275b). But in attributing cultural innovations to Egypt Plato is following Herodotus, who tells his reader how many marvels are to be found in that land. In fact he devotes a stretch of Book 2 of his *Histories* to cataloguing them. Egypt is Opposite Land. Greeks push the weft up when they weave but the Egyptians push it down, and so on (*Histories* 2.35–2.37).

And as if by way of conclusion to this review of Egyptian paradoxicalities, Herodotus describes how those people write, moving their hands from right to left (*Hist.* 2.36.4). He even adds, capping the exoticism of this land, that Egyptians do not consider their way to be reversed. "They say they move to the right and that Greeks go right to left" (whatever on earth that could mean). In the wake of Herodotus, Socrates' appeals to Egypt re-emphasize the possibility that ἀριστερός can carry opposite references, as you might expect from a word that points to the worse by meaning "very much the better."

The contrarian swerves of the word are even more visible when this apparent comparative to ἄριστος operates in a division in which the ἄριστος might appear on the other side. The word ἄριστος is common in Plato, and it is no more technical than "best" is in English. But on several occasions the *Phaedrus*

---

21   In Aristophanes, the phrase ἀγαθός δαίμων might mean exactly the opposite at *Knights* 85 and *Wasps* 525.

uses ἄριστος to identify the preferred element in an opposition. The word ἄριστος invokes the dialectical method when Socrates uses it for the best part of the soul (*Phdr.* 248b), or calls *eros* the best kind of inspiration (249e, 265b). Such uses of ἄριστος imply that carrying out a philosophical analysis will entail putting the best on one side and the other item on the side that is, you might say (in fact you *are* saying, like it or not) very much the best, ἀριστερός—as if language were baffling the task of sorting out terms. This one is excellent and its opposite is even more excellent, or bad.

(Here I also note one passage in which Socrates apparently etymologizes ἐραστὴς, "lover," into ἔρως and ἄριστος (*Phdr.* 249e). The etymology is so unpersuasive that it seems to be inviting its reader to combine "lover" and "best" in some other way; and when you do, the most natural product of ἄριστος and ἔρως is ἀριστερός.)

No wonder we wander, as Socrates says, when we use words like "just" and "good" whose meanings remain disputed (*Phdr.* 263a–b). No wonder a piece of writing rolls around, as he says, being understood in different ways and having to come back to its father seeking assistance (275e).

Incidentally, this fathering metaphor, so familiar today that it has become a cliché, is not a passing thought but recurs through the *Phaedrus*. People father words (*Phdr.* 257b, 261a, 275a). I mention fatherhood because Plato's father's name was Ariston. He has Socrates play on the meaning Ariston/*aristos* in the *Republic* (*Rep.* IX, 580b), and he would have observed the uses and inversions of ἄριστος/ἀριστερός if anything more automatically than we do. And as someone without human children Plato would have made Ariston the name of the child he did have, the philosophical dialogue, inscribed everywhere with what is best if also with what is still better.

V

When you use the world to map out the limits of the world and signs of the otherworldly, such limits on knowledge as I have been describing are inclined to reassert themselves. We've seen the point before, that the world might never allow reference to anything besides itself.

You might even prefer to read the *Phaedrus* as imparting this lesson consciously, by which we mean that Plato intends a lesson about the limits on human knowledge. In that case a protestation of ignorance is all that we can hope for and all that Plato wants us to see. The well-meaning philosopher and practitioner of a would-be rational rhetoric finds the soul that is full of right-handed love indistinguishable from the opposite soul. But then we find other psychological taxonomies stumbling over themselves in this dialogue too. There are eleven or twelve gods that souls follow around the top of heaven, but there are those nine rankings of soul that neither duplicate the differences among gods nor define an entirely different set. Depending on how you read those classificatory passages, the *Phaedrus* might be defining nine, eleven, twelve, 99, or 144 kinds of souls. (That is not even counting the division by Muses.)[22] In the end you just can't construct a philosophical psychology rich enough to inform good rhetoric, and the failed separation of good and bad kinds of love only reasserts the same limits to knowledge.

Maybe so—except that something else is also clear from the *Phaedrus*, and that is the threat of sexual abuse when love is not holy. Expertise about souls is for seducers to use, and obstacles to such knowledge matter to love mostly insofar as they interfere with the would-be lover's pursuit. The objects of seduction or abduction do not profit from distinguishing between demagogues and farmers, or telling Hermes-people from Demeter-people. They *would* benefit from knowing whether the pursuing lover is divinely touched or just one more of those predators the world is full of, and who are full of worldly thoughts.

Socrates seems able to tell the difference, for he feels the divinity at work in the spot they have come to. And everyone knows how attuned he was to the divine sign that would come to him, presumably sensing right away *that* it was divine. But even he would prefer to have a *techne* that told the difference, if only so that he can teach Phaedrus to distinguish the two kinds of love, and the two kinds of madness, from one another.[23]

Is this the problem of a school for articulating what a charismatic perceives inarticulately? Then the *techne* that Socrates lacks is the challenge to Plato. Philosophy must not only represent the good *eros* but also theorize the difference.

The threat of abuse enters this dialogue with Phaedrus's mention of Boreas and returns with other references to known myths, like that of Ganymede (*Phdr.* 255c). The first speech by Socrates portrays a predatory lover who'd like to have a defenseless young orphan in his sights (239e). And the thought of a

---

22   *Phdr.*: eleven or twelve gods and their retinues, 246e–247a; nine rankings 248d–e; classification by the Muse one follows, 259c–d. I speak of eleven *or* twelve companies of gods because I have found that some readers interpret the first of these passages to mean that eleven groups ride around heaven, while others take it to mean that there is the Jovian group plus eleven others.

23   This paragraph is only one point at which I have the comments of Gary Gurtler in mind, and where I specifically want to thank him for his thoughts.

protecting father brings us to abuse of the young as metaphor, in Socrates' description of the fate that writing faces as it rolls around vulnerable to all attacks (275e). When Socrates compares written philosophy to a garden of Adonis, he reinforces the link between that suffering misunderstood piece of writing and a beautiful doomed boy (276b).

Even the promise of erotic ennoblement that emerges from the great myth needs to be read with suspicion. The soul rides its chariot behind the god it resembles, and will later seek to bring the soul of the loved one into the same company. Socrates calls the group a "chorus,"[24] but it is hard to reconcile the image of these chariots with the performance of tragedy.[25] Nor is it quite a military image, when no Greek within living memory would have fought in a chariot. The awkward uses of chariots in the *Iliad* never depict them arrayed in a rank or order.[26]

The nearest referent to this allusion, as far as I know the *only* case Plato would have known of a human in a chariot following a god's chariot, comes from the days of Athenian tyranny. After his first exile, Pisistratus returned to power with a public relations gimmick that included a young woman in armor who purported to be Athena. She rode into Athens in a chariot, and it seems that Pisistratus rode in behind her, following his patron god. Plato would have read the story in Herodotus, but it also appeared again after his time, in the Aristotelian *Constitution of the Athenians*, in a manner that suggests it had become Athenian lore (as an apparent allusion in Aristophanes also does).[27]

---

24 *Phdr.*: procession called χορός, 247a, 250b; member is χορευτής, "chorus member, dancer," 252d.

25 The Nehamas/Woodruff translation develops the image of gods' companies into an elaborate dance-and-drama organized as if in a theater (Nehamas and Woodruff 1995, 32n72). It is a compelling extrapolation from Plato's language, though I fail to see how any of this graceful swerving and leaping up the rows of a theater would be possible for horse-drawn chariots.

26 Chariot: in regiment, *Phdr.* 246e–247b; as basis for choosing lover, *Phdr.* 252d; in *Iliad*, Cotterell 2004, 129.

27 *Hist.*: Pisistratus returning to power, 1.60; tall young woman Phua in armor, 1.60.4. The anecdote does not specify where Pisistratus was standing when "Athena" rode into town, but a herald was posted to announce that Athena κατάγει "is guiding, leading" Pisistratus into Athens, 1.60.5; this implies that he rode in behind. The story in Aristotle's *Constitution of the Athenians* 14.4, the almost identical tale, specifies that the woman παραιβατούσης Pisistratus, using a nearly technical word for standing next to the driver. On the other hand the Aristotelian version lends a kind of support to my reading, with its closing words that "those in the city worshiped and marveled as they received him [προσκυνοῦντες ἐδέχοντο θαυμάζοντες]," as the lover worships one he recognizes as previously having ridden with him. The allusion from Aristophanes appears at the end of *Birds*: Pisthetairos,

Stories of abusive or deviant sexuality attached themselves to this dynasty. Right after the return of Pisistratus to power, Herodotus says that his sexual relations with his new wife were not according to *nomos* "law or custom."[28] Thucydides, who otherwise rarely mentions *eros*, uses that word in spelling out a notorious tale from the same family's subsequent generation, when Hipparchus the son of Pisistratus pursued young Harmodius as if he were the bad lover that Lysias warned of, the result being the downfall of the tyranny.[29]

That the best image Socrates can muster for ennobling love is also an image of its tyrannical variety makes you wonder how the one being pursued is supposed to detect the difference. Here too we are thrust into the problem of Greek religion—a problem for Plato, who pursues the holy and yet has to work with such divinity as the problematic religion of his day has bequeathed to him. (And we remember that this religion's heaven holds young Ganymede, abducted for all eternity.)

The assurance that the object of love won't be abused is to come from the theory of ἀντέρως in Socrates' speech: "counter-love," "love in return" (*Phdr.* 255a–e). This is as optimistic as theories of love get, this idea that being overpowered by desire for another person makes you attractive to the one you desire. It is morally reassuring, too. You are not going to force the one you love into anything.

Plato is elusive about how love's reply actually happens. Evidently your mind is so taken over by thoughts of the one you love that when this loved one talks to you, an idealized version of that same person comes forward. It is as if the object of love is looking into your eyes, seeing a reflection of themselves there, and taking that reflected charm to be the beauty coming from your eyes. Less metaphorically your love makes you emulate one you love, and it is this emulated idealization that attracts the loved one.

Here is how Socrates puts it. He uses language that apparently rules out informed consent. "He [the loved one] loves [ἐρᾷ], but he is confused as to whom he loves" (*Phdr.* 255d). This verb for being confused is ἀπορεῖ. The beloved is in a state of ἀπορία, what the dialogues display as philosophical ignorance. Socrates says the loved one "neither knows what he is experiencing

---

whose name evokes that of Pisistratus, rides in a chariot with *Basileia* "dominion," 1536–1546.

28 *Hist.*: relations between Pisistratus and daughter of Megacles οὐ κατὰ νόμον "not in the customary way," 1.61.1. This practice was serious enough for the young woman's mother to have questioned her at some length, and for her father to be angry when he learned about it, 1.61.2.

29 Thucydides *The Peloponnesian War* 6.53.3–6.59.4. References to *eros* in this section: 6.54.1, 6.54.3, 6.59.1 (Vickers 1995).

nor possesses the means to tell what it is [οὐδ'ἔχει φράσαι]." So this object of affection calls what he is feeling φιλία (255e) not even knowing what the feeling is. "It has escaped his notice," Socrates says, "that he is seeing himself as in a mirror" (255d). We might say he is loved and taken and kept in a state of ignorance.

When all goes well the lover sees in the loved one an image of the ideal they both follow, and their shared confusion promises to lead to a higher insight, as they both emulate idealizations of each other. No doubt. But my question is how you ensure that all goes well, how you know philosophically at the time, how you could say, that all is going well—and right now, how the object of love knows such a thing. One already has to tell the difference between divine love and its rapacious tyrannical variety. And all the signs of one thus far have been signs of the other. From a distance, or after thousands of years, or from the perspective of the new mythologizing that lets human beings see what the gods are seeing, the difference will reveal itself. But in the midst of a desirous encounter—while desiring—one lacks a criterion for the difference.

Contrast this way of looking at one's lover with the similar image in *Alcibiades* I. That dialogue speaks of the eye regarding itself in the pupil of another eye, an analogy to the way a soul may contemplate itself as perceived in another soul. But we find one crucial difference, that in the account of love and self-knowledge articulated in the *Alcibiades* I, you are aware of seeing yourself reflected.[30] The *Phaedrus*'s loved one is said not to realize that the image of love is a reflection.

Looking into a mirror means seeing something a step further removed from reality, so the ἀντέρως will be something weaker than the instigating *eros*. And as Plato's *Sophist, Theaetetus*, and *Timaeus* all say, it also means seeing an image that has been reversed left to right.[31] Does this matter to what the loved one sees? When you know that it is your reflection you see in the mirror, you remind yourself that what looks like a right hand is the left. But if you do not know you're looking in a mirror, you will take it to be a right hand. And the objects of love, looking into the hazy shine of their lovers' desire for them, don't realize they are seeing reflected images. Which is to say, in the language

---

30 Plato *Alcibiades* I: Socrates and Alcibiades speak of knowing the soul, 132e; self-knowledge compared to eye's seeing itself, 132d; organ of sight sees itself in mirror but also contains a mirror, 132d–e; the ones looking know they are seeing themselves, 132e–133a. I am grateful to Nicholas Rynearson for returning me to this passage, and for many other insightful remarks about the *Phaedrus*.

31 Plato: replying love is weaker, *Phdr.* 255e; mirror images reversed left to right, *Sophist* 266c, *Theaetetus* 193c–d, and especially *Timaeus* 46a–b.

of this dialogue, that they will not be able to tell divine *eros* from the left-handed kind.

My point is not a jape or a manufactured paradox. The one who is loved faces a difficulty that can be articulated without the language of smoke and mirrors. In the confusion of being idealized you see a version of yourself, but under conditions that leave you not knowing whether you are seeing something mundane or holy, an earthborn Typho or something simpler. (What you can have seen of your lover's nature is anybody's guess.) All we are ever trying to do is tell the difference. When the divine derives its name and its appearance from something in the non-divine world, we are reminded how hard it is for that world to know the divine. Those who are divinely mad might create poetry and speak of the future. Maybe they will chant prayers to purge a city of impurities. Maybe they'll love someone obsessively. But people who are deranged in a humanly way do all the same things. Will we ever have a reliable sign to tell us what goes on the left? A reliable sign would require not merely the instinct possessed by someone who feels spirits guiding him, but something more appropriate to a philosophy that now dwells in institutions: a technology of the divine. No one yet has toppled over to the right into heaven, or flown up into it on wings, or seen it. To this degree we are all in Phaedrus's position, baffled about the object of our desire to know, and calling what we feel φιλία, sometimes φιλοσοφία, without understanding what that experience entails.

COLLOQUIUM 2

Commentary on Pappas

Deborah De Chiara-Quenzer
Boston College

Abstract

This commentary on Nicholas Pappas's paper, "Telling Good Love from Bad in Plato's *Phaedrus*," reflects on a number of Pappas's thoughtful observations and interpretations of features woven into the drama of the discussion (for example, Typho and Boreas, wings, left and right). However, unlike Pappas, who refrains from claiming that divinely inspired human love (good love) can be discerned by turning to the earthly, this commentary suggests that Pappas's contrasts of wings which conceal versus wings which elevate, of left and right, and my added contrast of traditional Greek mythology versus Platonic mythology, lay the groundwork to discern the divine in the earthly, and to distinguish concomitantly bad from good human love. Additionally, the commentary discusses how Plato's use of collection and division is used to distinguish good and bad human love.

Keywords

bad love – good love – soul – mythology – collection and division

Professor Pappas has written an interesting paper on Plato's *Phaedrus*.[1] One reason I found it to be interesting is that it drew my attention to a number of smaller features in the dialogue, which I might have overlooked. His reflections on those features inspired me to think more deeply about their relevance, and consequently, to enhance my own thoughts on one of Plato's central concerns in the *Phaedrus*, which is to distinguish human eros from divine eros. For example, as Socrates and Phaedrus are meandering to their place under the plane tree, Professor Pappas calls one's attention to their discussion of two

---

1 The original paper was delivered at the B.A.C.A.P. on 5 November 2015 at Boston College. This paper has benefitted from the thoughtful formal discussion that followed the presentation, and has been slightly revised in light of that discussion.

mythological deities. These are Boreas and the story of his seizing of the young girl Oreithuia; and the creature Typho (the many headed beast), and Socrates' concern about whether his own soul is worse or better arranged than Typho's (229b4–230a6).[2] The references to these deities serve many functions, but one important function is to prepare the audience for a discussion of a type of human soul where depraved erotic appetites rule—a type of soul that will do whatever is necessary to satisfy the beast it has become. Likewise, not until Professor Pappas mentioned it,[3] had I realized that when Socrates presents the ranking of souls in the Myth of the Charioteer (248b5–248e3), the lowest ranking soul, the tyrannical soul (248e3), manifests the abusive human love described in the first two speeches in the *Phaedrus* (that is, in the speech attributed to Lysias and Socrates' first speech). Socrates later in the discussion refers to this abusive human eros as left-handed love when divisions are given by employing the method of collection and division (265e1–266b1). Additionally, Professor Pappas helpfully points out that Plato's description of the tyrannical soul in Book 9 of the *Republic* exhibits the abusive left-handed love described in the *Phaedrus*.[4]

One significant issue that Professor Pappas raises is the substantial challenge that faces Plato in communicating his ideas on divine love. According to Professor Pappas, this is challenging to Plato because he is attempting to illuminate his conception of divine eros within the framework of the worldly. As Professor Pappas puts it, "the paradox of demarcating the otherworldly within the world."[5] Although Professor Pappas is doubtful about whether the divine can be found by turning to the worldly,[6] it seems to me that, in fact, he has laid the groundwork for providing just this solution to the problem. For as he moves through his paper and presents various subtle reflections on physical objects (such as the wing) or physical relational properties (such as left and right), these can be used to point to distinctions between human eros and divinely inspired eros. And in so doing, they show how the divine can be, if not found within the earthly, then at least illuminated by turning to the earthly. For example, Professor Pappas points to the winged part of the cuirass, which covers and helps to protect a man's genitalia during battle. This winged covering attracts our attention to a man's sexual organs,[7] which in turn reminds one of

---

2 Pappas, pp. 42–44.
3 Pappas, pp. 44–45.
4 *Republic* IX, 571a1–575a8, especially 572e4–573b4, 573c7–573c9, & 574e2–575a8.
5 Pappas, p. 46.
6 Pappas, pp. 53–54, 58.
7 Pappas, pp. 46, 47.

the sexual activity Plato rails against in the *Phaedrus*. Yet, a physical wing when attached to a bird or more notably to a soul as is presented in the *Phaedrus*, enables one to soar and is used as a reminder of the soul's potential upward mobility to the divine.[8] In another instance, Professor Pappas focuses on the locational markers of left and right, and explains how they can signify not only latitudinal left and right but also up and down.[9] Thus these locational markers can also serve as signposts in the world to the two types of madness: base erotic madness (abusive pederasty)—left-handed love; and the best erotic madness in human beings (divinely inspired love)—right-handed love. Moreover there seems to me an invaluable approach used both by Professor Pappas in his paper and Plato in the dialogue. That is to grasp one concept while simultaneously maintaining a vision of the other. Thus, while being focused on left-handed love, one also has right-handed love in sight, and likewise while being focused on right-handed love, one also has left-handed love in sight.

In reviewing the movements in Professor Pappas's paper, one sees how the mythological figures of Boreas and Typho are meant to prepare us for human left-handed love.[10] Boreas and Typho are exemplars of a love where gods are dominated not by reason, but by sexual desires, and gratify their appetites by overpowering human beings. These mythological references are meant to prepare us for their human counterpart presented in Lysias's and Socrates' first speech in which the soul of a human being is dominated by a sexual desire that uses reason instrumentally to help satiate the needs of the man while violating and emasculating the boy. Thus, once we have grasped base human love, we are not to leave it behind, but rather we are to keep it within our sights while also discerning a vision of its divine contrary, divine eros, or right-handed love, the love that operates between true friends. And so, contrary to the mythic madness of Boreas and Typho and contrary to the human madness of the abusive human lover in the first two speeches, Professor Pappas's many insightful observations can be used to discern divine eros in the earthly. He has done this through the distinction and simultaneous grasp of the wing that lifts one up from the wing that shields the body, and through the distinction of right as opposed to left. And I would add through the contrasting forms of mythology in the dialogue. For the traditional Greek mythology that includes deities such as Boreas and Typho, deities who exemplify the degradation of souls, can be contrasted with the Platonic mythology reflected in the Myth of the Charioteer,

---

8   Pappas, pp. 45–46.
9   Pappas, pp. 47–48.
10 Pappas, pp. 42–44 & 54–56.

a myth which gives a vision of a few rare human souls capable of soaring to the limits of the heavens. So too this contrasting mythology can serve to illuminate the divine for those within the world.

Professor Pappas has laid substantial groundwork to allow an interpretive approach to finding divinely inspired love by turning to the earthly. With the remaining time left, I would like to discuss how divinely inspired love can also be found by turning away from the earthly to the soul, its intellect, and its grasp of being through the use of the dialectical method of collection and division. For if I were to leave a talk on good and bad erotic love in the *Phaedrus* without discussing the method of collection and division that is used repeatedly to distinguish those two kinds of love, I believe, in the spirit of Socrates, I would be paid a visit by my daimon.[11]

What we see in the *Phaedrus* is Plato's first extended use of the method of collection and division in the dialogues,[12] which is also used elsewhere in the *Sophist*, *Statesman*, and *Philebus*.[13] For a thinker of Plato's caliber, who has been concerned so often with definition and with the one and the many,[14] this intellectual approach seems to fit his philosophical needs quite well. Through the method of collection and division one grasps the commonness (the one) that exists among similar things, and through division one distinguishes the distinct kinds, kinds which exhibit real differences. I would argue that this commonness is more than a universal, Plato is not Aristotle, the one collected is a Platonic Form, and the kinds divided from the one are also Forms.[15]

---

11   Professor Pappas makes a number of references in his paper to division, and I have found his interpretations to reflect Plato's views (Pappas, pp. 45–49). For example, I thought his remarks that the divisions are made at the natural joints was correct (p. 47), and though often enough these divisions are bifurcations as he points out, they are not always so, with which I too agree. Nevertheless, Professor Pappas's concern with division seems to focus more on linking the divisions of left and right with the physical, and not with viewing the method of collection and division as an approach which the dialectician can use (1) to discern divinely inspired eros, (2) to communicate that insight to others, and (3) to aid the dialectician in identifying its presence (or absence) in human souls in the world.

12   An extensive description of the method of collection and division is given in the *Phaedrus* at 265c5–266d4.

13   De Chiara-Quenzer 1998.

14   For instance, in the *Meno*, Meno suffers Socrates' criticisms because he attempts to provide the many instead of the one (e.g., 71d4–73c8).

15   Sometimes Plato will speak of the one-and-many; sometimes he will speak of the one-many-and-infinite. In the latter case, the one usually refers to the most general form, the many to specific forms distinguished from the one, and then the infinite, the particulars

A noticeable feature of Plato's use of collection and division in the *Phaedrus* is that, as it is employed in various passages of the dialogue, it highlights different relationships. Plato is neither being inconsistent with any of the divisions he presents, nor are any of the divided kinds arbitrary. Rather, Plato will sometimes include or exclude different kinds depending on the context and the needs of the conversation before him. Thus, even though a dialectician makes divisions at the natural joints (265c1–266b1), that need not mean that when a dialectician is engaged in division he/she is necessarily going to set forth all the sub-kinds, that is, not all the natural joints must necessarily be cut. However, when cuts are made, they are to be at the natural joints, and in so doing the kinds that are distinguished are natural kinds or true εἴδη as opposed to arbitrary εἴδη.

For example, in the preamble to Socrates' first speech (237a2–238d7), a speech that will emphasize the male lover who wants to keeps his boy weak in every way possible so that he can dominate the boy and more easily have his needs satisfied, Socrates' division highlights a soul where the ruling principle is sexual appetite and not reason (237d6–238c4).[16] In this division, once Socrates has distinguished the two kinds of souls, one ruled by appetite and the other ruled by reason, he concentrates the division on the type of soul ruled by appetite. He divides and distinguishes three specific kinds of appetite—gluttony, excessive drinking, and sexual love. In so doing, he identifies the human erotic soul as the one where the appetite for sexual pleasure rules. This is an effective introduction to Socrates' first speech about an abusive sexual lover dominated by appetite.

Similarly, after Socrates retracts his first speech (242b4–243e3) and before he gives his second speech, he again uses the method of collection and division, but in this case he illuminates divinely inspired love present in the divinely inspired lover. The division proceeds from the general category madness (μανία), it virtually ignores human madness, and instead proceeds to divinely inspired madness. Divinely inspired madness is distinguished into four kinds: Love (242b8–242e4 and 245b1–245c2), Prophetic Madness, Mystic Madness, and Muse-Inspired Madness (243e9–245a8). Here in the preamble to

---

things in this world which exhibit the nature of the specific forms. For a discussion of the different senses of the one-and-many for Plato, see De Chiara-Quenzer 1993.

16 The division begins from the ruling principle in the soul and divides it into two types. One ruling principle is an inborn desire for pleasure, which Socrates refers to as hubris (ὕβρις, 238a2). The other ruling principle is that which makes judgments about what is best for the entire soul referred to as sophrosune (σωφροσύνη, 238a1). Hubris in turn is divided into gluttony, excessive drinking, and sexual love. Other kinds (εἴδη) are alluded to but not mentioned. No further division of σωφροσύνη is given.

the Great Speech of Socrates, a speech where divinely inspired eros will be its centerpiece, a division is given which highlights types of divinely inspired madness, one of which is love.[17]

In Plato's extensive description of the dialectical method of collection and division at 265c5–266c1, we are told of the formidable power of a person gifted with the ability to engage in collection and division. As Socrates says, "I myself am a lover of these divisions and collections that I may gain the power to speak and think" (266b3–266b5).[18] As part of his description, Socrates reviews how his division of madness was reflected in the earlier speeches. Madness (μανία) was divided into left-handed madness, that is, human love (ἔρως) and human love was exhibited in Lysias's speech and Socrates' first speech. Madness was also divided into right-handed love (ἔρως), that is, divinely inspired love, which was exhibited in Socrates' second speech (265e3–266b1). Thus I am suggesting that when Plato (through Socrates) applies collection and division to love in the *Phaedrus*, he need not give an exhaustive accounting of the kinds that fall under a one, but the kinds he does distinguish are specific Forms grounded in Being and not arbitrary kinds.

Now that I am arriving at the end of my commentary, I will circle back to Professor Pappas's paper and see how my reflections on collection and division tie into it. Professor Pappas was hesitant to claim that Plato provides a way of seeking the divine in the earthly. As he says, "When you use the world to map out the limits of the world and signs of the otherworldly, such limits on knowledge as I have been describing are inclined to reassert themselves. We've seen the point before that the world might never allow reference to anything besides itself."[19] However, I believe the subtle and thoughtful distinctions Professor Pappas has made in his paper in regard to earthly objects (for example, wings, left and right, and my suggestion of two forms of mythological), focus one's attention both downward and upward, and allow one to seek the divine by

---

17 Similarly, after Socrates has given his second speech, and while he is engaged in discussing good and bad rhetoric, we again see collection and division at work. Once all three speeches have been given, and the two distinct forms of love have been described, Socrates reviews how madness was represented in those previous speeches on love (265a7–265c4). Madness (μανία) had been bifurcated into the madness produced by human sexual illness—this illness was exhibited in the abusive lover depicted in Lysias's speech and Socrates' first speech—and divinely inspired madness, which in turn was divided into four types associated with Apollo, Dionysios, the Muses, and Aphrodite. It was this divine love that Plato held up as the ideal love present and exchanged between a lover and his beloved in Socrates' second speech.

18 Hackforth 1979, 134.

19 Pappas, p. 53 (see also p. 58).

turning to the earthly. I do not think this should be so surprising given that in Plato we have a philosopher who believes there is a hierarchy and a connectedness in being.[20] Furthermore, I am proposing that by turning to Plato's method of collection and division and seeing how it is used to identify and to separate base human love from divinely inspired human love, and given Plato's high regard for its success when exercised in gifted dialectical minds, Plato gives us a way of seeking divine love. Thus Plato in the *Phaedrus* presents us with a dialectical approach that provides us with an alternative and complementary way to seek divinely inspired love by using the intellect and collection and division to grasp the unchanging. Here the intellect leaves behind the physical and embraces being; it frees itself from the earthly and communes with the transcendent. The dialectician can see the divine eros and separate it from the depraved eros.

---

20 In the *Republic*, Socrates' distinction of the lovers of sights and sounds who are dreaming from philosophers who are awake (476b–d), the divided line (509d1–511e5), and the description of the ruler's ascent out of and back into the cave (514a1–521b11) demonstrate the connectedness of being. We are told, for example, that the philosopher-king grasps the nature of things in the cave ten thousand times better than others who have not seen the Forms because he/she has seen the Forms and now sees in the world the things that participate in, and are images of, the Forms (517a8–c5, 520b5–d1).

COLLOQUIUM 2

Pappas/De Chiara-Quenzer Bibliography

Arafat, K.W. 1997. State of the Art—Art of the State: Sexual Violence and Politics in Late Archaic and Early Classical Vase-Painting. In *Rape in Antiquity: Sexual Violence in the Greek and Roman Worlds*, eds. S. Deacy and K.F. Pierce, 97–122. London: Duckworth/Classical Press of Wales.

Burnet, J., ed. 1973. *Platonis Opera*. Vol. II. Oxford: Clarendon Press.

Burkert, W. 1985 [1977]. *Greek Religion: Archaic and Classical*, tr. J. Raffan. Cambridge: Harvard University Press.

Cavell, S. 1979. *The Claim of Reason: Wittgenstein, Skepticism, Morality, and Tragedy.* Oxford: Oxford University Press.

Cotterell, A. 2004. *Chariot: The Astounding Rise and Fall of the World's First War Machine.* London: Pimlico.

De Chiara-Quenzer, D. 1993. A Method for Pleasure and Reason: Plato's *Philebus*. *Apeiron*. 26.1:37–55.

De Chiara-Quenzer, D. 1998. The Purpose of the Philosophical Method in Plato's *Statesman*. *Apeiron* 31.2:91–126.

Dover, K.J. 1974. *Greek Popular Morality in the Time of Plato and Aristotle*. Oxford: Basil Blackwell.

Forstenpointner, G. 2003. Promethean Legacy: Investigations into the Ritual Procedure of "Olympian" Sacrifice. *British School at Athens Studies* 9:203–213.

Gill, D. 1974. Trapezomata: A Neglected Aspect of Greek Sacrifice. *Harvard Theological Review* 67:117–137.

Hackforth, R, tr. 1979. *Plato's Phaedrus*. Cambridge: Cambridge University Press.

Halliwell, S. 2012. Amousia: Living without the Muses. In *Aesthetic Value in Classical Antiquity*, eds. Ineke Sluiter and Ralph M. Rosen, 15–46. Leiden: Brill.

Hannay, H.J., P.J. Ciaccia, J.W. Kerr, and D. Barrett. 1990. Self-Report of Right-Left Confusion in College Men and Women. *Perceptual and Motor Skills* 70:451–457.

Harris, L.J. and S.R. Gitterman. 1978. University Professors' Self-Descriptions of Left-Right Confusability: Sex and Handedness Difference. *Perceptual and Motor Skills* 47:819–823.

Kant, I. 1968 [1768]. Von dem ersten Grunde des Unterschiedes der Gegenden im Raume. *Kants Werke*, Akademie Ausgabe, vol. 2, 375–384. Berlin: Georg Reimer/de Gruyter.

Lloyd, G.E.R. 1962. Left and Right in Greek Philosophy. *Journal of Hellenic Studies* 82:56–66.

Nehamas, A. and P. Woodruff, trs. 1995. *Plato: Phaedrus*. Indianapolis: Hackett Publishing.

Thornton, B.S. 1997. *Eros: The Myth of Ancient Greek Sexuality.* Boulder: Westview Press.
Vickers, M. 1995. Thucydides 6.53.3–59: Not a "Digression." *Dialogues d'histoire ancienne* 21:193–200.
Yunis, H. 2011. *Plato: Phaedrus.* Cambridge: Cambridge University Press.

COLLOQUIUM 3

The Place of Perception in Plato's Tripartite Soul

Peter D. Larsen
Trinity College Dublin

Abstract

This paper considers the place of the capacity for sense perception in Plato's tripartite soul. It argues, against a common recent interpretation, that despite being a capacity of the soul's appetitive part, sense perception is not independent of the soul's rational capacities. On the contrary, the soul's ability to cognize the content that it receives through sense perception depends upon the objects and the activity of its rational capacities. Defending a position of this sort requires one to suppose that despite its partition, the soul, for Plato, is, with respect to the activity of its various parts, substantially unitary. There are, however, passages that suggest that the capacities of the non-rational soul parts, in general, and sense perception, in particular, enjoy a certain degree of autonomy and independence from reason such that they, without the input of reason, can form beliefs about and act on the basis of their content. These passages have been read as belying this supposition. It will be shown, however, that these passages are perfectly consistent with the idea that the content of the non-rational capacities of the soul depends, for its intelligibility, on the soul's rational capacities.

Keywords

Plato – sense perception – tripartition – soul – *Republic*

I

What is the relation between Plato's partition of the soul, especially in the *Republic*, and his account of perception? This is the question to which this paper is addressed. It is a common view, which has recently been forcefully defended, that, once Plato divides the soul into rational and non-rational elements, the capacity for sense perception belongs to the non-rational element, that is, the appetitive part, and is, to a great extent, independent of the rational element. If the argument of this paper is correct, then this view is mistaken.

What is true is, on the contrary, that perceptual states depend, for both the awareness of their content and for their overall intelligibility, on the rational capacity of the soul. Thus, whereas sense perception may be a capacity of the soul's appetitive part, we should not likewise understand it as independent of the capacities of the soul's rational part. To make sense of this view, we have to suppose that, notwithstanding the division of the soul, Plato conceives of the soul as substantially unitary; because we have to suppose, as I shall argue, that the subject of perception is the very same as the subject of rational thought.

Some critics have recently argued that between writing the *Republic*, on the one hand, and the *Theaetetus*, *Timaeus* and *Sophist*, on the other, Plato changed his view on the question of whether or not the non-rational elements in the soul can, on their own, form beliefs about their content.[1] Those critics who employ this interpretive strategy do so in order to explain the apparent contradiction between the way in which Plato characterizes perception and thought in those dialogues that are typically taken to be from the middle period (*Phaedo*, *Republic*), in contrast to the stance that he projects in the so-called later dialogues (*Theaetetus*, *Sophist*, *Timaeus*, *Philebus*). One of the aims of this paper is to resist this strategy and to do so by arguing that the dependence of perception on thought can be found not only in dialogues like *Theaetetus* and *Timaeus*, but also in the *Republic*. Thus, as we shall see, the apparent contradiction that these critics pick up on is no more than that, apparent.

In order to defend this view I begin by considering some of the basic features of Plato's account of perception.[2] In particular, I examine the role of the soul in Plato's account of perception with an eye to defending the following claims:

---

1 See Lorenz 2006, 95–7. Lorenz is, of course, not the first to defend such a view, which, can clearly be found in Burnyeat 1976, 34–6, and seems to be implied in Silverman's assertion: "Our perusal of the *late* dialogues [*Timaeus* and *Theaetetus*] reveals that Plato *had come to the conclusion* that αἴσθησις was an irrational capacity whose domain was quite limited" (Silverman 1991, 132 emphasis added).

2 One might object that conducting the inquiry in this way is to do so the wrong way round. We must first determine what the soul, and its various parts, is like and then see where and how perception fits into this conception. However, when Plato first introduces the partite soul at *Republic* 436a–d, he does so to explain the fact that a single individual can be the subject of different and, indeed, opposing, states—learning, desiring and getting angry (436a8–b4). Thus while the character of the mental states that belong to the different parts of the soul do not ground the soul's division, as such, these differences can and, on Plato's analysis, do determine where those mental states belong in the divided soul.

A. For Plato the soul (ψυχή), and not the body (σῶμα), or any of its organs, is the proper subject of perception.
B. The soul is also the subject of several other cognitive capacities, which are distinct from, but related to perception. None of these capacities are dependent upon the body in the way that perception is, and they are all, broadly speaking, rational.

I consider these claims in sections II and III respectively. Here I argue that Plato carefully distinguishes between two kinds of psychical states: (1) states that depend, in some way, on the body; and (2) states that can arise independently of the body. Defending these general, and relatively unproblematic, claims about the nature of the different kinds of cognitive states allows us to develop a conception of the soul as the locus for a wide variety of connected cognitive capacities, both perceptual/affective and rational. Furthermore, it gives us a firm basis from which to approach the question of the relation between these two kinds of capacities and their content.

In section IV I turn to this question of the relation between perception and the rational capacities. Here I examine the connection that Plato develops between the body-dependent capacities and the rational capacities by first examining the sorts of objects that comprise the content of each, that is, by considering what the objects of perception are, and how they differ from the objects of, at least some of, the rational capacities. And secondly, by considering what the content of the rational capacities contributes to perceptual awareness. On the question of the relation between these two kinds of capacities, I defend the following claim:

C. There is a close connection between the perceptual capacity and at least some of the rational capacities such that the perceptual states depend, for both the awareness of their content and for their overall intelligibility, on the soul's ability to reason.

This claim, as we shall see, emerges, in large part, from the way in which Plato narrowly circumscribes the content of perception. I further argue that when the perceptual content is considered in conjunction with the content of, at least some of, the rational capacities, it becomes clear that the soul's ability to identify perceptual content as the very content that it is, is dependent upon the soul's ability to reason about that content. Based on this, I conclude that there is a strong connection between these two kinds of capacities such that in a fully developed rational soul αἴσθησις is always thought-involving.

That this is Plato's view can, I think, be shown from the way in which he characterizes perception and the rational capacities in a number of dialogues that are, on a traditional view, considered to be from a later period in his development. In some of the so-called middle dialogues, however, Plato has been read as affording perception and the other capacities associated with the soul's non-rational element a significant degree of autonomy from the rational element, and its capacities, such that, first, they can, on their own, generate beliefs about their content, and, secondly, they can, on their own and without the input of reason, generate action (Lorenz 2006, 49–51). In the final section of the paper I argue that the *Republic*, in general, and Plato's argument for tripartition in Book 10, in particular, need not be read in this way. I argue that the alternative reading that this paper defends coheres well with Plato's more general account of the structure of the soul and the relation between the non-rational parts and reason. In particular, I argue that Plato's account of the downward directed activity of reason provides a model for understanding the dependence of the appetitive and spirited parts on reason. Taking seriously the idea that the rational capacities can be directed either upward or downward allows us to make better sense of Plato's account of cognitive conflict in Book 10—the conflict between beliefs based on perception and beliefs based on reason. For, as we shall see, all of these beliefs are, in the end, formed through the involvement of the soul's rational capacities. If this is correct, then it shows that there is reason to think that the dependency of perception on thought, which I am defending in this paper, is already present in the *Republic*.

Defending the position that, for Plato, the content of perception depends on the soul's awareness of the objects of its rational capacities, and on the rational capacities, in general, is part of defending a larger, more general, view about the connection between Plato's metaphysics and his cognitive psychology. It is clear that, for Plato, the physical world and its objects depend both for their existence and their character on the forms. Absent forms, the physical world is radically indeterminate (*Timaeus* 29b1–d3 and 48e2–51d1). There is some reason to think that Plato envisions a strong isomorphism between the metaphysical relation that forms bear to sense perceptible particulars and the cognitive relation between the soul's awareness of the physical world and its rational awareness through its rational capacities. If this is correct, then we may infer that, like the physical world without the forms, the content of perception is, on its own, radically unintelligible. The coherent and integrated cognition of the physical world, then, depends on the soul's rational capacities. While I do not argue for this broader view in this paper, I do think that the position defended here goes some way toward supporting it.

II

My thinking about these issues began with the relatively clear and, I hope, uncontroversial observation that, for Plato, the soul is the proper subject of perception. That is to say, in a sentient creature it is that creature's soul, and not, strictly speaking, its body, that perceives. That this is indeed Plato's view can, I think, be shown by examining the comments that he makes about perception, and, in particular, the language that he uses to express those comments, across a number of dialogues. In order to demonstrate this point, let us begin by looking at two passages in which Plato considers the role of the soul in sense perception. In a well-worn passage from the *Theaetetus* (184b7–d5), Socrates, in an effort to correct an error in Theaetetus's understanding of the perceptual process goes out of his way to impress upon his young interlocutor that perception is carried out *with* the soul (expressed by the word for "soul" in the dative case) *through* the sense organs (expressed by the preposition διά accompanied by the word for the sense organ in the genitive case).[3] This text is particularly germane to our purpose because it carefully specifies the roles that both the soul and the body play in perception. The former is here presented as that which carries out the act of perceiving, while the latter serves an important causal role in bringing about perceptual awareness.[4]

For corroboration and clarification of this point we may turn to the *Philebus*. Here Plato, in the course of examining the question of whether or not genuine pleasure can arise through mere anticipation, indicates that an answer to this question will necessarily involve an appeal to memory. Socrates and his interlocutors, therefore, must first examine the nature of memory and since memory, he says, is nothing other than the preservation of perceptions, it is necessary for this inquiry that they first consider how perception works. Plato begins his general account of perception here by dividing the affections (παθήματα) of the body into two types: (1) those that are extinguished (κατασβενύναι) within the body before they reach the soul; and (2) those that shake (σεισμός) body and soul each individually (ἴδιον) and both in common (κοινόν) (33d2–6). He then goes on to specify the conditions under which these bodily affections either give rise to perception or not. When the body is moved,

---

3 I accept most of Myles Burnyeat's now standard reading of the grammar of this passage (1976, 29–30, 33–34 & 36–39).

4 See Burnyeat 1976, 37–38 where he argues that the sense organs in this passage are presented as inanimate causes in the production of perception—merely the equipment for the job. While I do not entirely agree with Burnyeat in his assessment of the precise causal role that the senses play, I do think that he is right to analyse Plato's use of διά with the genitive case here as picking up the causal, as opposed to spatial, sense of the English preposition "through."

he says, if the affection that moves it does not penetrate through to the soul, no perception occurs. Socrates initially characterizes this condition as one in which the soul is oblivious (using a form of the verb λανθάνειν). He, however, thinks better of referring to it in this way and revises the term he uses from one that means obliviousness to a more specific term indicating a complete absence of perception (ἀναισθησία). The point here is that when the soul is unaffected, it remains in a state of non-perceiving. In contrast, Socrates identifies perceptions with those affections that disturb the body and soul in common (33d8–34a7).

The passage just described shows two things. First, it shows that, for Plato, the mere disturbance of the body is not sufficient to produce perception; at the very least perception requires a movement of the soul. Secondly, it shows that the body is, at least typically, the medium through which perception-producing affections are communicated to the soul. The first point indicates that, for Plato, it is the soul and not the body that is the subject of perceiving and is, therefore, not only consonant with, but also confirmatory of the view from the *Theaetetus* that the soul and not the body, or any of its organs, is what is, properly speaking, percipient—our CLAIM A from above.[5] The second point, however, shows that perception, for Plato, despite being a state of the soul, depends on the body. This, as we shall see in the next section, distinguishes perceptual states in an important way from certain other psychical states, which are construed as rational and which are characterized as arising in the soul through its own activity and independently of the body.

At this stage we must consider a potential objection to the claim that Plato held, or consistently held, that the soul and not the body is the subject of perception. For one might suggest that while the view we have imputed to Plato is one that he expresses later in his philosophical development it is not one that he held throughout his work.[6] In support of such an objection, one might cite

---

5   One might object that what this passage shows is not that the soul *in contrast to* the body is the subject of perception, but rather that the soul *together with* the body is the subject of perception. Because, our objector maintains, it is those very affections that are communicated through the body that produce perceptions in the soul. There is, however, some reason to think that this is not the conclusion that Plato wishes us to draw from this passage. For in characterizing those affections that penetrate through the body to the soul, Socrates indicates that they move body and soul both in common (κοινόν) but also each in an individual way (ἴδιον). It is not entirely clear what is special, or private, about the way in which the body and soul are moved in these interactions, but it is clear that Plato wanted to defend the view of our objector, all he would have needed to say is that in perception body and soul are moved in common.

6   According to the traditional account, both of the dialogues we've considered are generally agreed to be either firmly from Plato's so-called late period or, in the case of the *Theaetetus*, on the border between middle and late.

dialogues generally agreed to be earlier than *Theaetetus* and *Philebus* in which Plato uses precisely the same locution—namely, the dative case construction, that in the *Theaetetus* he uses to carefully specify the role of the soul in perception—for the body and its organs. Thus, for example, at *Phaedo* 65d7 Socrates asks Simmias the following question: "Have you ever seen any of the things of this sort [the just itself, the beautiful itself, the good itself] *with* your eyes (τοῖς ὀφθαλμοῖς)?" By phrasing this question as he does and by putting "the eyes" in the dative case, Plato, following our analysis above, signals to the reader that were it possible to perceive the forms, it would be the eyes themselves that would do the seeing. To add fuel to the fire of this objection, we find the same locution used in the very same way somewhat later in the *Phaedo* when, in distinguishing forms from sense perceptible things, Socrates says to Cebes: "you can touch (ἅπτεσθαι) and see (ὁρᾶν) and perceive (αἰσθάνεσθαι) these things [the many beautiful things, the many equal things, etc.] *with* all the other senses (ταῖς ἄλλαις αἰσθήσεσιν)" (79a1–2).

The language used in these passages from the *Phaedo* is striking when we consider it against the backdrop of the section from the *Theaetetus* just discussed; for there Plato has Socrates make a special point about the need for precision in the language he uses to refer to the different elements in the perceptual process (*Theaetetus* 184c1–7). The exactness (ἀκρίβεια) that Socrates seeks in this instance concerns precisely the way in which one designates the role of the senses in perception. Thus, Socrates chooses the διά + genitive construction rather than the dative case in order to flag, as he says, something that is incorrect in Theaetetus's understanding of perception. With respect to our view, these lines from the *Phaedo* indicate that, at best, Plato is not consistent in his use of the dative case construction to refer to the soul when talking about perception. For in these instances, as well as others, he uses it to refer to the body and its organs (*Republic* 352e6–8). And at worst, they show that Plato, at the time of writing the *Phaedo*, held that the bodily sense organs were the subjects of perception.

While these passages certainly seem to be evidence against my reading, it seems to me that we should not take them as conclusive evidence. In fact, they seem to provide fairly weak evidence. The reason for this is that in conjunction with both of the aforecited passages, Plato also uses the other grammatical construction—namely, διά with the genitive—to refer to the body. Recall that this was precisely the formulation that in the *Theaetetus* he had applied to the bodily sense organs for the express purpose of designating them as the means to, as distinct from the subject of, perception. Just two lines after the first *Phaedo* passage in which Socrates had asked Simmias if he has seen the forms with his eyes, he expands the question and asks whether he has grasped them through any other bodily sense (Ἀλλ' ἄλλῃ τινὶ αἰσθήσει τῶν διὰ τοῦ σώματος ἐφήψω αὐτῶν; 65d11–12). This phrase is then repeated two lines later when, after clarifying that his question is about *all* of the entities that populate the realm of forms, Socrates restates the question as follows: "Is what is most true in them [the forms] considered (θεωρεῖσθαι) through the body (διὰ τοῦ σώματος)…?" (65e1–2)

The application of the διά + genitive construction to the bodily sense organs occurs in conjunction with the second passage mentioned above as well. Here Socrates claims that the soul is more akin to the imperceptible forms, while the body is like in nature to perceptible, mutable things. He concludes from this that whenever the soul attempts to investigate something (σκοπεῖν τι) through sight or hearing or any of the sensory powers (διὰ τοῦ ὁρᾶν ἢ διὰ τοῦ ἀκούειν ἢ δι' ἄλλης τινὸς αἰσθήσεως) it is constantly dragged by the body (ὑπὸ τοῦ σώματος) toward that which is perceptible and changeable (*Phaedo* 79c2–8). In addition to showing that Plato uses the διά + genitive construction for the body here, this passage also indicates that it is the soul that perceives through the body, because it is the soul that is constantly dragged down toward the changeable things when it considers things through sense perception.

Thus, we can see that while these passages from the *Phaedo* do provide a potential counter example to our claim that, for Plato, the soul is the subject of sense perception, they do not constitute a definitive assertion of the opposite view—namely, that the body and its organs are the subjects of perception. For in each case we find also the διά + genitive construction applied to the body. The reason for this lack of precision, I think, is that in these passages, and in the *Phaedo*, and other so-called middle dialogues, more generally, Plato is not interested in making specific points about the perceptual process; he is rather concerned to argue that there is a distinction in kind between perceptible, changeable things and imperceptible, unchanging forms. Furthermore, he aims to show that the ontological distinction between these kinds of beings also has an epistemological/cognitive element, but in that regard, he seems in dialogues like *Phaedo*, *Republic*, *Symposium* to be more concerned with the soul's mode of access to forms than with its awareness of perceptible things.

III

So far I have, in an effort to motivate CLAIM A, argued that the soul, and not the body or any of its organs, is, according to Plato, the proper subject of perception. Further I have argued that it is reasonable to assume that Plato remains consistent on this position through dialogues from both his so-called middle and late periods. This is an important point because it shows that Plato conceives of the soul as the common subject of both the cognitive states that arise through the body and, as we shall see presently, those that it arrives at on its own and independently of the affections that it receives through the body. In this section I consider the evidence for, and defend, CLAIM B: this is the claim that *the soul is also the subject of several distinct but related cognitive capacities none of which are dependent upon the body in the way that perception is, and which are all, broadly speaking, rational.* As in the discussion of CLAIM A, I begin by considering a number of dialogues in which Plato discusses the cognitive capacities of the soul and show that they can be grouped into two broad kinds: (1) body-dependent capacities; and (2) a number of capacities, which, while they may be closely related to capacities that depend on the body, are not, themselves, so dependent and to which, I refer collectively as rational.

Toward the end of the section I begin to lay the groundwork for defending CLAIM C, by considering how these two kinds of psychical states—perceptual/affective and rational—are related to one another. I argue that despite the distinction in the objects they are set over and in the way in which they arise in the soul, Plato conceives of the body-dependent capacities and the rational capacities as closely connected and he does so not only in the so-called later dialogues, but also in dialogues generally taken to be from the middle period. This argument requires us to consider what the objects of these different kinds of capacities are and what, if anything, the objects of the rational capacities contribute to those of which the soul becomes aware through the body-dependent capacities. Here I argue that the objects of perception are so narrowly conceived that, on its own, the perceptual capacity lacks the resources to generate an integrated, coherent experience. This shows, I argue, that the perceptual capacity must work closely together with, at least some of, the rational capacities. Defending this claim will provide us with a firm basis from which we may approach the questions raised by Plato's account of soul partition.

It is appropriate to begin here, as before, with the *Theaetetus*. For in this dialogue, more than any other, Plato concerns himself with carefully distinguishing and circumscribing the function and content of different psychical activities. Thus, at *Theaetetus* 185a4–6, after having established that soul is the proper subject of perception and having elicited Theaetetus's agreement that that which is perceived through, or by means of, one sensory power, for example, hearing, cannot be perceived through, or by means of, another such power, for example, sight, Socrates infers from this that when someone thinks (διανοεῖσθαι) something in common about both of the objects of two distinct sense modalities, the content of that thought is not arrived at through either of the individual sensory powers.[7] That is to say, a thought that is about an object of sight and an object of hearing together is not a perception of either or both.[8] This passage shows two important things. First it distinguishes between two kinds of psychical states: *aisthetic* and *dianoetic*. Secondly, it provides a *prima facie* criterion for differentiating between the mental states generated by these two kinds of capacities; namely, by considering whether the content of the state in question can be ascribed to one, and only one, sense modality. If it can, then it is an *aisthetic* state, if it cannot, then it is, at least a candidate for, a *dianoetic* state.

Further on in this argument, after clarifying this distinction by going through some of the objects specific to the *dianoetic* capacity with Theaetetus, Socrates asks the following question: through *which* power (δύναμις) does one become aware of the common features of all things (τό τ' ἐπὶ πᾶσι κοινὸν) ... which (sense) organs (ὄργανα) do you designate for all of the things of this sort [the common features] through which that which perceives in us, perceives each one (ἕκαστον)?" (185c3–8). Before answering, Theaetetus restates Socrates' question and, in so doing, he picks up on Socrates' reference to *that which perceives in us* (ἡμῶν τὸ αἰσθηνόμενον) and supplies the unnamed subject. Thus, as a point of clarification he says: "... through which of the bodily senses the soul (τῇ ψυχῇ) perceives them all?" (185d3–4). Theaetetus then answers this question by saying that it does not seem to him that there is any special organ (ὄργανον ἴδιον) like there is for the others. It seems rather to be the case that the soul considers the things that are common to all things itself through itself (αὐτὴ δι' αὑτῆς) (185d7–e2). Here we have a clear application of the idea that it is the soul to which these two distinct types of states belong. The soul perceives (αἰσθάνεσθαι) through or by means of the bodily sense organs and the soul thinks (διανοεῖσθαι) through or by means of itself.

This idea—that the soul is the subject of two different kinds of mental activity—is, of course, the specification of a common Platonic principle. We find it, perhaps paradigmatically, in the *Phaedo*. At 65a9 after having

---

7 That Plato understands this point to be the conclusion of an argument is signalled by his use of ἄρα to introduce it.

8 This is taken to be excluded by the previous claim that what is perceived by means of one sense cannot be perceived by means of another (184e8–185a3). Whether or not this claim is strong enough to ground this further point is an interesting question. For the view that the principle is, as stated, far too weak to ground the conclusions Plato draws from it, see Bostock 1988 112–114. My own view is that the principle, as stated, is strong enough to ground the conclusions that Plato derives from it and this because it is prepared for by a careful argument. Unfortunately pursuing this now would take us too far afield, so I must leave it for another occasion.

established that death is nothing other than the separation of the soul from the body, Socrates claims that the true philosopher, above all, should desire to be in this condition. He argues for this in two ways. First he considers what is lost with the departure of the body—namely, the pleasures associated with food, drink and sex. The philosopher, because she does not care about these pleasures (64c10–65a8), ought, therefore, to have no particular attachment to the body and should be untroubled when she is finally separated from it. Secondly, he looks at what the philosopher gains in being free from the body. This, he says, is precisely a more direct path to what she truly desires—namely, the acquisition of knowledge (τὴν τῆς φρονήσεως κτῆσιν). For the possession of a body, Socrates argues, is a hindrance to the full satisfaction of the desire for knowledge acquisition.[9] The senses, moreover, are forever misleading the soul; therefore, whenever it attempts investigate (ἐπισκοπεῖν) anything by means of them it is unable to attain truth (65a9–65b11). It is, rather, through reasoning (λογίζεσθαι) that the soul becomes aware of truth and the soul reasons best when it is most by itself (65c2–9). At the conclusion of this argument Socrates is satisfied that it has been shown that if one is ever to have pure knowledge (καθαρῶς εἴσεσθαι) then one must rid oneself, to the greatest degree possible, of the perceptions that come through the body.

In this argument we find a clear illustration of the idea that the soul is the subject of awareness for at least two different kinds of states. One perceptual, which it arrives at by means of the body, and the other rational, and which it pursues on its own and, ideally, without the influence of the body. This passage, however, adds two important elements to this view. First, it shows that whereas perception depends upon the body—only souls in an embodied state are troubled by the conveyances of the senses—reasoning does not so depend. The soul, in fact, reasons (λογίζεσθαι) best, Plato tells us, when it is most by itself (μάλιστα αὐτὴ καθ' αὑτή) and is not troubled by the senses (65c5–9). Secondly, the way in which Plato describes the interplay between perception and reason here indicates that these states are frequently at odds with one another. The senses are presented as misleading (ἐξαπατᾶσθαι) reason and as, generally, inimical to the acquisition of knowledge. This idea—that perception and reason are, at least in many cases, opposed to one another—is a characterization that we find elsewhere in Plato (*Rep.* 440a8–e6).

---

9   It is a good question whether Plato thinks that it is possible for a soul to acquire knowledge in an embodied state. For if the mode of cognition that arises through the body is always misleading and if it is impossible to sever completely the soul from the body during life, then there is some reason to think that this might not be possible. Gerson 2003, 279 argues, based primarily on the *Phaedo* and on *Republic* 10, that it is not possible.

We have now seen that the soul is the subject of two different kinds of mental states; one that arises through the body and one that is arrived at through the soul's own activity and independently of the body. What remains unclear, however, is which psychical capacities are correlated with these states and what the specific objects of these states are. I turn to these issues now as a first step toward showing that despite the difference, and indeed the often antagonistic relationship, between the capacity for perception and the rational capacities, Plato also develops a close connection between them such that the former depend, for their intelligibility on at least some of the latter.

Let us begin with the body-dependent capacities. Included on this side of the distinction are clearly the capacity for perception, in general, along with its sub-categories—sight, hearing, smell, taste and touch. So too, however, are pleasure and pain and the bodily desires whose satisfaction or abnegation produce them.[10] The inclusion of pleasure and pain in the body-dependent capacities is made clear in the *Phaedo* where Plato argues that the philosopher is not troubled by death because she does not care about the pleasures associated with the body (64c10–65a8). This view is corroborated and expanded slightly in the *Timaeus*. At 69cd Plato describes the creation of the human body and mortal soul—seat of the body-dependent capacities—not by the demiurge, but by the younger gods. These gods began, Plato tells us, by encasing the immortal soul in a round mortal body—the head—and they placed within that body a mortal soul, which serves as the subject for the affections (παθήματα) that come to the soul through it. These affections are identified as: pleasure (ἡδονή), pain (λύπη), reckless courage (θάρσος), fear (φόβος), spirit (θυμός) and hope (ἐλπίς); these, he says, were bound with sense perception (αἴσθησις) and lustful desire (ἔρως).

We find, therefore, relative agreement between the *Phaedo* and *Timaeus* that the body-dependent capacities are perception and the capacity for bodily pleasure and pain. The *Timaeus*, however, adds to this list the following: courage, fear, spirit, hope and erotic desire. We need not, I think, be terribly troubled by these additions; for it seems that most of them can be accommodated if we class them among the bodily desires—fear: the desire to avoid bodily harm;

---

10   It is not entirely clear that pleasure and pain form a class of affective states distinct from perceptual states. There is, in fact, evidence that Plato thinks they do not. At *Timaeus* 64a2–65b3 Plato seems to group pleasures and pains with the objects of tactile sensations. It isn't immediately clear, however, that understanding pleasure and pain in this way can accommodate the feelings associated with the bodily fillings and emptyings that Plato discusses at *Gorgias* 496c7–e4, and the body's departing from and returning to a natural state as in the *Philebus* (31e6–32a4).

and ἔρως: the desire for sexual satisfaction. The two additions that do not neatly fit into the class of bodily desires are reckless courage, the desire for honor; and spirit, the desire to right a perceived wrong. Elsewhere Plato identifies these states as belonging to the spirited element of the soul (θυμοειδής) (*Rep.* 442b11–c2). Despite Plato's characterization of the θυμοειδής as the ally of the rational element in the soul in its civil war with desire, it is also grouped with the desiderative element as being non-rational. Based on this, I think that we have good reason to class all of these states among those generated by the body-dependent capacities. If it is correct to read these as body-dependent states, then the list of body-dependent capacities in the *Timaeus* is consonant with the one presented in the *Phaedo* passage considered just above. For there Plato includes, in a blanket statement, the other desires associated with the body (τὰς ἄλλας τὰς περὶ τὸ σῶμα θεραπείας). Based on this, one could plausibly identify the body-dependent capacities as the capacity for pleasure and pain, the capacity for perception and the desiderative capacity, when those desires pertain to the body, or to the embodied person.

Now let us turn to the rational capacities—those that do not depend upon a body. In the *Theaetetus* passage considered above, Plato makes reference to the capacity for thought (διάνοια). Here he indicates that when one considers a property that is true of more than one object of perception, this property is not an object of perception, but is rather an object of thought, and the capacity employed in arriving at that mental state is not the *aisthetic* capacity, but is, rather, the *dianoetic* capacity (185a4–c2). This shows, at the very least, that διάνοια is a distinct capacity with a distinct set of objects.[11] Furthermore, the fact that, when questioned, Theaetetus cannot identify a specific bodily organ through which the soul becomes aware of these objects, but, as he says, it seems to him that the soul investigates the common features of all things through itself (ἀλλ' αὐτὴ δι' αὑτῆς ἡ ψυχὴ τὰ κοινά μοι φαίνεται περὶ πάντων ἐπισκοπεῖν) indicates that διάνοια is not body-dependent in the way that perception is. What this passage also shows, however, is that despite these distinctions between perception and thought, there is clearly also a close connection. As Plato says, to be aware of something that is a feature of the objects of two distinct sense modalities is to think something about those objects. This means that at least some of the objects of thought apply to, in the sense that they are true of, the objects of perception.

---

11   This coheres with Plato's criterion for individuating powers in *Republic* 5 (477c1–d7). Here Plato indicates that powers (δυνάμεις) are differentiated by the objects they are set over and what they do.

Thought is, of course, only one among many of the capacities that Plato presents as not dependent upon the body. The *Phaedo*, as we have seen, also provides a nice illustration of the relation between perception and certain rational capacities. At 65b9–c9 Plato claims that whenever someone attempts to investigate something through the body he is deceived by it; he then clarifies that it is through the reasoning capacity (λογισμός) that one is best suited to consider reality. Furthermore, the soul reasons best when it is not disturbed by sight, hearing, pleasure or pain, that is, when it is most by itself. We can see from this passage that λογισμός certainly does not depend on the body because, ideally, it carries out its work on its own and, as far as possible, apart from the body. However, it is possible for it to conduct an inquiry by means of the body and the body-dependent capacities. Later in this argument Socrates wonders how it is, if not through perception, that one comes to cognize the forms. In the course of this discussion, and in a passage we considered above in a different context, Socrates asks Simmias whether he has ever "grasped (ἐφάπτεσθαι) any of these [the forms] with his eyes ... is what is most true (ἀληθέστατος) contemplated (θεωρεῖσθαι) through the body?" (65d11–e4). And just a couple of lines later he uses the verbal form of διάνοια (διανοεῖσθαι) to describe the sort of activity that leads to knowledge of the forms.

For corroboration and expansion of these points, we may turn to the *Republic* and the divided line. At the end of the sun analogy, and as an explication of that image, Plato divides things into two kinds (διττὰ εἴδη): visible (ὁρατός) and intelligible (νοητός). He then illustrates the soul's mode of awareness of these two kinds of things through the image of a line divided into two unequal parts, one corresponding to the visible and the other corresponding to the intelligible. Each of these is then divided again unequally in the same ratio as before. The things that correspond to the four parts of the line increase in clarity (σαφήνεια) as one ascends from the bottom to the top, as, precisely, does one's cognition of the things that populate each of the levels. The bottom of the visible part consists of images (εἰκόνες), like shadows and the appearance of reflections in water (τὰ ἐν τοῖς ὕδασι φαντάσματα) (509d10–510a3); these are cognized by the imaging capacity (εἰκασία). The next rung of the visible contains the things of which the images are images, such as animals, trees, and manufactured things; these are grasped by conviction or belief (πίστις). On the intelligible level, the first step contains geometrical and other mathematical objects, and thought (διάνοια) is the cognitive capacity corresponding to these. The top section of the line is reserved for the forms, which are grasped by understanding (νόησις).

There are many interesting questions raised by this image, but I would like to flag two points of relevance for our topic. First, it is notable that perception (αἴσθησις) is absent from the line. It is not mentioned as responsible for grasping any of the objects that appear on the line. While I admit that Plato's aim here is not to give a full account of the mental states that are associated with the objects at the different levels of the line, one would think that if he considers the capacity for sense perception to be capable, on its own, of cognizing its content, he would have associated it with the upper level of the visible where the medium-sized objects that we generally take to comprise the visible world reside; but here instead we find conviction or belief (πίστις). The capacity that comes closest to perception is the image making capacity (εἰκασία), but it is not at all clear what connection there is between εἰκασία and αἴσθησις. I think the reason why perception does not appear on the line is that the whole line is taken to be concerned with objects the cognition of which requires a higher level of complexity than that afforded by αἴσθησις alone. I do not, however, want to argue for this now. I shall return to it later. For the moment, all I wish to have established is that the capacities corresponding to the objects on the two intelligible parts of the line—διάνοια and νόησις—are not body-dependent. This is evident from the fact that their objects can be accessed independent of any of the body-dependent capacities of the soul.

IV

The aim of the foregoing discussion has been to establish that, for Plato, the soul is the joint subject of two kinds of capacities: perceptual/affective and rational. Furthermore, as we have seen, the capacities of the former type—the capacity for bodily desires and perception—are body-dependent. The capacities of the latter kind—among which are thought (διάνοια), reason (λογισμός), contemplation (θεωρία) and understanding (νόησις)—while not body-dependent may be related to bodily affections as demonstrated by Plato's claim in the *Theaetetus* that one can think (διανοεῖσθαι) something common about the content of two distinct sense modalities and that the content of such a thought is not arrived at through either of the individual sense modalities. This indicates both that these two kinds of capacities are distinct, but also that this distinction is not so sharp that they are completely unrelated to one another; on the contrary, as we have seen, there are certainly times at which they work together. Thus, at *Phaedo* 65e1–2 Socrates asks Simmias if what is most true is contemplated (θεωρεῖσθαι) through the body (διὰ τοῦ σώματος), the implication being that something is *contemplated* through the body, just not that which is most true. In fact, the account that Plato develops of these capacities in a number of places indicates that they work together much of the time in normal everyday experience. We can see this clearly if we return to the *Theaetetus* passage. If, as Plato says, thinking the common things about the objects of sense requires the employment of a distinct capacity, we may assume that this is because the requisite objects lie outside of the scope of the perceptual capacity. If this is correct, then there is reason to think that the perceptual capacity depends upon thought at least to the extent that thought is capable of revealing things that are true of its content.

This conclusion—namely, that the body-dependent capacities and the rational capacities work together most of the time—could use some further defense. I propose to provide this by considering the content of these different kinds of capacities. My aim in doing this is to shed further light on what the cooperation between them consists in and to see what benefit it is. This is part of the wider aim of defending CLAIM C: the claim that *there is a close connection between the perceptual capacity and at least some of the rational capacities such that the perceptual states depend, for both the awareness of their content and for their overall intelligibility, on the soul's ability to reason.* For if we can show that the perceptual capacity and, at least some of, the rational capacities work together most of the time, then it would be reasonable to conclude that they are closely connected. Furthermore, in considering the content of the different capacities we will lay the groundwork for defending the claim that the soul's awareness of the content of its perceptual states depends upon the exercise of its rational capacities.

Let us begin with the content of perception. *Timaeus* 61c3–68d3 is the primary source for Plato's account of the content of perception. Here Plato goes through each of the sensory powers, identifying its content and the physical interaction or interactions that give rise to that content. We may begin, as Plato does, with touch. The objects of touch are: hot (θερμός), cold (ψυχρός), hard (σκληρός), soft (μαλακός), heavy (βαρύς), light (κοῦφος), smooth (λεῖος), rough (τραχύς), the pleasant (ἡδύς) and the painful (ἀλγεινός). The objects of taste are: sour (στρυφνός), bitter (αὐσηρός), pungent (πικρός), salty (ἁλυκός), sharp (δριμύς) and sweet (γλυκύς). Smell has for its objects odors (ὀσμή) within which there are no discrete categories aside from pleasant (ἡδύς) and disturbing (λυπηρός). The objects of hearing are sounds (φωναί), which, similar to smell, are not categorized but rather exist on a continuum of pitch and a volume. Finally, the objects of sight are colors (χρώματα), which, Plato tells us, are many and various, but he does give, as examples, some of the most common. Some of these are: black (μέλας), white (λευκός), bright (λαμπρός), red (ἐρυθρός), yellow (ξανθός), purple (ἁλουργής), and grey (ὄρφνινος).

The interesting thing about these lists is that they are composed entirely of simple qualities. That is to say, the objects that Plato identifies as comprising the content of the perceptual capacity are not the medium-sized objects that we typically take to be the things we see, hear and smell on a daily basis: things like trees, birds and automobiles. They are the qualities that belong to those things, in some way or other. Furthermore, if we return to the divided line, this idea that the objects of perception are the qualities that belong to medium-sized objects, might provide us with some explanation of why αἴσθησις is missing from it—namely, because the objects specific to the perceptual capacity do not, themselves, feature on the line. Even at the lowest level of the divided line—the level of images—some sort of integration and combination beyond the mere sensory qualities themselves is assumed.

This idea that the objects of perception, for Plato, are only simple sense qualities is corroborated by the *Theaetetus*. If we return to the argument at 184–7, we see that the only objects specified as comprising the content of perception are either specific sensory qualities like white, black, hot, hard, light and sweet (184d8–e6), or generic terms for sets of qualities like color and sound (185a8–9). This makes perfect sense within the context of the argument in which it appears; for if it is the case that the objects perceived by means of one sense cannot be perceived by means of another, then one would expect the content of perception to be limited to only those features specific to the five senses. Furthermore, since the medium-sized objects that populate the second section of the divided line are perceptible by more than one sense—one can perceive an automobile by seeing it, or by hearing it, or by touching it, or, I suppose, if one were so inclined, by tasting it!—they do not qualify as objects of sense *per se*. If this account of the perceptual qualities is correct, then there are two conclusions we can draw. The one is that the purview of the *aisthetic* capacity is very narrowly circumscribed. The second is that if one is going to have an experience of an integrated world composed of the sorts of complex objects that correspond to the objects that populate the second level of the divided line, then αἴσθησις alone will not be sufficient. If this second conclusion is too quick, then let us consider the content of the rational states in order to provide it with some further plausibility.

Unfortunately, Plato does not provide us with a nice list of the objects of the rational capacities like he does for the objects of perception. However, through bringing together a number of sources, such a list can be constructed. Clearly the paradigmatic (no pun intended) objects of reason are the forms. This is clear from the divided line on which they occupy the top position as the true objects of νοῦς. The process of dialectic at the highest level of the line is presented as an inquiry that starts with forms themselves, proceeds through forms and ends in forms (513c1–2). This is a good start, but it is hardly specific. What does Plato mean when he refers to forms here? It seems reasonable to assume that what Plato has in mind here are the sorts of entities that he refers to elsewhere in the *Republic*, and in other dialogues, by using the locution "*the x-itself*" to describe them.[12] The *Theaetetus* also provides a list of objects that are cognized through, or used in the activity of, διάνοια, but in this case the list is larger and more specific than that provided in the *Republic*. Here we have *being, sameness, difference, number, likeness, unlikeness, beautiful, ugly, good, bad*. Is it a problem for this comparison between *Republic* and *Theaetetus* that Plato uses the term νοῦς in the *Republic* and διάνοια in the *Theaetetus*? I don't think so. It is clear in the *Republic* that Plato uses the term διάνοια in both a narrower and a wider way: the narrower way specifying our cognition of the objects on the lower section of the upper portion of the line; the wider way including (at least) the whole upper portion of the line.[13]

It is this last set of objects that I would like to focus on here. The knowledge of the forms, if it is achieved at all, is something achieved by only a very few, but the ability to think about and employ these concepts seems to be something far more common. In fact, I would like to suggest that these are concepts that any perceiver must be able to deploy if she hopes to have an integrated, coherent sensory experience.[14] Recall that in the argument from the *Theaetetus* these objects are never spoken of in the abstract, they are always considered in relation to some object, or set of objects, of perception. In fact, when Theaetetus suggests a more generalized application of these concepts by claiming that when the soul considers objects like *beautiful, ugly, good*, and *bad* it examines their being in relation to each other (πρὸς ἄλληλα) and makes a calculation about the past and present in relation to the future, Socrates reins him back in and reminds him that the properties they are discussing are, specifically,

---

12 See, for example, *Rep.* 476a5–8, *Phd.* 65d4–7, *Sym.* 211a8–b2.

13 I say "at least," because it can be argued that when Plato uses διάνοια in the wider sense, he intends it to include the objects on the lower two sections of the line. While I cannot argue this point here, it appears to be a direct consequence of what he says at *Republic* V: "Would we not be correct, then, in saying that the thought (διάνοια) of the one person is knowledge since this is the person who knows, and that the thought of the other person is opinion since *he* is the person who opines?" (476d4–5). For a defense of the claim that διάνοια is, deliberately and significantly, used in this wider way by Plato, see Gosling 1968.

14 It has been suggested to me several times that if this is, indeed, Plato's view, then he must deny that non-human animals, though they are perceivers, possess coherent sensory experiences and this seems implausible. I agree that this seems implausible, but it need not be something to which Plato is committed on the view I have been defending. The validity of inferring that Plato is committed to such a view depends on his denial that non-human animals possess any and all ability to reason. It is not clear that Plato ever makes such a denial.

properties of sensory qualities (186a9–b9). This is important because it shows that Plato's focus here is precisely on what the capacity of thought contributes, specifically, to perception.[15]

There is widespread disagreement in the scholarship on this passage about how to construe the scope of αἴσθησις here. In particular, this debate centers on whether the *aisthetic* capacity, on its own, has the ability to form beliefs, even very simple beliefs, about its content.[16] The focus of this debate has, for good reason, been almost exclusively on how to interpret Plato's exclusion of *being* (οὐσία) from the content of perception. The debate surrounds whether *being* here should be construed narrowly such that it refers only to an awareness that the perceptual quality in question exists, or more widely such that it covers both existence claims and predications. I do not have any new insights to contribute to the debate on how we should read Plato's use of οὐσία here; I think that Lorenz has persuasively argued that we should read Plato here as denying that αἴσθησις has the resources to make any predications and, thus, lacks the ability to form beliefs of any kind (2006, 79–86). As part of his argument Lorenz also flags Plato's exclusion of *opposition* from the scope of perceptual content as showing that αἴσθησις is unable to identify, label, or form any beliefs about its content. For the ability to predicate, Lorenz argues, is, for Plato, essentially linked to the ability to differentiate one property from another and this, he says, requires an awareness of *opposition* (2006, 87–91).

Lorenz is right to call our attention to features other than *being* as evidence that Plato's exclusion of them from perceptual content shows that perception lacks the necessary resources to form beliefs of any kind. I think there is another of these features, which also speaks to the conceptual poverty of αἴσθησις, and which has not received the attention it deserves—namely, *number* (ἀριθμός). An awareness of *number*, and the number one, which apparently Plato uses also to refer to unity, in particular, seems to be necessary for individuating perceptual content. That is, the soul's ability to assess a particular perceived color or sound as a single thing, and/or as a unitary thing, depends upon its capacity to apply the concept *one* to that perception. Furthermore, it seems that the ability to individuate is a precondition for differentiating. For if

---

15   The middle Platonist Alcinous seems to make this very point when in section IV of the *Didaskalikos* he refers to that by means of which what is judged is judged as the rational capacity operating on the physical level—λόγος φυσικός. This passage indicates that while it is the intellect (νοῦς) in us that, properly speaking, judges, the intellect also has a downward directed activity, which is what allows it to distinguish (κρίνειν) things on the physical level (Alcinous, *Didaskalikos*, IV. 10–18).

16   For a defense of the view that in this argument Plato conceives of αἴσθησις as capable of forming simple beliefs about its content see Cooper 1970 and Modrak 1981.

one cannot even identify a quality as a single quality, how can one hope to differentiate that quality from others? Plato makes this very point in the *Republic* when, in considering those instances in which sense perception summons the understanding (νοῦς), he says that the soul must first (πρότερος) determine whether the perceptual quality is one or two. If it is determined that it is two, then it will be evident to the soul that the two things are distinct from each other (524b3–c1). This indicates that the application of number is preliminary to differentiating. If this is correct, then it only reinforces the idea that αἴσθησις is dependent on διάνοια for without the latter, the soul is unable to individuate, differentiate and recognize the contents of perception as the objects that they are.

In this section I have argued that despite the distinction that Plato develops between the body-dependent capacities of the soul and those that it exercises through its own rational activity and without the input of the body, he also considers there to be a close connection between the former capacities and, at least some of, the latter. This connection, I have argued, is such that the soul's ability to individuate and differentiate the content that it receives through the body depends on its awareness of certain objects of the rational capacity. If true, this is an important finding because it shows that, for Plato, at least some basic rational capacity is necessary to produce a coherent perceptual experience. Furthermore, it goes some way toward showing that, for Plato, there is a strong isomorphism between the ontological dependence that sense perceptible particulars have on forms and what we might call the intellectual dependence that the objects perception have on the objects of some of the rational capacities. While we have gone some way toward defending these ideas, there is certainly much that needs to be filled in and objections that must be addressed. In the remainder of this paper, I intend to address one of these objections by considering Plato's account of the tripartite soul and whether this represents an insuperable stumbling block for the view that I have defended above.

V

What I hope to have shown thus far is that in a number of dialogues Plato distinguishes between two kinds of psychical capacities—those that depend on the body and those that do not so depend—but that, at the same time, he develops an account the relation between the body-dependent capacities and, at least some of, the rational capacities, according to which the soul's awareness of the objects of reason contributes substantially to its ability to make sense of the objects of perception. This connection is particularly relevant, as we have seen, for understanding Plato's account of sense perception. The argument at *Theaetetus* 184–7 in which Plato specifies precisely what the content of thought (διάνοια) contributes to perception shows, at least on the reading I have been pressing, that without the input thought, the soul would be left unable to individuate, differentiate and label the content that it receives through the senses.

One potential difficulty for this view, however, is Plato's division of the soul into rational and non-rational elements in the *Republic*. For there is some evidence to suggest that in dividing the soul Plato endorses the idea that one, or both, of its non-rational parts has the ability, on its own and without the necessary aid of reason and/or the rational capacities, to form beliefs about its content.[17] If this is correct, then it presents a serious problem for our reading of the status of the perceptual capacity as dependent upon, at least some of, the rational capacities. The problem is this: if Plato, in dividing the soul, affords the non-rational parts a degree of autonomy such that they can, on their own, produce not only beliefs about their content, but also behaviour based on those beliefs, then there is no reason to think that perception depends on any of the capacities of the rational part of the soul in the way that we have suggested. In what follows I consider Plato's account of the partite soul in Book 10.[18] I argue that there is nothing in this passage that is inconsistent with the account of perception defended above, and indeed it can be read in such a way that it coheres well with this position. This reading involves taking seriously Plato's references to the downward directed activity of reason in Book 5. Furthermore, the account of soul partition in Book 10, I argue, is not about αἴσθησις *per se* but is rather about perceptual appearance (φαντασία), which, for Plato, always involves the input of something beyond perception. Taken together, these considerations allow us to make sense of the conflicting beliefs that Plato ascribes to the best thing and an inferior thing, in the soul, in Book 10.

Before we turn to Plato's defense of soul partition, it would be apposite of us to look at a preceding passage in which Plato discusses the relation between perception and thought—the finger passage (523a10–525a14). For here Plato considers carefully two different kinds of perceptual experiences and, in so

---

17 This view has been ably defended by a number of recent critics including Lorenz 2006, Moss 2008, and Storey 2014.

18 I have decided to leave the first account of tripartition (436a8–443a2) out of the discussion because it is concerned almost exclusively with the relation between reason, spirit, and bodily desire. While this account does reveal much about the structure of the divided soul, it does not consider perception or belief in any serious way.

doing, addresses the relation between αἴσθησις and certain rational capacities. In an effort to uncover the topics of study that lead the learner toward truth and understanding, Socrates considers the relation between perceiving, on the one hand, and reasoning about the things one perceives, on the other. Some critics have identified this passage as demonstrating that Plato holds, or at least held at the time of writing the *Republic*, that perception, on its own, is sufficient to generate beliefs about its content.[19] The passage begins by distinguishing between perceptions that do not summon the understanding (νόησις) and those that exhort the understanding to investigate (ἐπισκοπεῖν). The perceptions of the first kind do not require the understanding because, as Socrates says, the judgments (κρίσεις) that arise as a consequence of sense perception (ὑπὸ τῆς αἰσθήσεως) are sufficient (ἱκανῶς). Plato then gives examples of the kinds of perceptual experiences he has in mind. Considering the non-problematic case first, he says that when one perceives a finger from a close distance, one is not, generally, induced to ask, through the understanding: what is a finger (τί ποτ' ἐστὶ δάκτυλος)? This is because, as he says, sight does not, at the same time, signify (σημαίνειν) that it is both finger and the opposite of finger (523c10–d6). The problematic cases, Plato says, concern properties with opposites such as bigness and smallness or hardness and softness. In these instances the sensory capacity that is set over the pair of opposite properties is liable to transmit (παραγγέλλειν) perceptions that indicate, of the same thing, that it is, for example, both hard and soft. In these cases the soul is puzzled (ἀπορεῖν) and summons the reasoning capacity (λογισμός) and understanding (νοῦς) to investigate, first, whether each of the things reported are one or two (524b3–5).

In this passage, Plato distinguishes between two types of perceptual experience: one in which the judgment arrived at by means of perception is sufficient to produce an awareness that is clear and unproblematic; the second in which the quality, or qualities, indicated by perception leads to an apparent contradiction that requires the employment of the understanding to resolve. The question we must ask is: Does this passage clearly affirm that in the first kind of experience αἴσθησις is all that is required for the soul to achieve a clear awareness of the object? Let us consider this question, first, with respect to the specific sorts of experiences that Plato identifies here. The non-summoning experiences, I take it, are those in which the judgments arrived at by means of the information provided by perception is sufficient.[20] The reason why the understanding is not summoned to consider these judgments is that, in these

---

19 See Lorenz 2006, 88 and Storey 2014, 110–112.
20 I realize that my rendering of these lines as referring to the sufficiency of the judgments *caused by* perception is tendentious. I defend this rendering below.

cases, no contradiction arises from the information presented to the soul by perception. But, surely, it does not follow that in other cases the understanding need not be involved; Plato is simply not addressing this issue here. To make plain what I mean: the following is a logical fallacy: "if sense perception is presented with an apparent contradiction, then there is a need to summon the understanding; therefore if it is not the case that sense perception is presented with an apparent contradiction, then it is not the case that there is a need to summon the understanding." Plato makes it clear that his intent is not to make this point when he says, of the non-summoning perceptions that they do not induce the soul of the many, or the common soul (τῶν πολλῶν ἡ ψυχή), to ask questions of the form: τί ποτ' ἐστὶ Φ; (523d3–5). This indicates that there are some for whom even the non-summoning perception does, in fact, summon. This, as we shall see, is because the reasoning that Plato has in mind here occurs at a high level.

In order to get a clearer view on what Plato has in mind here, let us consider the language of the passage. Although Plato clearly does not mention any other capacities when discussing the non-problematic cases, the language that he uses to describe the way in which αἴσθησις makes the perceptual features available to the soul does not indicate, in one way or another, that αἴσθησις is sufficient for generating the relevant judgments. The first telling phrase, in this regard, is Plato's reference at 523b1–2 to the fact that in the non-summoning cases the judgments (κρίσεις) that come from sense perception (ὑπὸ τῆς αἰσθήσεως) are sufficient. The ὑπό + genitive construction is often used to designate the cause of some action or condition, but not necessarily the agent that carries out the action or is the subject of the condition. Thus in the *Sophist* Plato says of the Sophist's art that it causes our souls to believe what is false (τότε πότερον ψευδῆ δοξάζειν τὴν ψυχὴν ἡμῶν φήσομεν ὑπο τῆς ἐκείνου τέχνης) (*Sophist* 240d2–4). What Plato means here, I take it, is that it is through or by means of, as a cause, the sophists' τέχνη that our souls come to believe what is false. Similarly, our current passage can be read as indicating that the judgments in question are caused by αἴσθησις, but not that it is αἴσθησις that believes. Furthermore, it is the judgments, not αἴσθησις that are sufficient in the non-summoning cases. Such a reading is perfectly consistent with there being a capacity distinct from αἴσθησις that is involved in making those judgments on its basis, or under its power.

The verbs that Plato uses in this passage to describe how αἴσθησις makes the soul aware of its content have been read by some critics as indicating that his underlying assumption is that αἴσθησις is capable of generating these non-problematic judgments.[21] Through the course of this argument Plato uses a

---

21   See Lorenz 2006, 88 and Storey 2014, 110.

number of different verbs for this purpose,[22] but there is one verb that he uses three times—signify (σημαίνειν). As one might expect, Plato uses this verb most frequently in the *Cratylus*. Here he uses it to refer to the relation between a name and what it names, or the things to which those names refer. This verb is also used, at *Theaetetus* 191d7 for example, to describe how the impression of a signet ring functions. The impression puts one who sees it in mind of the owner of that particular symbol. The act of signifying typically involves a signifier, which stands in for a thing signified and causes that thing to be present to the mind of one who encounters it. Based on this, it is reasonable to assume that applying this verb to the work of αἴσθησις in this context Plato means to indicate that the capacity transmits or reflects or somehow communicates a quality to something else, but not that it cognizes that quality and certainly not that it judges it.

The two verbs that Lorenz specifies as demonstrating that in this passage αἴσθησις is credited with cognizing a wide variety of objects are λέγειν (524a8) and εἰσαγγέλλειν (524b5). To say that αἴσθησις "says" that the same thing is both hard and soft certainly could indicate that αἴσθησις is reporting to the soul the quality of a thing that it has already cognized, but it need not. There is a perfectly colloquial use of the term according to which it means only to indicate. Thus, an anthropologist studying the skull of a prehistoric human might say something like, "the degree to which these teeth are degraded says to me that this person ate a meat-heavy diet." In saying this, the anthropologist means that the condition of the teeth serve as evidence for the conclusion that the skull's owner ate a lot of meat; she certainly does not impute any awareness or cognition to the teeth, let alone ascribe to them the ability to speak.[23]

We can see, therefore, that while one might read this argument as an endorsement of the position that perception cognizes and makes judgments about its content, and that it only requires the rational capacities to adjudicate problem cases, it need not be read in this way. There is reason to believe that the questions that are asked in attempting to resolve the problem cases— τί ἐστὶ questions—signal that the reasoning involved occurs at a fairly high level. This leaves open the possibility that some form of lower-level reasoning is involved in producing the judgments that are characteristic of the

---

22 cf., δηλοῦν (523c3), παραγγέλλειν (524a3), λέγειν (524a8), σημαίνειν (523d5, 524a6, 524a9), εἰσαγγέλλειν (524b5).

23 Plato himself uses the term in this way when, for example, he personifies the outcome of the argument that Socrates and Protagoras have engaged in through the course of the dialogue at the end of the *Protagoras* (361a3–c2). Such a use is also evident when Socrates personifies the Athenian laws in the *Crito* (50a6ff.).

non-summoning experiences. Furthermore, the language that Plato uses to describe the process of perception and its relation to thought is perfectly consonant with the idea that αἴσθησις, even in the good cases, only provides the soul with qualities that must then be integrated into a coherent experience.

Let us now turn to perhaps the most challenging passage for our reading, Plato's argument for soul partition in *Republic* 10. In Plato's reprisal of the argument for tripartition he moves from the motivational conflicts of Book 4 to conflicting appearances and, eventually, to conflicting beliefs. Before we look at the argument it is important to first consider the context in which it occurs. Socrates has been engaged in a defense of the view that poetry should be excluded from the kallipolis on the basis that its products are a third remove from reality. The poet, like the painter, is an imitator who presents, as truths, things that are merely imitations, and who makes knowledge claims about things of which he knows nothing. Imitators know only about the way things appear (φαινόμενα) and nothing about the way they really are (601b9–c2). The poet imitates without the knowledge of whether his imitations are good or bad; he imitates what appears (φαίνεσθαι) to be fine to the many who know nothing (μηδὲν εἰδόσιν) (602b1–3).

After establishing these things about the poet's art—namely, that its products are at a third remove from reality, that it imitates appearances and that it is done without any knowledge of the things imitated—Socrates gets to the important question: Toward which element of a person does imitation direct its power? (602c4–5) In an effort to come to an answer to this question, Socrates gives the following argument.

1. Optical illusions put the soul in a state of confusion (602c7–d4).
2. In these cases calculating, measuring and weighing offer welcome relief (602d6–10).
3. Calculating, measuring, and weighing are the work of the rational element in the soul (602e1–2).
4. It is possible, however, that even after having measured and indicated that some things are bigger, smaller or the same size as others, those things may appear, at the same time, in the opposite way to the soul (602e4–6).
5. They had agreed previously that it is impossible for the same thing to believe opposites about the same thing at the same time (602e8–9).[24]

---

24 This refers back to the principle of opposition upon which Plato grounds his initial division of the soul (436b9–c2). According to this principle, the same thing cannot do or suffer opposites in the same respect, toward the same thing, at the same time.

6. Thus, the thing in the soul that believes contrary to measurement and calculation cannot be the same as the thing that believes in accordance with it (603a1–2).
7. The thing that trusts in measurement and calculation is the best element (βέλτιστος) in the soul, while the thing that opposes it is one of the inferior elements (φαῦλοι) (603a4–7).

The point that I was making about painting and imitation, as a whole, says Socrates, is this: Imitation appeals to something in us that is far from reason (φρόνησις) and that the outcome is never sound or true (603a9–b3). This applies both to imitations in respect of sight—paintings—and to those in respect of hearing—poetry.

This concludes Plato's argument that, like painting, imitative poetry also exerts its power on an inferior element in the soul. The first thing to notice about this argument is that nowhere in it does Plato refer to αἴσθησις. The talk of optical illusions is cast entirely in terms of appearings (φαίνεσθαι). In this argument Plato attempts to explain how it is possible that, in cases of optical illusion, the illusion persists even after one has come to the right view of the matter through measurement and calculation.[25] Thus, how is it that, for example, the Müller-Lyer lines still appear to be different sizes even after one has measured them? In such cases, Plato says, the observer is the subject of two simultaneous opposing beliefs about the same thing; and based on the principle, established at 436b9–c2, that the same thing will not be willing do or suffer opposites in the same respect, toward the same thing at the same time, it cannot not be the same thing in the observer that is the subject of these opposing beliefs. The question that we are concerned with is whether Plato, in this argument, ascribes belief formation to one, or both, of the non-rational elements in the soul, and if he does, does this necessarily impugn our claim that the content of αἴσθησις depends, for its intelligibility, on, at least some of the rational capacities.

The discussions of this issue in the literature have mainly focused on whether Plato's reference to the subjects of the opposing beliefs as the best thing (βέλτιστος) in the soul and an inferior (φαῦλον) thing signal a division within reason or an ascription of the capacity for belief-formation to a non-rational soul part.[26] Unfortunately, Plato gives us very little to go on here. While it would suit my view well if Plato were dividing reason here, I do not find the

---

25   Storey 2014, 84 makes this point.
26   Storey provides an excellent and very helpful account of the strategies employed by many of the protagonists in this debate (2014, 94–98).

arguments in favor of this view to be convincing. For one thing, at the end of the argument in Book 4 Socrates seems content that the rational element (λογιστικόν), the spirited element (θυμοειδής) and the appetitive element (ἐπιθυμητικόν) are the only parts of the soul (441c4–6). Furthermore, he employs the same principle that he had used in the earlier argument to ground the division of the soul here as well. This indicates, I think, that we are meant to have that argument, and those elements, in mind.

Others have tried to make sense of this passage by arguing that it does not generate a conflict that necessitates ascribing these particular mental states to different parts of the soul. Taking the example of the stick in water appearing bent, this strategy relies on reading the distinction as a distinction between, on the one hand, the *belief* that the stick is straight and, on the other, the *appearance* that it is bent. If the distinction that Plato is making can be read in this way, then the problem dissolves because belief and appearance are different psychological states.[27] Thus, there can be no contradiction that contravenes the principle of opposition because the subject does not suffer opposites in the same respect. This reading also seems to be a non-starter. Plato clearly thinks that not only are the two mental states in question belief states, but they are opposing belief states (602e8–9).[28] This point also obviates the strategy that would attempt to resolve the problem by claiming that the beliefs do not, in fact, conflict because they do not have the same content: one is the belief that the stick *is* straight, the other is the belief that the stick *appears* bent, but not that it is bent.

I would like to propose a different reading; one that allows us to remain true to Plato's text, while at the same time resolving any potential uneasiness caused by ascribing to Plato the view that non-rational soul parts can, on their own, form beliefs. Let us begin by reminding ourselves of the context in which the argument arises. As mentioned above, the question is raised here as part of a discussion of imitation (μίμησις) and, in particular, the value and impact of the work of those who engage in the *mimetic* arts—painters and poets. The details and the language of this discussion are very similar to Plato's account of the sophist's art in the eponymous dialogue. There, Plato identifies the sophist as an imitator (235a8). He then divides the expertise of imitation into likeness-making (εἰκαστικὴ τέχνη) (235d6) and appearance-making (φανταστικὴ τέχνη) (236c3–4). The practitioners of both of these arts are presented as visual artists; the former produce likenesses that are true to the proportions of the

---

27 For an example of this strategy see Reeve 2013, 84.
28 Moss 2008, 41–49 and Storey 2014, 87–94 have argued persuasively that the inferior part of the soul is one, or both, of the non-rational parts of the soul.

original, while the products of the latter do not maintain the proportions of the original, but appear beautiful if viewed from a certain perspective. The Eleatic Visitor and Theaetetus are unsure, at this point in the dialogue, about which of these classifications is most appropriate to the sophist, so they leave the question unanswered. Toward the end of the dialogue, however, they raise the issue again, but only after they have established that false speech and false belief are possible (264b5–d1). Had it been the case that false speech and false belief were impossible, imitation, and its corresponding effects, would have also been impossible. To show that false speech and false belief are possible, the discussants must look into the natures of speech, belief and appearance. Here it is argued that thought (διάνοια) is a dialogue that the soul has with itself, belief (δόξα) is the result of thought and what we call "appearing" (φαίνεσθαι) is a blending (σύμμειξις) of perception (αἴσθησις) and belief (δόξα) (264a8–b3). This passage makes two things clear: (1) A belief is required to generate a perceptual appearance; and (2) belief involves thought. It seems reasonable, therefore, to infer from this that perceptual appearance involves thought.[29]

Returning to our passage, Plato clearly invokes the idea here that appearance involves belief. This is why he moves from the conflict between an appearance and a belief to a conflict between a belief and a belief.[30] There is also good reason to think that, because it is based on the distinctive resources of the λογιστικόν, the belief that accords with calculation and measuring is a belief of λογισμός. If this is the case, then the belief state involved in the appearance cannot be a state of the λογιστικόν and must, therefore, be a state of one of the non-rational parts of the soul, otherwise it would contravene the principle of opposition. This does not, however, mean that the belief associated with the appearance is *generated* by one or both of non-rational parts on its own. It could be the case that the belief is arrived at through the cooperation of one or more of the rational capacities with the non-rational part of the soul. The *Sophist* passage just discussed allows us to see this more clearly. For if,

---

29 Storey recognizes the relevance of this *Sophist* passage for understanding Plato's use of δόξα in *Republic* 10 and uses it to bolster his argument that the conflict of beliefs here should be understood as a conflict in the assertions that the soul makes to itself (2014, 112n43). Storey is absolutely right to point out that, in the *Sophist*, the δόξαι characteristic of appearances are assertions and denials that the soul makes to itself, but he doesn't mention one crucial element of Plato's account of this process—namely, that δόξαι are, precisely, the conclusions of *dianoetic* processes (δόξα δὲ διανοίας ἀποτελεύτησις). This shows, decisively in my view, that the δόξαι that issue in appearances, at least as they are understood in the *Sophist*, necessarily involve διάνοια.

30 For an in-depth discussion of the move from appearance to belief see Storey 2014, 98–109.

belief is the result of thought, and if appearance is a blending of perception and belief, then there is every reason to think that the capacity for thought is involved in generating the belief associated with the appearance. On this understanding, the belief could still be counted a belief of the non-rational element because the content of the belief is taken entirely from the material available to it; but it is arrived at through the joint activity of the non-rational part together with the capacity for thought.

One might object to this reading on the grounds that its justification comes from a dialogue that, on a traditional view, is firmly in Plato's later period. Thus, it may be the case that Plato held these views about the relation between thought, belief, and appearance later in his development, but that does not mean that he also held them when he wrote the *Republic*. It can be shown, however, that the idea that the rational capacities cooperate with the non-rational parts of the soul is present already in the *Republic*. After establishing the initial partition of the soul in Book 4 and introducing the division of all being into visible and intelligible and the corresponding modes by which the soul cognizes each in Books 5 and 6, Plato, in Book 7, discusses the way in which education must be conceived if it is going to successfully incline the learner toward being and truth—namely, it must involve turning the soul away from the realm of becoming and toward that which truly is. In this context, Plato indicates that everyone, by nature, possesses the capacity to learn, but that the difficulty is in ensuring that that capacity is directed upward toward being rather than downward toward becoming (519c8–d7). In the very next lines Plato gives an example of what can happen when the reasoning capacity remains downward turned. Here he says those who are vicious, but clever, have a keen ability to distinguish (διορᾶν) the things toward which their soul is directed, but that because of the nature of these objects, this causes them to serve evil or unworthy ends (518d9–519b5). Because the modes of cognition that are specific to the realm of becoming are those associated with the non-rational parts of the soul—perception, desire, pleasure and pain—it seems reasonable to assume that the downward-directed function of the rational capacities identified in this passage refers to reason's cooperation with these non-rational modes.

If the reading offered above is correct, then it shows that Plato, in the *Republic*, thinks that reason can, and frequently does, exercise its power very much in conjunction with the capacities of the non-rational parts of the soul. A further indication of this view comes at the end of the argument for soul partition in Book 10. After having conceded that the justification for excluding imitative poetry from the kallipolis should not be based wholly on the analogy with painting, Socrates says to Glaucon that in order to secure this independent justification, they must go directly to that element of our thought (τῆς διανοίας) with which imitative poetry cavorts (603b10–c3). The reference to thought in this passage is striking, especially coming directly after an argument in which Socrates had defended the view that imitative poetry exerts its influence on an inferior element in the soul. This reference shows, and the ensuing discussion about the war in the soul ignited by imitative poetry confirms, that, for Plato, there is something more than mere perception involved in the cognition of these imitations.[31] Furthermore, Plato's reference to thought here picks up on a line from the very beginning of Book 10 in which Socrates indicates that poetry is likely to distort (λώβη) the thought (τῆς διανοίας) of anyone who hears it and lacks the knowledge to counter its effects (595b3–7). These references to the idea that it is one's thought to which the power of poetry is directed also puts us in mind again of the *Sophist* passage in which it is, precisely, thought that is presented as the means by which the beliefs that enter into the appearances arise. Thus, I would like to suggest that, for Plato, thought (διάνοια) cooperates with the capacities of the non-rational parts of the soul, and it is this cooperation that generates the beliefs that conflict with those formed in accordance with measuring, weighing and calculation.

In this section I have argued that the account of the partite soul in Book 10 is not incompatible with the view that the intelligibility of the content of the body-dependent capacities relies upon the soul's awareness of the content of, at least some of, the rational capacities. Far from being incompatible, I have argued that Plato's account of the conflict between the beliefs of reason and the beliefs associated with appearance can be understood in terms of the distinction between the upward-directed and the downward-directed activity of reason. Furthermore, understanding the argument in this way makes good sense of its context—namely as part of a discussion of the deleterious effects that the imitative arts have on the soul. As we have seen, the concerns that Plato's voices about the imitative arts in *Republic* 10 bear a strong resemblance to his criticism in the *Sophist* of the nature and effects of the sophistic art. Finally, this reading has the interpretive advantage of allowing us to under-

---

31 Reeve 2013 has a similar overall reading of the role of reason and its relation to the non-rational elements: "Reason—the more divine element in the soul—always has sharp vision, but it can be controlled by vice, that is, by the rule in the soul of appetite or spirit…. The effect of such rule is to turn it downward toward the visible world of becoming, rather than allowing it to look upward toward the intelligible world of being and the forms to which it is akin…. But the psychological power concerned with becoming is belief…. Hence it should be the rational part (turned downward) that is responsible for it" (83).

stand Plato's argument here without attributing cognitive autonomy to a non-rational part of the soul. For, according to this reading, the non-rational part of the soul can be the subject of an appearance—a mental state, which, for Plato, clearly requires that it involve some belief—only if it receives the necessary assistance of thought, or one of the other rational capacities.[32]

---

32   I am grateful to all of the organizers of Boston Area Colloquium in Ancient Philosophy for inviting me to present this paper; I am particularly grateful to Sarah Glenn, my host at St. Anselm College, for her hospitality and stimulating discussion. I would like to thank my respondent, Jessica Moss, for her thoughtful and most helpful comments; the paper, in its present form, has benefitted substantially from her insight as well as from the criticism provided by the BACAP anonymous reader. Last, but not least, I am grateful to Vasilis Politis, in particular, and all of the members of the Trinity Plato Centre at Trinity College Dublin, in general, for their comments on this paper throughout its various stages of development.

COLLOQUIUM 3

Commentary on Larsen

Jessica Moss
New York University

Abstract

How does Plato draw the line between perceiving and reasoning? According to Peter Larsen, he gives perception only the power to perceive isolated proper perceptibles, and treats all other cognitive operations as reasoning. I show problems for this interpretation. I argue that in the *Republic*, non-rational cognition—perception, either on its own, or perhaps augmented by other non-rational powers Plato does not specify, along the lines of Aristotle's φαντασία (appearance or imagination)—can generate complex cognitions. Reason's job is not to integrate the raw data of perception into a coherent experience, for we can do that without reason. Instead reason's job is to question, criticize and correct non-rational experience. I argue that there are grounds for detecting a similar doctrine in the *Theaetetus* as well.

Keywords

perception – reasoning – cognition – *Republic* – *Theaetetus*

That Plato draws a sharp distinction between perception and reason, everyone will agree. As to exactly how he draws the distinction, how it aligns with his partition of the soul, and whether he is consistent in how he draws it between dialogues, there is much less clarity and much more dispute. In his paper, Peter Larsen argues for some intriguing new answers to these questions. He puts forth several particularly controversial theses, namely:[1]

---

[1] I present these theses rather than Larsen's A-C in order to highlight what I think are the most fundamental and also most controversial claims at work in his argument. I accept as correct Larsen's claim A—that according to Plato the soul is the proper subject of perception. I present what I see as a controversial assumption underlying claim B in my (2), and I present what I see as the basic idea underlying his claim C in my (1).

1. Throughout the dialogues, Plato holds that perception can only represent isolated proper perceptible qualities like red or cold.
2. Plato characterizes anything that goes beyond perceiving as reasoning.
3. Therefore, the *Republic*'s appetitive and spirited parts—since they cannot reason and hence, by claim (2), can only perceive—are drastically cognitively impoverished. They cannot generate beliefs (δόξαι) on their own, but rely on the rational part to work up their bare perceptions into complex representations such as beliefs.

In what follows, I will raise concerns for each of these theses.

I   The Poverty of Perception

Larsen claims that throughout the dialogues Plato presents perception as unable to generate "integrated experience" without the help of thought. He makes a compelling case that this may be the view of some later dialogues, but does not give us enough reason to think that it is the view of his main target, the *Republic*.

Let us begin with the most straightforward case for Larsen, the *Timaeus*. As he rightly notes, Plato's most elaborate account of the objects of the senses, at *Timaeus* 61c–68d, centers on proper perceptibles like colors, sounds, and temperatures. This is not however conclusive evidence for a restricted account of perception, for Plato may have in mind an account like the one Aristotle makes explicit—an account on which, while what strictly affects our perceptual capacity are the proper perceptibles, we are somehow thereby enabled to perceive other properties and indeed whole physical objects and their relations (see *De Anima* II.6). It is nonetheless a compelling basis for the claim that in the *Timaeus*, Plato has a narrow view of perception. What about other dialogues?

Larsen's only other direct evidence is *Theaetetus* 184–7. Here Plato distinguishes perception from thought and belief by their objects: through perception we access proper perceptibles (things that can be perceived only by one sense) like red or cold, while we use thought without perception to access "commons"—properties that are not the exclusive object of any one sense—like number, difference, benefit, and being. Larsen accepts wholesale a widespread interpretation on which Plato's claim is that perception on its own can only represent isolated properties, and cannot predicate properties of anything—that is, cannot generate what Larsen calls "integrated experience." This interpretation, which I will call the perceptual-impoverishment view, was very influentially defended by Burnyeat (see Burnyeat 1976), and has been accepted by many others. It is however neither obvious nor uncontroversial. Traditionally Plato's claim that perception has no access to being (οὐσία) was interpreted as a restatement of the familiar point that perception has no access to Forms; it has also sometimes been interpreted as the claim that perception makes no claims about how things objectively are, since it makes no distinction between appearance and reality.[2]

Larsen offers little direct argument for the perceptual-impoverishment interpretation of the *Theaetetus*, deferring instead to the arguments of Lorenz 2006. Assessing the merits of this interpretation as against its rivals is a whole project in itself: certainly there are serious challenges that have not been met.[3] Here I will only note a worry that is particular to Larsen's version of the perceptual-impoverishment interpretation—first because it arises from the one new argument he offers for it, and second because, unlike other defenders of the interpretation, he maintains that Plato's view of perception is consistent between the *Republic* and *Theaetetus*.

Larsen argues that by denying perception any access to number, the *Theaetetus* is denying it the ability to "individuate, differentiate, and recognize the contents of perception as the objects they are"—in other words, the ability to have any contentful experience without the aid of thought. Through perception alone we cannot even be aware that we are seeing red, let alone that we are seeing a red apple. He supports this interpretation by saying that Plato "makes this very point" in a passage in the *Republic,* the famous summoners passage (*Republic* VII, 524a–c). This passage, however, is usually and very plausibly taken to be making quite a different point, granting to perception the ability to generate contentful experience while arguing that its content is inherently self-contradictory. Plato argues:

a. Perception sometimes says (παραγγέλλει, λέγει, σημαίνει; compare ἑρμηνεῖαι) that the same finger is big and small (*Rep.* VII, 524a–b).
b. We need reasoning to tell us whether the Big and Small are one or two, the same or different; this leads us to ask what *is* the Big and what *is* the Small—that is, to ask about the intelligible Forms (*Rep.* VII, 524b–c).

Larsen takes this passage to be making the same point he finds in the *Theaetetus*. On the standard reading, however, Plato's point in (a) is not that perception is

---

2 For the traditional Forms view see especially Cornford 1957; for the objectivity view see Paton 1922, Cooper 1970, Lott 2011, and Moss 2014.

3 Lott 2011 mounts a particularly detailed and compelling case against interpretations like Burnyeat's.

incapable of delivering judgments of any kind, but that the judgments it delivers—the reports it makes—are contradictory, because perception has access only to flawed physical objects, which are full of contradictions. Perception itself *does* predicate properties of objects, albeit in a confused and limited way: sight says that the same finger is big and small, touch says that it is hard and soft, and so on.

Larsen rejects this standard reading, arguing that we can give metaphorical or otherwise deflationary readings of Plato's claims about what perception says, signifies, or announces. Perhaps we can, but in the face of so many semantic verbs, and so little sign of metaphor or deflation, why should we? Larsen's motive is his unitarianism: the thesis that Plato's view of perception is consistent across the dialogues. If we accept this, however, we can simply turn the tables on him, and read the account of perception traditionally found in the *Republic* into the *Theaetetus* instead. And this is in fact a promising strategy in its own right.

On a straightforward reading of *Republic*'s summoners passage, perception delivers contentful reports about the world, but ones that are confused and contradictory. Reasoning corrects these confusions by discovering the underlying truths about number (the Big and Small are two distinct things, not one), sameness and difference (the Big and Small are different), and ultimately *being* (asking "what at all the Big is, and the Small" (524c). Like the *Theaetetus*, then, the *Republic* correlates proper perceptibles with perception, and a list of commons—number, sameness, and being—with reasoning. Perception delivers reports about proper perceptibles; reasoning gets at the truth by thinking about commons. Perhaps then the *Theaetetus* is drawing the very same contrast we have found in the *Republic* (and that we very plausibly also find in another passage Larsen discusses, *Phaedo* 65a–c): perception on its own does supply complex, contentful representations, but very confused ones; reason appeals to the commons to figure out how things really are. (Note that this would not entail that the *Theaetetus*'s commons are Forms: Plato's claim could be that perception accesses only how physical things appear, while reason tells us how physical things really, objectively are.)

This may be a hard fit with the first part of the *Theaetetus*'s argument about proper perceptibles, but arguably no harder than the fit between Larsen's reading of the *Republic* and the summoners passage's many descriptions of perception's pronouncements. Meanwhile, it is a strikingly *good* fit with remarks later in the *Theaetetus* about the contrast between reasoning and perception, where the idea seems to be that perception provides experience which reason then scrutinizes:

> The soul investigates the being [of the commons] in relation to one another, calculating in itself (ἀναλογιζομένη) past and present things in relation to the future. (*Theaetetus* 186a–b)

> Whatever affections (παθήματα) reach the soul through the body are present to humans and beasts as soon as we are born, while the calculations (ἀναλογίσματα) about these things, regarding both being and benefit, scarcely arrive to those to whom they do arrive even after a long time, and through a lot of effort and education. (*Tht.* 186d)

Perception says that a body is hot or wine sweet (thereby delivering "integrated experiences"); reason determines whether these things really are so, or will be so, or whether, regardless of appearances, they will do us good. Of course these passages can be (and have been) read in ways compatible with the perceptual-impoverishment interpretation of the *Theaetetus*; my point is simply that if we approach them with our minds on the contrast we saw in the *Republic* between confused perception and critical reasoning, they are very easily read as making the same point.

Thus an argument for perceptual impoverishment in the *Republic* that relies on comparison with the *Theaetetus* is problematic. Are there independent reasons to accept this reading of the *Republic*? Larsen mentions two that I find promising, although inconclusive. First, perception is absent from Plato's official catalogues of what we might call cognitive powers in both the Divided Line and Cave passages. Δόξα must make use of perception, insofar as it is set over perceptibles, but perception itself appears nowhere in these catalogues, and a plausible explanation is that perception on its own is not enough to deliver a full mental representation. To make this case more fully we would need an account of what precisely the cognitive items in the Line and Cave passages are supposed to be—powers of mental representation? varieties of belief?—and why perception falls short, but it is indeed a promising suggestion. Second, Larsen makes an intriguing comparison between the ontological dependence of perceptible objects on Forms and the putative epistemological dependence of perception on thought. This seems to me an original and promising idea well worth developing. It will however encounter some at least *prima facie* obstacles: is the idea that we can only have contentful representations about perceptibles if we have already had thoughts about Forms? If so, what about lovers of sights and sounds—emblematic of non-philosophers in general—who do not recognize and cannot think about Forms (476b–c), but have lots of beliefs (δόξαι) about perceptibles? Perhaps an appeal to something like the doctrine of Recollection would solve this puzzle—their beliefs about perceptibles are possible only because they have implicit awareness of Forms—but such a doctrine is notably absent from the *Republic*.

I conclude that Larsen's case for perceptual impoverishment in the *Republic* is intriguing but in need of considerable further development. Now on to his second fundamental claim, which operates in the paper mostly as an implicit assumption, but is crucial to his overall interpretation of the *Republic*:

II The Exhaustive Division between Perception and Reason

Larsen wants eventually to argue that the non-rational parts of soul in the *Republic* are incapable of generating "integrated, coherent experience" on their own, and thus rely on the rational part for the content of the beliefs Plato associates with them (Claim 3). To show this, however, it is not enough to show that perception is thus unable (Claim 1), for even if we grant this we might think that the non-rational parts have other cognitive resources at their disposal. Here Larsen is implicitly appealing to Claim 2: anything that goes beyond bare perceiving counts as reasoning.

This assumption underlies what Larsen calls claim B—that all the soul's cognitive capacities other than perception are "broadly speaking rational." It also, crucially, underlies his contention that the non-rational parts of the soul operate only with perception: being non-rational, they can have no rational capacities; if everything other than perception is rational, they must have only perception. Finally, it underlies his main argument for Claim 3, the thorough dependence of the lower parts on the rational part: any cognitive activity that goes beyond bare perception, even the forming of very simple beliefs, must involve some kind of reasoning. (This last thought is most explicit in Larsen's comment on the summoners passage: although Plato only mentions a role for reasoning (λογισμός) in criticizing the reports that the finger is big and that it is small, Larsen argues that given the putative poverty of perception even those reports must involve "some form of lower-level reasoning.")

It is however far from obvious that these are Plato's views. Plato's central psychological project in the *Republic* is to distinguish between superior rational (λογιστικόν) and inferior non-rational (ἀλόγιστον) forms of psychic activity—in the service of his central ethical project, defining and defending justice. He is fairly explicit about the nature of rational cognition: the rational part of the soul is capable of calculation, thought, and understanding (λογισμός, διάνοια, νόησις, νοῦς). In a number of passages he sharply contrasts the rational part's judgments with judgments that he seems to attribute to the non-rational parts of the soul, and certainly treats as arising independently of λογισμός. Not only do reports like "The finger is small" and "The finger is big" arise *before* the soul "summons reasoning and thought" (*Rep.* VII, 524a–b), but also illusory-appearance-based beliefs like "The stick is bent" and "The distant object is small" are contrasted with the beliefs based on reasoning and belonging to the rational part, in a passage from *Republic* x to which we will return below (602e). And although Larsen does not mention the fact, there are also whatever representations underlie and guide the non-rational desires that are contrasted with those that arise from reasoning in *Republic* IV, representations like "The drink is pleasant," "The corpses are intriguing," "Revenge is sweet." To repeat, all these are explicitly contrasted with λογισμός-based thoughts: the very natural interpretation is that none of them count as operations of λογισμός, διάνοια, νόησις, or νοῦς.

What resources does Plato think go into the formation of such cognitions? He has little to say on the subject in the *Republic*. Certainly perception, but possibly something else as well. Given the sharp contrast between such cognitions and those based on reasoning, however, we should try hard to find an interpretation on which whatever they involve does not count as reasoning. Either perception alone is enough to generate them—in which case it cannot be the impoverished kind of thing Larsen thinks it is—or the lower parts have resources beyond perception. It is in fact open to Plato to say that lower parts of the soul are capable of *any* kind of cognition, perceptual or otherwise, that allows them to form complex, contentful cognitions, so long as this cognition falls short of reasoning. For one such model consider Aristotle's notion of φαντασία (imagination or appearance-reception), and also of perception of common and incidental perceptibles: all these are explicitly attributed to the non-rational, perceptive part of the soul, and are contrasted with reasoning and thought (again λογισμός, διάνοια, νόησις, νοῦς), but they go far beyond the perception of proper perceptibles. Together they allow for very complex cognitions akin to some that Plato calls δόξα, cognitions which are enough to generate locomotion and other complex behavior with no contribution from reasoning. Is Aristotle contradicting himself, attributing rational cognition to a non-rational part of the soul? Surely not: instead, he understands reasoning in a particular way which excludes the kind of thing he is describing as perception and φαντασία.

There is sometimes a tendency in Plato interpretation to think that we know what counts as rational and what does not, and can use this knowledge to go beyond what is explicit in the texts—or even to go against what is strongly implied in them. The fact is however that it is Plato who introduces into our philosophical tradition the idea of λογισμός (reasoning), and therefore our task in the first instance should be to determine how *he* uses that idea to classify mental phenomena, leaving open the possibility that we may count as rational some things that he does not.[4]

Indeed the comparison with Aristotle is enough to suggest that Plato *must* allow for complex, contentful experience that has no contribution from reason, for like Aristotle he denies reason to animals, and yet clearly recognizes that they are capable of sophisticated behavior that would be very mysterious were they to lack any integrated experience. In the next section I will argue that a similar conclusion is implied by Plato's treatment of Larsen's main subject in the paper, the non-rational parts of the human soul.

III   The Dependence of the Non-Rational Parts of the Soul

On Larsen's account, a part of the soul that lacks reason has only perception (claim 2); given the very bare nature of perception (claim 1), any reason-lacking part of the soul must be incapable of generating its own contentful experiences, let alone its own beliefs, without assistance from a rational part. The non-rational parts of the soul are thoroughly dependent on the rational part.

Although Larsen does not point out these implications, the result is that his non-rational parts of the soul are not the independent, although foolish, agents suggested by Plato's analogies with social classes in the city (*Rep.* IV, VIII and IX) or with sub-human animals (*Rep.* IX, 588c). On their own they can provide only raw information (and presumably conation—Larsen does not discuss this) to be put to use by a more sophisticated creature: they are more like psychic capacities than agents. In arguing for this Larsen is taking sides in a long-standing debate over which of these pictures of the soul is Plato's in the *Republic*. It is also worth noting that Larsen's interpretation, although he does not explicitly address the issue of the lower parts' desires, has much in common with that of Penner and others, on which the appetitive part is the seat only of "blind drives," because only reason can focus it on complex objects (like cold drink instead of just plain drink)—or indeed on any particular objects, so

---

[4] I have in mind for example the arguments that the non-rational parts of the soul rely on the rational part to give them complex objects of desire since grasping these requires reasoning (see Penner 1990), or complaints that Plato should not or could not have meant to attribute evaluative beliefs to the non-rational parts since such beliefs require reasoning. For arguments against these, and an alternative account of Platonic rationality as the ability to criticize and transcend appearances, see Moss 2008; for another account see Ganson 2009.

that without help from reason it cannot prompt action.[5] Again these debates are entire topics in their own rights, and I will not try here to settle them here.[6] I will however point out some difficulties for Larsen's particular way of handling obstacles to these positions.

Larsen recognizes that many think the non-rational parts "can, on their own, produce not only beliefs about their content, but also behaviour based on those beliefs." In arguing against this view however he explicitly sets aside Plato's characterizations of the parts of the soul in *Republic* IV (as well as ignoring VIII and IX), on the grounds that these discussions have little to say about perception and belief (see his footnote 18). In fact however these discussions have very strong implications for the cognitive make-up of the non-rational parts. On a widespread and compelling interpretation they show that these parts are independent, agent-like creatures, whose complex desires and ability to generate autonomous behavior must be underwritten by an ability to generate rich cognitions. If this is correct then, like Aristotle's perceptive part of the soul, Plato's appetitive and spirited parts must have mental states that are very like what we might call beliefs, although ones that rely not at all on reasoning. The discussions of the soul's desires and conflicts in *Republic* IV, VIII and IX thus provide rich fodder for the view that the non-rational parts must have beliefs.

There are of course strategies for arguing against this interpretation—dismissing the implications of autonomous agency as misleading or as metaphor—but without employing them Larsen leaves a major objection to his view untouched. Moreover, given his extremely stark account of non-rational cognition, the objections to such strategies will be particularly forceful against him. In particular, he owes us an account of how Plato can allow for the possibility of animal behavior. If animals lack the rational part of the soul, as Plato strongly implies, and are thereby left only with bare perception of proper perceptibles, how do we account for the complex behavior, emotions, and even quasi-beliefs that Plato clearly acknowledges in animals? Surely animals must have some resources for "integrated, coherent experience" although they lack reasoning—and if this is so for animals, why should it not be so for the non-rational parts of the human soul?

Now to turn to the argument Larsen does give in defense of Claim 3. He targets a passage on the division of the soul in *Republic* X (602c–603a) which is usually thought explicitly to attribute beliefs to the lower parts; he proposes a

---

5 See Penner 1990 and Anagnastopoulos 2006.
6 I have defended the view that the parts are all agent-like, in my 2008, and argued against Penner's view of non-rational desire in my 2016.

novel interpretation on which the beliefs in question are in fact generated by the rational part, using the raw material available to the lower part. This is an inventive strategy, and I doubt there is anything in the text directly to contradict it; neither however is there is anything to suggest it, since the *Republic* is simply silent on the question of how beliefs (δόξαι) are formed. Why then should we accept Larsen's interpretation?

The argument Larsen gives for his interpretation of the passage is parallel to the one he gave us for Claim 1: a later dialogue (this time the *Sophist*) construes δόξα as rational; Plato is a unitarian (tacitly implied); therefore so too does the *Republic*.[7] It is certainly true that the *Sophist* very explicitly describes δόξα as the product of thought (διάνοια); moreover, this dialogue, along with its probable contemporaries the *Theaetetus* and *Philebus,* describes δόξα as resulting from processes of active reflection, questioning, and discussing that the *Republic* would presumably assign to the rational part of the soul. Does this show that the *Republic* would agree? It does not: indeed, the unitarian assumption in this case—the assumption that we can read Plato's later account of δόξα back into the *Republic*—is particularly problematic, and this for two reasons.

First, the passage in *Republic* x attributes one of the opposing beliefs to the rational part of the soul on the explicit grounds that this belief arises from measurement, weighing, and calculation, "surely the work of the calculating [or rational—λογιστικόν] part of the soul" (602d–e). The strong implication is that the opposing belief, since it is based directly on how things appear without any measurement, weighing, or calculation, is *not* the work of the rational part. As I argued above, here as in various places in the *Republic* Plato seems concerned to assign mental phenomena that involve reasoning to the rational part, and to oppose these to mental phenomena that involve no reasoning and hence belong to the non-rational part—a picture very different from that on which both opposing states (beliefs here, desires in *Republic* IV) are generated at least in part by reasoning.

Second, and perhaps more decisively, it is notoriously difficult to give a unitarian reading of δόξα across the *Republic* and later dialogues, for Plato seems to change his mind on the question of the rationality of δόξα. In the *Republic*, as we have just seen, and as Larsen himself agrees, the non-rational parts of the soul can have δόξα (although on Larsen's account they need help from the rational part). In the *Timaeus*, Plato argues that the appetitive part has no δόξα,

---

7 Larsen's actual argument goes by way of the *Sophist*'s definition of φαντασία as perception-based δόξα, but the *Republic* does not use the term φαντασία, and it would suffice for his purposes to point out that the *Republic* calls the view formed in accordance with appearances a δόξα.

reasoning (λογισμός), or thought (νοῦς), but only perception (77b–c); the strong implication is that it has no δόξα precisely because it has no reasoning or thought. Why does Plato change his mind about the appetitive part's capacity for δόξα? A compelling thought is that he has changed his mind about the nature of δόξα (or has come to use the word in a more narrow, technical way): in the *Republic* mental states generated without the aid of λογισμός counted as δόξαι, whereas now, given the later dialogues' account of δόξα as arising from thought and reflection, they do not.[8] If this is so, however, then we simply cannot assume that in the *Republic* Plato already had in mind an account of δόξα as essentially rational. Indeed, if he did hold this view at the time of writing the *Republic*, and therefore thought, as Larsen argues, that the non-rational parts can only achieve δόξα through the help of the rational part, then why would he change his mind in the *Timaeus*—why couldn't appetite there inherit δόξα in just the same way?

Thus Larsen's argument for the dependence of the lower parts of the soul upon the rational part is problematic. Perhaps the root cause of the difficulty is the unitarian assumption. Reading the *Republic*'s psychology through the lens of the later dialogues is an uphill battle: in the case of perception as well as of belief it is very natural to think that Plato changes his mind, with the *Republic* allowing a richer account of perception, and a richer account of non-rational cognition in general, than the later dialogues —and hence allowing real autonomy to the non-rational parts of the soul.

Nonetheless, Larsen's experiment is one well worth trying, for he invites us to question assumptions about the *Republic*'s psychology that are deeply entrenched, and to test whether the dialogue can be read instead as advancing a very different, and in some ways more modern, picture of the human soul.

---

8   For this account see Lorenz 2006 and Ganson 2009. Bobonich 2002 defends a different account, on which the main change is in Plato's assessment of the capacities of the lower parts of the soul, but he too would deny that in attributing δόξα to the appetitive part of the soul the *Republic* means to be attributing to it something rational.

COLLOQUIUM 3
Larsen/Moss Bibliography

Anagnostopoulos, M. 2006. The Divided Soul and the Desire for Good in Plato's *Republic*. In *The Blackwell Guide to Plato's* Republic, ed. G. Santas, 166-188. Oxford: Blackwell Publishing.

Bobonich, C. 2002. *Plato's Utopia Recast*. Oxford: Oxford University Press.

Bostock, D. 1988. *Plato's Theaetetus*. Oxford: Oxford University Press.

Burnyeat, M.F. 1976. Plato on the Grammar of Perceiving. *Classical Quarterly* 26:29-51.

Cooper, J.M. 1970. Plato on Sense-Perception and Knowledge (*Theaetetus* 184-186). *Phronesis* 15:123-146.

Cornford, F.M. 1957. *Plato's Theory of Knowledge: the* Theaetetus *and the* Sophist *of Plato*. New York: Harcourt, Brace and Company

Dillon, J. 1993. *Alcinous: The Handbook of Platonism*. Oxford: Oxford University Press.

Ganson, T. 2009. The Rational/Non-Rational Distinction in Plato's Republic. *Oxford Studies in Ancient Philosophy* 36:179-197.

Gerson, L. 2003. *Knowing Persons: A Study in Plato*. Oxford: Oxford University Press.

Gosling, J.C.B. 1968. *Doxa* and *Dunamis* in Plato's *Republic*. *Phronesis* 13:119–130.

Lorenz, H. 2006. *The Brute Within: Appetitive Desire in Plato and Aristotle*. Oxford: Oxford University Press.

Lott, T. 2011. Plato on the Rationality of Belief: *Theaetetus* 184-7. *Trames* 15:339-64.

Modrak, D. 1981. Perception and Judgment in the "Theaetetus." *Phronesis* 26:35–54.

Moss, J. 2008. Appearances and Calculations: Plato's Division of the Soul. *Oxford Studies in Ancient Philosophy* 34:35-68.

Moss, J. 2014. Plato's Appearance-Assent Account of Belief. *Proceedings of the Aristotelian Society* 114:213-38.

Moss, J. Forthcoming. Against Bare Urges: Appetites in *Republic* IV. *Proceedings of the Ninth Keeling Colloquium* 2011.

Paton, H.J. 1922. Plato's Theory of EIKASIA. *Proceedings of the Aristotelian Society* 69-104.

Penner, T. 1990. Plato and Davidson: Parts of the Soul and Weakness of Will. *Canadian Journal of Philosophy* 16: 35-74.

Reeve, C. 2013. *Blindness and Reorientation: Problems in Plato's Republic*. Oxford: Oxford University Press.

Shields, C. 2001. Simple Souls. In *Essays on Plato's Psychology*, ed. E Wagner, 137–156. Boston: Lexington Books.

Silverman, A. 1991. Plato on "Phantasia." *Classical Antiquity* 10:123–147.

Storey, D. 2014. Appearance, Perception, and Non-Rational Belief: *Republic* 602c–603a. *Oxford Studies in Ancient Philosophy* 47:81–118.

COLLOQUIUM 4

The Stoics on Identity, Identification, and Peculiar Qualities

Tamer Nawar
University of Groningen

Abstract

In this paper, I clarify some central aspects of Stoic thought concerning identity, identification, and so-called peculiar qualities (qualities which were seemingly meant to ground an individual's identity and enable identification). I offer a precise account of Stoic theses concerning the identity and discernibility of individuals and carefully examine the evidence concerning the function and nature of peculiar qualities. I argue that the leading proposal concerning the nature of peculiar qualities, put forward by Eric Lewis, faces a number of objections, and offer two constructive suggestions which turn upon reconsidering the nature and function(s) of peculiar qualities. Finally, I examine a simple but potent Academic argument against the view that identification requires detecting some attribute(s) unique to the relevant individual. Such an argument is, I argue, largely successful and may have encouraged later Stoics not to think that peculiar qualities enable identification.

Keywords

Stoics – academics – identity – identification – metaphysics

I Introduction

Stoic theorising about identity, discernibility, and identification had implications for questions in ethics, metaphysics, logic, and epistemology. However, reconstructing Stoic thought concerning identity is difficult. Most of our surviving evidence comes from piecemeal and often hostile reports describing metaphysical and epistemic disputes between the Stoics, Academics, and others, or else reports by later philosophers concerned primarily with other matters (such as expounding Aristotle's *Categories*). While the evidence concerning Stoic thought on identity is vexed, it is usually agreed that the so-called peculiar quality (ἰδία ποιότης) was central to Stoic thinking about identity from Chrysippus onwards and that the Stoics took the peculiar quality of an individual to be: (α) unique; (β) lifelong (that is to say, borne throughout the individual's existence); (γ) of use in epistemically identifying the individual; and (δ) something which grounded an individual's unity and identity. In this paper, I aim to clarify the Stoic account of peculiar qualities and some central aspects of Stoic thought about identity, discernibility, and identification. I carefully examine the textual evidence on these issues with the aim of making more precise our understanding of the Stoics' claims and in so doing challenge a number of existing views concerning the function and nature of peculiar qualities.

In what follows, I first examine the metaphysical background to Stoic thought about issues concerning identity and discernibility (section II) and then turn to consider our evidence concerning the function of peculiar qualities (section III) and the nature of peculiar qualities themselves (section IV). It has been argued, notably by Eric Lewis (1995), that the Stoics took an individual's peculiar quality to be a pneumatological quality and that such an account satisfies desiderata (α)—(δ). I raise several objections to Lewis's account and suggest that the Stoic account of how predications are made true presents us with two principal options. Either peculiar qualities are predicated in a sense such that something is literally posited in the relevant individual—in which case Lewis's proposal may be adapted so as to no longer fall prey to some of the objections I raise, though this leads to other problems—or peculiar qualities are not predicated in this sense, in which case peculiar qualities might more straightforwardly be lifelong and unique but should not be taken to ground an individual's identity. Finally (section V), I reconstruct an Academic argument against the view that identification requires detecting some attribute(s) unique to the relevant individual and argue that the Academic argument is largely successful and may have encouraged later Stoics not to think that peculiar qualities enable identification.[1]

II The Metaphysical Background

Much Stoic thought about identity and discernibility seems to have taken place in response to the so-called "Growing Argument" (αὐξανόμενος λόγος).[2]

---

[1] Thanks to: the organisers; Sarah Byers (my respondent); reviewers; an audience at Utrecht; and to Matthew Duncombe for comments.

[2] The four so-called "categories" were: (1) ὑποκείμενον ("subject" or "substrate") or οὐσία ("substance" or "matter"); (2) ποιόν ("qualified"); (3) πως ἔχον ("somehow disposed"); and (4) πρός τί

The argument traces its roots back to the fifth-century playwright Epicharmus and was seemingly often invoked by the Academics (Anonymous, *In Platonis Theaetetum* 60.5–26 = LS 28 B). I will first give a brief account of the argument and some Stoic responses to it, highlighting what I take to be pertinent for understanding Stoic thought about identity and discernibility.

A   *The Growing Argument*

Our fullest report of the Growing Argument is as follows:

> The argument about growth is an old one, for, as Chrysippus says, it is propounded by Epicharmus. Yet when the Academics hold that the puzzle is not altogether easy or straightforward, these people [namely the Stoics] have laid many charges against them and denounced them as destroying and contravening our conceptions. Yet they themselves not only fail to save our conceptions but also pervert sense-perception. For the argument is a simple one and these people grant its premises: all particular substances are in flux and motion, releasing some things from themselves and receiving others which reach them from elsewhere (τὰς ἐν μέρει πάσας οὐσίας ῥεῖν καὶ φέρεσθαι, τὰ μὲν ἐξ αὐτῶν μεθιείσας τὰ δέ ποθεν ἐπιόντα προσδεχομένας); the numbers or quantities which these are added to or subtracted from do not remain the same but become different as the aforementioned arrivals and departures cause the substance to be transformed; the prevailing convention is wrong to call these processes of growth and decay: rather they should be called generation and destruction, since they transform the thing from what it is into something else, whereas growing and diminishing are affections of a body which serves as substrate and persists. (Plutarch, *De Communibus Notitiis* 1083a7–c2 = LS 28 A1–2)

As presented here, the crucial premises may be rather roughly characterized as follows. First, all things are agglomerations or sums of matter (or "substance," οὐσία).[3] Second, for any sum, if one adds to or subtracts away from that sum, then—after the addition or subtraction—the sum is "transformed into some-

---

πως ἔχον ("somehow disposed relative to something"). For an influential reconstruction of the development of Stoic thought on the issue (especially the third and fourth categories), see Menn 1999.

3   That individuals in the world are identical to these agglomerations of matter is not explicitly claimed in the text, but this tacit premise (or one to a similar effect) is required. While I have sometimes adapted the translations, I have followed Long and Sedley in rendering οὐσία as "substance." However, one should avoid thinking of Aristotelian substance. For the Stoics,

thing else" (and there is no underlying subject which persists throughout the change).[4] Third, growth and diminution require the addition and subtraction of matter. Fourth, growth or diminution requires an underlying subject which persists throughout the relevant change. Since the growth or diminution of a thing requires both the persistence of an underlying subject and the addition or subtraction of matter, but all things are sums of matter and the addition or subtraction of matter to a thing "transforms a thing into something else" (that is to say, is such that there is no persisting subject), it follows that there is no growth or diminution. Instead, there is generation and destruction (and it is these processes which people incorrectly call "growth" and "diminution"). When one also takes into account the degree of flux in the material world, it turns out that there are no persisting individuals in the material world.

B   *Stoic Responses to the Growing Argument and the Appeal to Peculiarly Qualified Individuals*

In broad outline, it seems that the response of Chrysippus to the Growing Argument was to claim that the world is populated by many peculiarly qualified individuals and that peculiarly qualified individuals may not be straightforwardly identified with mere agglomerations or sums of matter. Furthermore, while the agglomeration of matter does not grow, the peculiarly qualified individual does grow. As Plutarch puts it, for the Stoics:

> Each of us is a pair of twins, two-natured and double—not in the way the poets think of the Molionidae, joined in some parts and separated in others, but two bodies sharing the same colour, the same shape, the same weight, and the same place, <yet nevertheless double even though> no man previously has seen them. But these men alone [the Stoics] have seen this combination, this duplicity, this ambiguity, that each of us is two substrates (ὑποκείμενα), the one substance (οὐσία), the other <[a peculiarly qualified individual]>;[5] and that the one is always in flux and motion, neither growing nor diminishing nor remaining as it is at all, while the other remains and grows and diminishes and undergoes all the

---

οὐσία in the relevant sense here is matter (ὕλη) (cf. Diogenes Laertius, 7.134; Plutarch, *Comm. not.* 1085e7, f2–3; Stobaeus, 1.132.27 = LS 28 Q).

4   The premise may be made plausible by considering arithmetic addition or subtraction: if one adds to or subtracts away from some number, one no longer has the same number (Sedley 1982, 255–9).

5   There is a gap. Wyttenbach supplies ποιότης, but Sedley instead suggests ἰδίως ποιός (1982, 273n26).

opposite affections to the first one—although it is its natural partner, combined and fused with it, and nowhere providing sense-perception with a grasp of the difference ... Yet this difference and distinction in us no one has marked off or discriminated, nor have we perceived that we are born double, always in flux with one part of ourselves, while remaining the same from birth to death with the other. (Plutarch, *Comm. not.* 1083c5–d7, e3–6 = LS 28 A3–5)[6]

On the account offered here, "each of us is a pair of twins" and what is apparently one is in fact in some way two or double (compare Simplicius, *In Aristotelis Physica* 48.11–12 = LS 28 E; Dexippus, *In Aristotelis Categorias* 23.25–6 = SVF 2.374). Although always being added to or subtracted from, the agglomeration of matter neither grows nor diminishes. Instead, it perishes from one moment to the next and is replaced by another agglomeration of a different quantity (Plutarch, *Comm. not.* 1083d2–4 = LS 28 A4). The second thing (named in the Oxyrhynchus Papyrus as the ἰδίως ποιὸν but not explicitly named in Plutarch's report) persists and does undergo growth and diminution (Plutarch, *Comm. not.* 1083d4–5 = LS 28 A4; compare LS 28 D8).[7] While the agglomeration of matter does not survive but is instead replaced from one moment to another, we "remain the same from birth to death with respect to the second thing [the presumed ἰδίως ποιὸν]" (τῷ μὲν ἀεὶ ῥέοντες μέρει τῷ δ' ἀπὸ γενέσεως ἄχρι τελευτῆς οἱ αὐτοὶ διαμένοντες, Plutarch, *Comm. not.* 1083e5–6 = LS 28 A5; compare Simplicius, *In Cat.* 217.36–218.2 = LS 28 I).

Plutarch complains that this flies in the face of common sense and is in fact absurd. After all these purported *two* things each "share the same colour, the same shape, the same weight, and the same place" and not even the keenest

---

6 ἕκαστον ἡμῶν δίδυμον εἶναι καὶ διφυῆ καὶ διττόν—οὐχ ὥσπερ οἱ ποιηταὶ τοὺς Μολιονίδας οἴονται, τοῖς μὲν ἡνωμένους μέρεσι τοῖς δ' ἀποκρινομένους, ἀλλὰ δύο σώματα ταὐτὸν ἔχοντα χρῶμα, ταὐτὸν δὲ σχῆμα, ταὐτὸν δὲ βάρος καὶ τόπον <τὸν αὐτὸν ὅμως δὲ διπλᾶ καίπερ> ὑπὸ μηδενὸς ἀνθρώπων ὁρώμενα πρότερον· ἀλλ' οὗτοι μόνοι εἶδον τὴν σύνθεσιν ταύτην καὶ διπλόην καὶ ἀμφιβολίαν, ὡς δύο ἡμῶν ἕκαστός ἐστιν ὑποκείμενα, τὸ μὲν οὐσία τὸ δὲ <...>, καὶ τὸ μὲν ἀεὶ ῥεῖ καὶ φέρεται, μήτ' αὐξόμενον μήτε μειούμενον μήθ' ὅλως οἷόν ἐστι διαμένον, τὸ δὲ διαμένει καὶ αὐξάνεται καὶ μειοῦται, καὶ πάντα πάσχει τἀναντία θατέρῳ, συμπεφυκὸς καὶ συνηρμοσμένον καὶ συγκεχυμένον καὶ τῆς διαφορᾶς τῇ αἰσθήσει μηδαμοῦ παρέχον ἅψασθαι ... ταύτην δὲ τὴν ἐν ἡμῖν ἑτερότητα καὶ <δια>φορὰν οὐδεὶς διεῖλεν οὐδὲ διέστησεν, οὐδ' ἡμεῖς ᾐσθόμεθα διττοὶ γεγονότες καὶ τῷ μὲν ἀεὶ ῥέοντες μέρει τῷ δ' ἀπὸ γενέσεως ἄχρι τελευτῆς οἱ αὐτοὶ διαμένοντες.
7 "In the case of peculiarly qualified individuals they say that there are two receptive parts, the one pertaining to the presence of the substance, the other to that of the qualified individual. For it is the latter, as we have said several times, that is receptive of growth and diminution" (LS 28 D8).

perceivers have been able to discern two distinct things—namely, the peculiarly qualified individual and its matter —where apparently there is only one (Plutarch, *Comm. not.* 1083d8–e4).[8] A later anonymous treatise expands upon this complaint:

> ... since the duality which they say belongs to each body is differentiated in a way unrecognizable by sense-perception. For if a peculiarly qualified thing like Plato is a body, and Plato's substance is a body, and there is no apparent difference between these in shape, colour, size and appearance, but both have equal weight and the same place,[9] by what definition and mark shall we distinguish them and say that now we are grasping Plato himself, now the substance of Plato? For if there is some difference, let it be stated and demonstrated. (Oxyrhynchus Papyrus 3008 = LS 28 C = FDS 843 B)[10]

This report also speaks explicitly of the two items in question as being indistinguishable and of their sharing a great number of properties (shape, colour, weight, and spatial location) in common. It attempts to highlight an apparent absurdity by asking which of the two things a perceiver who is looking in someone's direction might be perceiving: are we perceiving Plato, or his matter?

On the basis of these reports, we can see that, in response to the Growing Argument, the Stoics distinguished between a (peculiarly qualified) thing and its matter, but were faced with the challenge of saying precisely what the difference between a (peculiarly qualified) thing and its matter was.[11] If the Stoics

---

8   Plutarch does not, however, mention the fact that Plato was seemingly reproved in a similar manner by Antisthenes (Simplicius, *In Cat.* 208.30–4).

9   There is a hole in the manuscript. Following a recent suggestion by David Sedley (not yet in print), I offer "place" (τόπος) instead of "outline" (τύπος).

10]σαι δ' εἶναι, τῆς περὶ ἕκαστον | λεγομένης τῶν σωμάτων | δυάδος ἀδιάγνωστον αἰσθή|σει τὴν δ[ι]αφορὰν ἐχούσης. | εἰ γὰρ σῶμα μὲν ἰδίως ποιὸν οἷον Πλάτων, σῶμα θ' ἡ | οὐσία τοῦ Πλάτωνος, διαφορὰ | δὲ φαινομένη τούτων οὐκ ἔ|στιν οὔτε σχήματος οὔτε | χρώματος οὔτε μεγέθους οὔ<τε> | μορφῆς, ἀλλὰ καὶ βάρος ἴσον | καὶ τ[ό]πος ὁ αὐτὸς ἀμφοτέ|ρων, τίνι διαιροῦντες ὅρῳ | κ[αὶ] χαρακτῆρι νῦν μὲν | φήσομεν αὐτοῦ Πλάτωνος | νῦν δὲ τῆς οὐσίας ἀντιλαμ|βάνεσθαι τῆς Πλάτωνος; | εἰ μὲν γάρ ἐστίν τις διαφο|ρά, λεγέσθω μετὰ ἀποδεί|[ξεω]ς·

11 One may wonder whether there was a real *difference* between these two apparently coextensive and indistinguishable things or some other kind of difference (e.g., merely a conceptual difference or a difference in description). Most interpreters, adverting to what they take to be the nature and function of the Stoic categories, have assumed that a peculiarly qualified individual and its matter differ in description (or "aspect") but that there is

could not point to a difference between the two, then their interlocutors would have good grounds for saying that the two were not truly distinct and that the Stoic account of the manifold nature of things was fictitious. A report from Stobaeus seems to preserve a later Stoic reply to such criticisms:

> That what concerns the peculiarly qualified is not the same as what concerns the substance, Mnesarchus says is clear. For things which are the same must have the same properties. For if, for the sake of argument, someone were to mould a horse, squash it, then make a dog, it would be reasonable for us on seeing this to say that this previously did not exist but now does exist. So what is said when it comes to the qualified thing is different. So too when it comes to substance, to hold universally that we are the same as our substances seems unconvincing. For it often comes about that the substance exists before something's generation, before Socrates' generation, say, when Socrates does not yet exist, and that after Socrates' destruction the substance remains although he no longer exists. (Stobaeus, 1.20.7.29–40 = LS 28 D10–12)[12]

According to the report, Mnesarchus (a leading figure in the Stoa after the death of Panaetius, c. 110 BC) thought that a peculiarly qualified thing and its matter typically have different histories. Thus, for instance, there are points in time when the agglomeration of matter associated with an individual (for instance, Socrates' body) exists, but the peculiarly qualified individual (Socrates) does not—as, for instance, after Socrates has died. Accordingly, Socrates' matter might have one age, but Socrates himself another. The logic of the Growing Argument and the details of the Stoic response(s) deserve more attention than I can grant them here, but it seems that Mnesarchus is indicating that certain

---

no real difference and there are not, in fact, two numerically distinct items (e.g., Sedley 1982, 259–260; Brunschwig 2003, 228). However, if that is indeed the case, then it is hard to make sense of the claims being made in our sources about identity and distinctness (for which see below). This issue deserves further attention, but I cannot discuss it in greater detail here.

12 τὸ δὲ μὴ εἶναι ταὐτὸ τό τε κατὰ τὸ ἰδίως ποιὸν καὶ τὸ κατὰ τὴν οὐσίαν, δῆλον εἶναί φησιν ὁ Μνήσαρχος· ἀναγκαῖον γὰρ τοῖς αὐτοῖς ταὐτὰ συμβεβηκέναι. εἰ γάρ τις πλάσας ἵππον, λόγου χάριν, συνθλάσειεν, ἔπειτα κύνα ποιήσειεν, εὐλόγως ἂν ἡμᾶς ἰδόντας εἰπεῖν ὅτι τοῦτ' οὐκ ἦν πάλαι, νῦν δ' ἔστιν· ὥσθ' ἕτερον εἶναι τὸ ἐπὶ τοῦ ποιοῦ λεγόμενον. τὸ δὲ καὶ ἐπὶ τῆς οὐσίας καθόλου νομίζειν τοὺς αὐτοὺς ἡμᾶς εἶναι ταῖς οὐσίαις ἀπίθανον εἶναι φαίνεται· πολλάκις γὰρ συμβαίνει τὴν μὲν οὐσίαν ὑπάρχειν πρὸ τῆς γενέσεως, εἰ τύχοι, τῆς Σωκράτους, τὸν δὲ Σωκράτην μηδέπω ὑπάρχειν, καὶ μετὰ τὴν τοῦ Σωκράτους ἀναίρεσιν ὑπομένειν μὲν τὴν οὐσίαν, αὐτὸν δὲ μηκέτ' εἶναι.

things can be said of the peculiarly qualified thing that cannot be said of its matter.

C Stoic Views concerning Identity and Dicernibility

In attempting to show that a peculiarly qualified thing and its matter are in some sense distinct, Mnesarchus appealed to their different properties or predicates while claiming that "things which are the same must have the same properties" (Stobaeus, 1.177.21–179.17 = LS 28 D9–10). Putting aside the precise relation between a peculiarly qualified thing and its matter (which is not my focus here),[13] we may observe that Mnesarchus appeals to a general thesis—which presumably would have been widely agreed upon—concerning the indiscernibility (that is to say, perfect qualitative identity)[14] of numerically identical individuals.[15] Supposing that indiscernibility or perfect resemblance (that is to say, x "being just like" y) may be construed in terms of individual subjects sharing all their attributes (by "attributes" I mean properties or predicates), we may put the claim thus:

> **Indiscernibility of Identicals (INDISC):** $\forall x \forall y([x = y] \supset \forall F[Fx \equiv Fy])$.
> That is to say: for any x, for any y, if x is numerically identical to y, then for any attribute F, x is F *iff* y is F.

Thus construed, (INDISC) claims that (numerically) identical things are perfectly similar. If a and b are numerically identical, then any attribute a has, b has. We saw how Mnesarchus attempted to distinguish between the agglomeration of matter and the peculiarly qualified individual by pointing to

---

13 Just before the quoted passage, there is a discussion of the relation between a thing and its matter—which seems to be the sort of relation that is instantiated between a whole and (one of) its (proper) parts. In addition to (numerical) identity and non-identity, the Stoics discussed other relations, notably *not being other than* (οὐχ ἕτερον), which was taken to be the relation between a part and the whole of which it was a part (Stobaeus, 1.77.21ff = LS 28 D; *M.* 9.336, 11.24 [= LS 60 G3]; cf. Plato, *Parmenides* 146b2–5; *Sophist* 257b3–4). For discussion, see Barnes 1988, Lewis 1995, 101–106.

14 I should emphasise that I use the term "indiscernibility" to denote perfect qualitative identity—and "discernibility" to denote the lack thereof—regardless of whether it is discoverable by epistemic subjects or not. Accordingly, "indiscernibility" and "discernibility" are not epistemic terms.

15 I say "presumably" because if the thesis were controversial there would seem to be little dialectical point in Mnesarchus appealing to it (cf. Oxyrhynchus Papyrus 3008 = LS 28 C).

attributes which held of one but not of the other.[16] This, presumably, would show that there is not numerical identity between a peculiarly qualified thing and the relevant agglomeration of matter.

In our sources, we also find reported a related view, namely that:

> Everything has its own kind, nothing is identical with something else, you say. It's certainly the Stoic view, and not a particularly credible one, that no strand of hair in the world is just like another, nor any grain of sand. (Cicero, *Academica* 2.85, trans. Brittain)[17]

The view attributed to the Stoics (no particular Stoic is named) by Cicero (and by Plutarch elsewhere; compare Plutarch, *Comm. not.* 1077c; 1083f; cited below) is that among distinct things, there is always some difference to be found.[18] This claim seems to reflect a general thesis concerning the discernibility of numerically distinct individuals. Supposing that discernibility should be construed as the lack of perfect resemblance, we may suppose that the Stoics were committed to something like the following view:

Discernibility of Non-Identicals (DISC): $\forall x \forall y ([x \neq y] \supset \exists F[Fx \wedge \neg Fy])$. That is to say: for any x, for any y, if x is numerically distinct from y, then there is some attribute F such that x is F and y is not F.

(DISC) offers a necessary condition for one individual being numerically distinct to another. It claims that, for any two (numerically) distinct individuals, there is some attribute or other such that one individual has it while the other does not.[19]

While (INDISC) seems to have been treated as obviously true or else assumed without comment, (DISC) was contested by the Academics (Cicero, *Acad.* 2.85

---

16 To be clear, I am not claiming that the attribute in question (which a peculiarly qualified thing has and its matter lacks or vice versa) is a peculiar quality (on peculiar qualities see below). The attribute in question is merely some predicate or property which holds of one but not of the other.

17 *Omnia dicis sui generis esse, nihil esse idem quod sit aliud. Stoicum est istuc quidem nec admodum credibile, nullum esse pilum omnibus rebus talem qualis sit pilus alius, nullum granum.*

18 Compare Leibniz: "it is not true that two substances can resemble each other completely and differ only in number [*solo numero*]" (*Discours de Métaphysique* §9, trans. Ariew and Garber).

19 It is possible that a stronger claim is in fact being presented: (DISC*) $\forall x \forall y ([x \neq y] \equiv \exists F[Fx \wedge \neg Fy])$. However, the points I go on to make about (DISC) apply equally to (DISC*).

[cited above]; compare Plutarch, *Comm. not.* 1077C [cited below]). The plausibility of (DISC) depends upon how precisely it is understood; in particular, much depends, in our (modern) terms, upon which individuals one takes to be within the domain of discourse of (DISC), and upon which attributes (or sorts of attributes) one takes quantifications of the predicate variable "*F*" to quantify over.[20]

As regards the former question, the reports indicate that humans, doves, bees, figs, hairs, grains of wheat, and grains of sand were thought to fall under the scope of (DISC) (Cicero, *Acad.* 2.84–6; Plutarch, *Comm. not.* 1077C; compare 1083f). Accordingly, we may plausibly suppose that any naturally formed, organic unit—even minute ones (such as grains of sand)—falls under its scope (compare Galen, *De Causis Contentivus* 1.1–2.4 = LS 55 F).

As regards the latter question—concerning which attributes (or sorts of attributes) one takes quantifications of the predicate variable "*F*" to quantify over—our sources are less clear, but it is generally thought that, for the Stoics, what I have termed "(DISC)" should be interpreted in one of the more substantive (and least plausible) ways possible, so as to quantify over what we would regard as intrinsic attributes of objects.[21] Accordingly, no two distinct grains of sand are perfectly similar insofar as they will differ in some intrinsic attribute or other (such as mass, shape, or so forth). Understood this way, (DISC) seems implausible. That (DISC) was indeed understood this way by at least some ancients seems clear from Plutarch, who complains: "And yet there is nobody who does not think this and consider that on the contrary it is extraordinary and paradoxical if one dove has not, in the whole of time, been indiscernible

---

20 If (DISC) is understood to quantify over what we would regard as only intrinsic properties, then (DISC) is substantive but does not seem especially plausible (especially for smaller individuals). Broadening (DISC) to include extrinsic properties within its scope gains it plausibility, but even here one might raise worries concerning duplicates which—according to some—instantiate even the same extrinsic properties (cf. Black 1952). However, it does seem that the committed defender of (DISC) will always have one fairly secure avenue of defence should they seek to take it—appealing to impure properties (these are or include relations to a particular individual, e.g., the property expressed by "being a student of Socrates"), or else to non-qualitative identity properties (think, for instance, of Scotus's notion of *haecceitas*, a purported non-qualitative property of a thing). For instance, if *a* and *b* are numerically distinct but instantiate all the same *pure* properties, nonetheless, upon pain of tautology, only *a* will instantiate the property of being (numerically) identical to *a*. This last option secures a defence of (DISC) but at the cost of rendering it trivial. Taking (DISC) to be true in such a way, the principle will merely assert that numerically distinct things are numerically distinct by way of not instantiating the property of being numerically identical to each other.

21 E.g., Sedley 1982, 262–3; 1999, 406–410; Long and Sedley 1987, i.174.

from another dove, and bee from bee, wheat-grain from wheat-grain, or fig from proverbial fig" (Plutarch, *Comm. not.* 1077C = LS 28 O2).[22]

From our surviving evidence, it is not entirely clear what the Stoic motivations for maintaining (DISC) were or what support they offered in its defence.[23] So far as I can tell, it seems that the Stoics sought to defend (DISC) by pointing to the facility of qualified experts to tell apart even *seemingly* exact duplicates (Cicero, *Acad.* 2.20, 56–7, 84–6; Sextus Empiricus, *Adversus Mathematicos* 7.409–10) and perhaps they might have appealed to the difficulty of finding empirical evidence which falsifies (DISC).[24] However, whereas later thinkers attracted to such notions could appeal to precise instrumentation to discern differences between seeming duplicates (for instance, "Two drops of water or milk, viewed with a microscope, will appear distinguishable from each other," Leibniz, *Fourth Letter to Clark* §4), the ancients lacked such precise instrumentation. Accordingly, it is hard to see how the Stoics might have provided warrant for their claims with regard to more minute individuals or with regard to large numbers of highly similar individuals (more on which in section V).

---

22 As I understand Plutarch here, he is *not* claiming that there are exceptions to (DISC) *across time* so that there exists some x-at-t_1 (e.g., a grain of sand many years ago) which shares all the same properties as y-at-t_2 (e.g., a grain of sand today). Instead, he is claiming that surely at some point in time, there have—at that point in time—been two individuals who shared all their properties, so that there exists some time t such that x-at-t shares all the same properties as y-at-t.

23 While Plutarch seems to understand (DISC) in the way described above, this seems to require taking quantifications of the predicate variable "F" to quantify over what the Stoics regarded as qualities in the more specific sense (Simplicius, *In Cat.* 213.24–37 = LS 28 M; *In Cat.* 212.12–213.1 = LS 28 N; for discussion of which see below). If (DISC) can be taken to concern what we would regard as impure properties (e.g., being-the-son-of-Sophroniscus) (compare my suggestion concerning peculiar qualities below in section IV) one might more plausibly defend (DISC).

24 Compare Leibniz: "An ingenious gentleman of my acquaintance, discoursing with me in the presence of Her Electoral Highness, the Princess Sophia, in the garden of Herrenhausen, thought he could find two leaves perfectly alike. The princess defied him to do it, and he ran all over the garden a long time to look for some; but it was to no purpose" (Leibniz, *Fourth Letter to Clark* §4, trans. Ariew and Garber). Note that Leibniz also thought that the identity of indiscernibles could be inferred from the principle of sufficient reason (e.g., Leibniz, *Fifth Letter to Clark* §21), for discussion of which see Rodriguez-Pereyra (2014). However, I know of no evidence indicating that the Stoics made such moves.

III The Function and Requirements of Peculiar Qualities

I have so far attempted to clarify some general theses concerning identity and discernibility put forward or otherwise assumed by the Stoics. I now turn to the Stoic thought that each peculiarly qualified individual (ἰδίως ποιόν) has a *peculiar quality* (ἰδία ποιότης).[25] It is usually agreed that the Stoics took a peculiar quality to be a quality which was: (α) unique;[26] (β) lifelong;[27] (γ) of epistemic use in identification;[28] and (δ) a ground of the unity and identity of the peculiarly qualified individual. In what follows I will examine the evidence in favour of these claims while also attempting to clarify and make more precise these claims where possible.

(α) Uniqueness

The first strand of thought I will discuss concerns the *uniqueness* of each peculiarly qualified individual's peculiar quality. Plutarch reports that the thought of a peculiarly qualified individual (ἰδίως ποιόν) occupying two distinct and

---

25 Notice two points. First, the claim is restricted to peculiarly qualified individuals. I am not claiming that, for the Stoics, *everything* has a peculiar quality. Thus, even if the matter of a peculiarly qualified thing and the peculiarly qualified thing are distinct, I am not claiming that the matter of a thing has a peculiar quality (assuming that the matter of a peculiarly qualified thing is not itself a peculiarly qualified thing). Secondly, in what follows a number of related terms shall appear including: "peculiarity" (ἰδίωμα); "peculiar characteristic" (ἴδιον); "peculiar nature" (ἰδιότης, e.g., Porphyry, *In Cat.* 129.8–10 = FDS 848); "individual peculiarity" (ἰδιοσυγκρασία, e.g., Sextus Empiricus, *PH* 1.80); and "individuating [feature]" (ἰδιάζον, e.g., Simplicius, *In Cat.* 229.16–18 = FDS 848).

26 "*Every individual object is qualitatively unique.* I shall call this the Uniqueness Thesis. It is, to be precise, the thesis that every individual has its own peculiar quality" (Sedley 1982, 264).

27 E.g., "they picked out the peculiar quality as alone capable of providing living things with continuity of identity. And they were adamant that a peculiar quality must last throughout a lifetime" (Sedley 1982, 261–2); "peculiar qualities must be lifelong, in order to make Dion the same person from birth to death" (Sedley 1982, 262); "only by possessing a fixed peculiar quality, they held, can a living individual retain an identity through time" (Sedley 1982, 265).

28 "What features must peculiar properties have? They need to have three features, each of which is related to a task which these qualities perform. 1. they must persist for as long as the individual they qualify persists (in the case of living things they must be lifelong) 2. they must be unique 3. they must be perceptible (under ideal conditions at least)" (Lewis 1995, 91). "The Stoics [required] for each individual, or at least for each living individual, a single lifelong individuating quality, which would (a) preserve its identity throughout its lifetime, and (b) make it recognisable as the individual it was" (Sedley 1982, 266–7).

presumably spatially separated agglomerations of matter (*at the same time*, we must add) was dismissed by the Stoics as absurd (Plutarch, *Comm. not.* 1077C = LS 28 O1). Accordingly, no two distinct, non-contiguous agglomerations of matter could share the same peculiar quality (ἰδία ποιότης).[29] In addition, a report of a Stoic discussion of the meaning and reference of the proper name or proper noun (ὄνομα κύριον) offers the following:

> According to Diogenes [of Babylon], an appellative (προσηγορία) is a part of language which signifies a common quality (σημαῖνον κοινὴν ποιότητα), for instance, *man, horse*; a name (ὄνομα) is a part of language which indicates a peculiar quality (δηλοῦν ἰδίαν ποιότητα), for instance, *Diogenes, Socrates.* (Diogenes Laertius, 7.58 = LS 33 M)[30]

On this account, which reports the views of Diogenes of Babylon (a successor of Chrysippus and part of the famous philosophical embassy to Rome in 155 BC), a common noun (for instance, "man") signifies (σημαίνειν) a common quality (κοινὴ ποιότης), such as *being human*. In contrast, a proper noun (for instance, "Socrates") indicates (δηλοῦν) a peculiar quality (ἰδία ποιότης).[31] What precisely this peculiar quality might be is not immediately clear, but it is strongly implied (even if not explicitly stated) that the peculiar quality is unique. In light of these pieces of evidence we may, I think, suppose that for the Stoics every peculiarly qualified individual has a unique peculiar quality. The thesis may be put thus:

---

29 There are complications concerning how, precisely, one should understand the notion of distinct and spatially separated agglomerations of matter and two difficulties are worth mentioning here. First, the famous discussion of Dion and Theon seems to concern the sort of case wherein two peculiarly qualified individuals occupy the same matter (Philo of Alexandria, *De Aeternitate Mundi* 47–51 = LS 28 P). Interpretation of the puzzle is difficult and the issue merits its own detailed treatment. For discussion, see Sedley 1982, 267–70; Irwin 1996, 467–70, 74–5; Bowin 2003. Secondly, if it is a problem that a proper part of a peculiarly qualified individual is *also* a peculiarly qualified individual (a worry *possibly* present in the discussion of Dion and Theon), then there are significant additional difficulties. This is because, according to the Stoics, all the observable peculiarly qualified individuals are proper parts of the cosmos which is itself a peculiarly qualified individual (Diogenes Laertius, 7.137–8 = LS 44 F). Again, this issue merits its own separate discussion.

30 Ἔστι δὲ προσηγορία μὲν κατὰ τὸν Διογένην μέρος λόγου σημαῖνον κοινὴν ποιότητα, οἷον Ἄνθρωπος, Ἵππος· ὄνομα δέ ἐστι μέρος λόγου δηλοῦν ἰδίαν ποιότητα, οἷον Διογένης, Σωκράτης·

31 For discussion of the fact that what is indicated is the peculiar quality (ἰδία ποιότης), rather than the peculiarly qualified individual (ἰδίως ποιόν), see Brunschwig 1984, 7ff.

Distinct Peculiarly Qualified Individuals have Unique Peculiar Qualities (UNIQ): $\forall x \exists F(Fx \land \forall y[(x \neq y) \supset \neg Fy])$. That is to say: for any x, there is some attribute F such that only x is F.

Whereas (DISC) (see above) claims that for any two distinct individuals there is always some attribute or other by which they differ (and seems to apply to all individuals), (UNIQ)—which takes as its domain of discourse peculiarly qualified individuals—claims that every peculiarly qualified individual instantiates some particular attribute which it, and no other individual, has.

(β)   *Permanence (or Being Lifelong)*

The most relevant pieces of evidence concerning peculiar qualities being lifelong (that is to say, instantiated by a peculiarly qualified individual throughout its existence) are as follows:

> The substance neither grows nor diminishes through addition or subtraction, but simply alters, just as in the case of numbers and measure. And it follows that it is in the case of peculiarly qualified individuals, such as Dion and Theon, that processes of growth and diminution arise. Therefore each individual's quality (ποιότης) actually remains from its generation to its destruction, in the case of destructible animals, plants and the like. (Stobaeus, 1.177.21–179.17 = LS 28 D5–7)[32]

> ... if in the case of compound entities there exists individual form—with reference to which the Stoics speak of something peculiarly qualified, which both is gained, and lost again, all together, and remains the same throughout the compound entity's life even though its constituent parts come to be and are destroyed at different times. (Simplicius, *In Libros Aristotelis De Anima* 217.36–218.2 = LS 28 I; compare Plutarch, *Comm. not.* e3–6 = LS 28 A5)[33]

---

32 τὴν γὰρ οὐσίαν οὔτ' αὔξεσθαι οὔτε μειοῦσθαι κατὰ πρόσθεσιν ἢ ἀφαίρεσιν, ἀλλὰ μόνον ἀλλοιοῦσθαι, καθάπερ ἐπ' ἀριθμῶν καὶ μέτρων. καὶ συμβαίνειν ἐπὶ τῶν ἰδίως ποιῶν, οἷον Δίωνος καὶ Θέωνος, καὶ αὐξήσεις καὶ μειώσεις γίνεσθαι. διὸ καὶ παραμένειν τὴν ἑκάστου ποιότητα [τα] ἀπὸ τῆς γενέσεως μέχρι τῆς ἀναιρέσεως, ἐπὶ τῶν ἀναίρεσιν ἐπιδεχομένων ζῴων καὶ φυτῶν καὶ τῶν τούτοις παραπλησίων.

33 εἴ γε καὶ ἐπὶ τῶν συνθέτων τὸ ἀτομωθὲν ὑπάρχει εἶδος, καθ' ὃ ἰδίως παρὰ τοῖς ἐκ τῆς Στοᾶς λέγεται ποιόν, ὃ καὶ ἀθρόως ἐπιγίνεται καὶ αὖ ἀπογίνεται καὶ τὸ αὐτὸ ἐν παντὶ τῷ τοῦ συνθέτου βίῳ διαμένει, καίτοι τῶν μορίων ἄλλων ἄλλοτε γινομένων τε καὶ φθειρομένων.

According to the report from Stobaeus, each individual's quality (ποιότης)—(presumably) their peculiar quality (ἰδία ποιότης)—remains (παραμένειν) throughout that individual's existence. The report from Simplicius claims that the peculiarly qualified thing (ἰδίως ποιὸν) persists (διαμένειν) *the same* throughout the relevant entity's existence (compare Plutarch, *Comm. not.* 1083e3–6 = LS 28 A5).[34]

The evidence that peculiar qualities are lifelong seems fairly clear but two cautionary points should be observed. First, while it is suggested that we retain the same peculiar quality what is actually said in Simplicius is that we retain or remain the same peculiarly qualified individual. This *might* allow for an individual (for instance, Socrates) remaining the same peculiarly qualified individual throughout his existence even if his peculiar quality does not remain the same throughout his existence. Secondly, even if we suppose that the peculiar quality does remain the same throughout the relevant peculiarly qualified individual's existence (as Stobaeus's report claims), due to certain idiosyncrasies concerning the Stoic account of qualities, it is not entirely clear whether the peculiarly qualified individual's peculiar quality remains qualitatively the same diachronically or numerically the same diachronically. This last point will sound highly odd to modern ears, but turns upon the corporealist account of qualities according to which qualities, in the more specific sense, are quite literally *bodies*. I return to this issue below in section IV.

(γ)   *Identification*

As far as the purported role peculiar qualities play in allowing us to identify individuals is concerned, matters are slightly more complicated. Little in the way of explicit textual evidence has been invoked by those scholars who think that peculiar qualities played a role in helping epistemic agents identify individuals. Instead, scholars have typically reasoned that peculiar qualities must play this role due to their construal of Stoic epistemology and their reasoning typically runs thus. First, a form of infallible cognition was central to Stoic epistemology. Secondly, the relevant infallible cognition required identifying

---

34   "Yet this difference and distinction in us no one has marked off or discriminated, nor have we perceived that we are born double, always in flux with one part of ourselves, while remaining the same from birth to death with the other" (... ταύτην δὲ τὴν ἐν ἡμῖν ἑτερότητα καὶ <δια>φορὰν οὐδεὶς διεῖλεν οὐδὲ διέστησεν, οὐδ' ἡμεῖς ᾐσθόμεθα διττοὶ γεγονότες καὶ τῷ μὲν ἀεὶ ῥέοντες μέρει τῷ δ' ἀπὸ γενέσεως ἄχρι τελευτῆς οἱ αὐτοὶ διαμένοντες. Plutarch, *Comm. not.* e3–6 = LS 28 A5). As we saw above, the report from Plutarch does not here name the ἰδίως ποιὸν explicitly, but it seems to be discussing it and what it says seems to closely resemble what we find in the (slightly more detailed) report by Simplicius. Here too the ἰδίως ποιὸν is treated as a part of a compound entity, and it is said to remain the same in spite of flux.

individuals as the precise individuals they were. Thirdly, the need to identify individuals encouraged the Stoics to posit the existence of peculiar qualities.[35] However, it is not clear that this reasoning is entirely sound.

That the Stoics, in their discussions of apprehension (κατάληψις)—a form of cognition which occurs as the result of giving assent to a kataleptic appearance (φαντασία καταληπτική, Sextus Empiricus, *M.* 7.151; 8.397)—were interested in a form of infallible cognition seems reasonably clear (though several features of the Stoic account and the precise nature of this infallibility are controversial).[36] However, it is not at all clear (contra, for instance, Lewis 1995, 90–1) why one should think that infallible cognition requires identifying particular individuals. Consider, for instance, infallibly cognising only something like "This is white." Such items of apprehension seem far more secure than items with content like "This is Socrates" (or, perhaps more securely, "This *seems* white to me"; compare Cicero, *Acad.* 2.21; Augustine, *C. Acad.* 3.11.26).[37] Indeed, it is

---

35 "First, the epistemological motivation. In order to ensure the possibility of infallible knowledge, and so preserve the possibility of the existence of a sage, the Stoics needed to preclude the possibility of two qualitatively indistinguishable individuals" (Lewis 1995, 90). "The Stoics had an epistemological motive for rejecting a criterion of identity that might not remain unchanged throughout an individual's lifetime" (Sedley 1982, 263). "[According to the Stoics] there is never any need to misidentify an external object, because every individual object is qualitatively unique. I shall call this the Uniqueness Thesis. It is, to be precise, the thesis that every individual has its own peculiar quality" (Sedley 1982, 264). "On the epistemological front, the criterion required was one by which individuals could be infallibly recognised" (Sedley 1982, 266).

36 For the Stoics, an appearance is kataleptic *iff* it: (i) ἀπὸ ὑπάρχοντος ("arises from what is"); (ii) κατ' αὐτὸ τὸ ὑπάρχον ἐναπομεμαγμένη καὶ ἐναπεσφραγισμένη ("is stamped and impressed exactly in accordance with what is"); and (iii) ὁποία οὐκ ἂν γένοιτο ἀπὸ μὴ ὑπάρχοντος ("is of such a kind as could not arise from what is not") (Sextus Empiricus, *M.* 7.248; 11.183; *PH* 2.4; Diogenes Laertius, 7.46, 50). Precisely how to understand this—especially (iii) (which, presumably, is the clause which reveals apprehension to be *infallible* in some suitable sense)—is contentious. I have elsewhere defended an account according to which in order to apprehend an agent must stand in an appropriate causal relation to the object apprehended and the agent's appearance of the object must be *clear* (and I understand this in an internalist manner according to which the clarity of the appearance is accessible to the epistemic agent). For detailed discussion, see Nawar 2014.

37 Sedley appeals to one's conceptions needing to be built upon appearances free from error: "it was not until Chrysippus appeared on the scene that a full scale defence of infallible perception was launched. A lot was at stake. Our very rationality, the Stoics held, depended on our development of a set of universal conceptions, and these they took to depend on numerous recollected sensory perceptions during the first years of life, the conception of "horse," for example, being constructed out of a series of individual perceptions of horses. If those sensory perceptions might after all be erroneous, our universal

plausible that infallible cognition requires *not* identifying individuals for the cognition in question (see section V).

While it should not simply be assumed (as some do), that infallible cognition requires identification of individuals, the textual evidence from discussions of Stoic epistemology does in my eyes strongly suggest that—whatever the reasons behind this might have been—the Stoics do indeed often seem to have envisioned the identification of a particular individual as the salient content of kataleptic appearances.[38] Not all of our evidence fits this pattern (sometimes it seems that the so-called "identification" occurs at the level of species rather than at the level of the individual),[39] but the preoccupation in many of our

---

conceptions, and hence our very rationality, could prove to be vacuous. No understanding of the world could rest on so shaky a foundation" (Sedley 1982, 263–4). However, *even if* that is right, it is not clear why developing a concept (e.g., the concept HORSE) requires (infallibly) identifying individual horses as the particular horses they are (e.g., Bucephalus, Brunellus, etc.).

[38] Thus, for instance, when confronted with twins, it seems that the salient content of a kataleptic appearance was expected to have been something like "this is twin *a*" (e.g., "this is Quintus Servilius Geminus," Cicero, *Acad.* 2.84; "this is Polydeuces," Sextus Empiricus, *M.* 7.410) as opposed to "this is one of the twins" or "this is twin *a* or *b*." Similarly, in discussing Menelaus having a kataleptic appearance of Helen upon seeing her on the isle of Pharos, the relevant content of the kataleptic appearance (one which Menelaus, due to his mistaken beliefs, did *not* assent to) must surely have been something like "this is Helen" or "you are Helen" (*M.* 7.180, 255). Something similar applies to the examples of Admetus (e.g., "this is Alcestis," *M.* 7.254), Orestes (who mistakenly gives assent to "you are one of my furies," *M.* 7.249 [cf. Euripides, *Orestes* 264]), and Heracles (*M.* 7.249). The thought was not confined to apprehending human beings (e.g., "this is snake *a*," Sextus Empiricus, *M.* 7.410; "this is egg *a*," Cicero, *Acad.* 2.56–8).

[39] Thus, for instance, it seems that when confronted with a Sorites the relevant content of a purported kataleptic appearance should have been something like "this is a heap" or "ten are few" (e.g., Cicero, *Acad.* 2.92–4; cf. Diogenes Laertius, 7.82). One might also adduce certain other cases where the pertinent content would seem to be "this is a horse" (*Acad.* 2.21), "this is a snake" (*M.* 7.187–8; *PH* 1.227–228; cf. *M.* 7.409–410), or "that is white" (*Acad.* 2.21). However, these may not be examples of (potential) kataleptic appearances as they are of Academic rather than Stoic provenance (though *Acad.* 2.21, which is Antiochean, is less clear cut) and are seemingly examples of *persuasive* appearances. Furthermore, if these are indeed meant to be kataleptic appearances, one might still see these as being concerned with identification but see the identification as occurring at the level of types (e.g., "this is a cat") rather than that of individuals (e.g., "this is Tibbles"). The Stoics may have been interested in both types of identification (or failed to clearly distinguish between the two). I here speak of identification primarily as identifying an individual qua individual.

sources with identifying the individual one is perceiving is striking.[40] However, *even if* one thought that particular individuals should be identified in apprehension, it is not entirely clear that the Stoics thought that peculiar qualities (as opposed to something else) were the means by which individuals might be identified.

The most explicit direct textual evidence of which I am aware which speaks in favour of the role of peculiar qualities in enabling identification of an individual comes from Sextus's discussion of Stoic epistemology:

> Not to mention its being stamped and impressed, so that all the peculiarities of the things that appear are skilfully stamped on (πάντα τεχνικῶς τὰ ἰδιώματα τῶν φανταστῶν ἀναμάττηται). For just as carvers tackle all the parts of the things they are completing, and in the same way as seals on signet rings always stamp all their markings exactly on the wax, so too those who get an apprehension of the underlying things ought to focus on all their peculiarities ... For the Stoics say that the person who has the kataleptic appearance skilfully gets in touch with the hidden difference in the objects, since this kind of appearance has a certain peculiarity, compared with other appearances, like what horned snakes have compared with other snakes. But the Academics say, on the contrary, that it would be possible for a falsehood that was indistinguishable from the kataleptic appearance to be found. (Sextus Empiricus, *M*. 7.250–2, trans. Bett)[41]

---

40 This is compounded by the fact that when the sceptic appealed to duplicates, the Stoic might have responded by saying: "well, this may not be Socrates, but it is certainly a man" (identification at the level of species) *or* "well, while this may not be *x*, it certainly looks like *x*" *or* "it appears to me that it is *x*." Given that such responses are straightforward enough and other ancients seem to have made them without much fuss (e.g., Augustine, *C. Acad.* 3.10.23ff; Sextus Empiricus, *M*. 7.191 [which discusses the Cyrenaics]), it is surprising that, with as far as I am aware only one possible exception (the idiosyncratic case of Sphaerus, *Ath.* 8 354e = SVF 1.624; Diogenes Laertius, 7.177 = SVF 1.625), there is little evidence the Stoics made such moves in response to the Academic arguments.

41 οὐ μὴν ἀλλὰ καὶ ἐναπομεμαγμένην καὶ ἐναπεσφραγισμένην τυγχάνειν, ἵνα πάντα τεχνικῶς τὰ ἰδιώματα τῶν φανταστῶν ἀναμάττηται. ὡς γὰρ οἱ γλυφεῖς πᾶσι τοῖς μέρεσι συμβάλλουσι τῶν τελουμένων, καὶ ὃν τρόπον αἱ διὰ τῶν δακτυλίων σφραγῖδες ἀεὶ πάντας ἐπ' ἀκριβὲς τοὺς χαρακτῆρας ἐναπομάττονται τῷ κηρῷ, οὕτω καὶ οἱ κατάληψιν ποιούμενοι τῶν ὑποκειμένων πᾶσιν ὀφείλουσιν αὐτῶν τοῖς ἰδιώμασιν ἐπιβάλλειν.... γάρ φασιν ὅτι ὁ ἔχων τὴν καταληπτικὴν φαντασίαν τεχνικῶς προσβάλλει τῇ ὑπούσῃ τῶν πραγμάτων διαφορᾷ, ἐπείπερ καὶ εἶχέ τι τοιοῦτον ἰδίωμα ἡ τοιαύτη φαντασία παρὰ τὰς ἄλλας φαντασίας καθάπερ οἱ κεράσται παρὰ τοὺς ἄλλους ὄφεις· οἱ δὲ ἀπὸ τῆς Ἀκαδημίας τοὐναντίον φασὶ δύνασθαι τῇ καταληπτικῇ φαντασίᾳ ἀπαράλλακτον εὑρεθήσεσθαι ψεῦδος.

Sextus is here attempting to elucidate the second and third conditions necessary for an appearance to be kataleptic. He claims that just as a signet ring impresses all its markings into the indentation it makes upon a piece of wax, so too when one has a kataleptic appearance of an object, *all* (*M.* 7.248, 250–1)[42] the object's "peculiarities" (ἰδιώματα)—which have presumably been faithfully represented in the kataleptic appearance—ought to be grasped by the epistemic subject having the kataleptic appearance.[43] However, it is not clear that this piece of evidence shows that the Stoics thought that peculiar qualities served to identify individuals.

Scholars have expressed puzzlement over how to render ἰδίωμα.[44] Given the Stoic interest in identifying individuals, one *might* think that ἰδιώματα serve to identify the individual and they express some unique feature of the object in question. One might further suppose that, since a peculiar quality (ἰδία ποιότης) is also meant to be unique, Sextus is here speaking of peculiar qualities albeit by means of a different term. However, so far as I can tell, in our principal sources (such as Sextus and Simplicius) ἰδιώματα are usually spoken of as features of *kinds* of objects or classes of thing rather than as features of particular individuals (Sextus Empiricus, *M.* 1.156; 6.44; 7.408, 411; Simplicius, *In Cat.* 22.6–

---

42 That a kataleptic appearance should capture *all* the object's peculiarities is repeated up to three times in *M.* 7.250–1 (and was also previously asserted at *M.* 7.248). This, it has been complained, places unreasonable demands upon the Stoic theory (e.g., Frede 1999, 305) and some scholars (e.g., LS 2, 255; Annas 1990, 191) take it to conflict with Cicero's parallel account (Cicero, *Acad.* 1.42). Cicero offers that: "[Zeno] thought that an apprehension caused by the senses was true and reliable—not because it apprehended all the features of its object, but on the ground[s] that it omitted nothing detectable by it" (*comprehensio facta sensibus et vera esse illi et fidelis videbatur, non quod omnia quae essent in re comprehenderet, sed quia nihil quod cadere in eam posset relinqueret*; *Acad.* 1.42, trans. Brittain). However, it is not clear that one need see a conflict here. According to the first part of Cicero's report, a kataleptic appearance does not have to capture "all the features of its object" (*omnia quae essent in re*), but this does not conflict with Sextus's account. Having to capture all of *x*'s peculiarities (as per Sextus) is perfectly compatible with not having to capture all of *x*'s features (as per Cicero). A more difficult question concerns whether there is a conflict between the second part of Cicero's report and what we find in Sextus. This is unclear because it is not entirely perspicuous (at least to me) precisely what *sed quia nihil quod cadere in eam posset relinqueret* means. Cf. Frede 1983, 76; 1999, 307–8.

43 In the latter part of the passage, Sextus claims that not only must kataleptic appearances capture all the *peculiarities* (ἰδιώματα) of their object, but also that kataleptic appearances, as a class, have their own *peculiarity* (ἰδίωμα): being clear/evident (*M.* 7.252, 408–11). For discussion, see Nawar (2014).

44 For instance, see Frede 1999, 307–8. It has also been rendered simply as "feature" or "property" (Frede 1983, 77; Annas 1990).

9; 121.29–122.1; 143.1–5).[45] More concretely, peculiarities (ἰδιώματα) seem to be *purportedly* unique attributes of the class of object in question. Thus, for instance, one might talk of plants having the common peculiarity (τὸ κοινὸν ἰδίωμα, Simplicius, *In Cat.* 238.14) of being rooted to the earth. Accordingly, we may suppose that *F* is a peculiarity (ἰδίωμα) of *G* iff *G* is *F* and nothing else is *F*.[46]

If such remarks are any guide, then Sextus is probably not here saying either: (i) that in order to have a kataleptic appearance of some plant one has to grasp the peculiar quality of the individual plant; or (ii) that in order to have a kataleptic appearance of some plant one must grasp the unique attribute(s) of the individual plant; but merely (iii) that in order to have a kataleptic appearance of some plant, one must grasp the peculiarities of plants (for instance, that plants have the attribute of being rooted in the earth).

In sum, the evidence considered reveals that the Stoics do seem to have been interested in the identification of individuals qua individuals and of individuals qua members of species, but insofar as I can tell it is not clear that they thought peculiar qualities were the means by which epistemic agents identified individuals.

(δ)   *Unity and Grounding*

The point that peculiar qualities ground an individual's unity and identity (or otherwise perform some important metaphysical role) in some strong sense is not—as far as I am aware—explicitly stressed in our ancient sources in any detail (compare Irwin 1996, 479n24). However, the Stoics do attribute such a role to qualities when spoken of in the more specific sense. Thus, the Stoics maintain that when (accurate) predications are made in the most specific (εἰδικός) sense the subject is qualified by the qualities quite literally within (or coextensive with) the relevant subject (Simplicius, *In Cat.* 213.24–37 = LS 28 M; *In Cat.* 212.12–213.1 = LS 28 N; see below). For instance, when one says "Socrates is prudent," it seems that the presence of the relevant quality *in* the individuals is what makes such claims true. "Socrates is prudent" is true because there is, quite literally, some prudence in him. This prudence is a corporeal item within a prudent person and is such that it makes that person act prudently (compare Plato, *Charmides* 160d5–e1, 161a8–9). Equally, the soul affects the body in such

---

45   Do notice however that the late evidence I consider below in section IV from Basil of Caesarea speaks of the ἰδιώματα of an individual.

46   It may be that this claim is too strong and ἰδιώματα are merely important features of the class of objection in question. Epicurus, who seems to be the originator of the term (LSJ s.v., I; cf. Diogenes Laertius, 10.72) seems to use ἰδίωμα almost interchangeably with ἴδιον (Diogenes Laertius, 10.72–3; cf. Aristotle, *Topics* 102a19–22).

a way that it makes it alive and causes the predicate "alive" to hold of it (Stobaeus, 1.138.14–139.14 = LS 55 A; Tertullian, *De Anima* 5; Sextus Empiricus, *M.* 9.211).

In general then, when things are qualified in the more specific sense, qualities cause objects to be qualified in the way that they are. As Plutarch attests:

> Yet they maintain that matter, which is of itself inert and motionless, is everywhere the substrate for qualities, and that qualities are breaths and aeriform tensions which give form and shape to the parts of matter in which they come to be. (Plutarch, *De Stoicorum Repugnantiis* 1054a9–b2 = LS 47 M2)[47]

Qualities (ποιότητες)—when spoken of in the relevant sense—are thus corporeal items or bodies inside (or coextensive with) the objects relevantly qualified (Galen, *Quod Qualitates Incorporeae Sint* 19.464.1–3).[48] More concretely, qualities are portions of πνεῦμα—seemingly taken by most of the Stoics to be some sort of mixture of air and fire (Alexander of Aphrodisias, *De Anima* 26.13–17 = SVF 2.786; Galen, *Quod Animi Mores Corporis Temperamenta Sequuntur* 4.783–4 = SVF 2.787; *De Placitis Hippocratis et Platonis* 5.3.8 = LS 47 H; compare Cicero, *Tusculan Disputations* 1.19 = SVF 1.134)—which give form to the things in which they inhere (Galen, *CC* 1.1–2.4 = LS 55 F).[49] Qualities are active while the matter, in which they inhere and which they act upon, is passive.[50] Through its so-

---

47 καίτοι πανταχοῦ τὴν ὕλην ἀργὸν ἐξ ἑαυτῆς καὶ ἀκίνητον ὑποκεῖσθαι ταῖς ποιότησιν ἀποφαίνουσι, τὰς δὲ ποιότητας πνεύματ' οὔσας καὶ τόνους ἀερώδεις, οἷς ἂν ἐγγένωνται μέρεσι τῆς ὕλης, εἰδοποιεῖν ἕκαστα καὶ σχηματίζειν.

48 ὁ περὶ | τῶν ποιοτήτων λόγος καὶ τῶν συμβεβηκότων ἁπάντων, <ἅ> φασιν εἶναι Στωϊκῶν παῖδες σώματα· For the Stoics, the incorporeal neither acts nor is acted upon (Cicero, *Acad.* 1.39 = LS 45 A; *M.* 8.263 = LS 45 B; Nemesius, 78.7–79.2 = LS 45 C). Accordingly, given its causal influence, and the fact that the Stoics apparently took the qualities of bodies themselves to be corporeal, it is unsurprising that πνεῦμα was thought to be corporeal (σωμᾰτικός), or, indeed, a body (σῶμα) (Seneca, *Ep.* 117.2; Simplicius, *In Cat.* 217.32–3 = LS 28 L; Eusebius, *Praeparatio Evangelica* 15.14.1 = LS 45 G).

49 I say "seemingly" because the evidence concerning the Stoic elements and composition of πνεῦμα is complex and there seem to have been disagreements within the Stoa on the issue. It seems that some Stoics, such as Cleanthes, took πνεῦμα to be heat or fire (cf. Cicero, *De Natura Deorum* 2.23–30 = LS 47 C); however, Chrysippus, perhaps in attempting to account for the contrary motions and actions of πνεῦμα, may have taken πνεῦμα to be composed of air and fire (Galen, *De Placitis Hippocratis et Platonis* 5.3.8 = LS 47 H; *CC* 1.1–2.4 = LS 55 F).

50 As Plutarch's account indicates, for the Stoics, matter (οὐσία, ὕλη) was a passive principle (ἀρχή), fit to be acted upon but itself devoid of form, features, or causal power (cf. Sextus Empiricus, *M.* 9.75; Calcidius, 292 = LS 44 D) (seemingly akin to the quality-less account of

called "tension" (τόνος) or "tensility" (εὐτονία), the relevant πνεῦμα acts upon matter and provides structure, unity, form, and stability to the matter which it informs (Alexander of Aphrodisias, *De Mixtione* 216, 14–17 = LS 48 C1; Galen, *De Plenitudine* 7.525.9–14 = LS 47 F).[51] In addition, we also find that qualities (again, presumably when spoken of in the most specific sense) are credited with a role in *individuating* individuals:

> The Stoics say that what is common to the quality which pertains to bodies is to be that which differentiates substance, not separable *per se*, but delimited by a concept and a peculiar nature (ἰδιότης), and not specified by its duration or strength but by the intrinsic "suchness" (τοιουτότης) in accordance with which a qualified thing is generated. (Simplicius, *In Cat.* 222.30–3 = LS 28 H)[52]

However, given their preoccupation with ambiguity (famously, Aulus Gellius, *Noctes Atticae* 11.12.1 = LS 37 N1), it is not surprising to find the Stoics drawing attention to the fact that the term "qualified" (ποιόν) is not univocal and that there are different ways in which predications are made true (Simplicius, *In Cat.* 212.12–213.1 = LS 28 N; for negative predications, compare Simplicius, *In Cat.* 396.3–27).[53] Things are not always qualified in the more specific sense and not every veridical predication is made true by the presence of the quality— some πνεῦμα—expressed or signified by the predicate being "inside" the subject. Something might satisfy a predicate without having the relevant quality (ποιότης) and thereby being the relevant qualified thing (ποιόν) in the

---

so-called "prime matter" which some readers find in Aristotle). Matter—the passive principle—is acted upon by the active principle taken to be the λόγος in it, which is identified with God (Diogenes Laertius, 7.134) and seemingly taken to be self-moving (Sextus Empiricus, *M.* 9.76 = LS 44 C) and deemed to be coextensive with and mixed in with matter (Alexander of Aphrodisias, *Mixt.* 225.1–2 = LS 45 H). While matter is without qualities *per se*, it is always found connected with some quality or other and serves as the substrate of these qualities (Calcidius, 292 = LS 44 D).

51   "The chief proponents of the sustaining power, such as the Stoics, make what sustains one thing, and what is sustained something different: the breathy substance is what sustains, and the material substance what is sustained. And so they say that air and fire sustain, and earth and water are sustained" (Galen, *Plen.* 7.525.9–14 = LS 47 F; cf. Plutarch, *St. rep.* 1053f2–a1 = LS 47 M1).

52   Οἱ δὲ Στωικοὶ τὸ κοινὸν τῆς ποιότητος τὸ ἐπὶ τῶν σωμάτων λέγουσιν διαφορὰν εἶναι οὐσίας οὐκ ἀποδιαληπτὴν καθ᾽ ἑαυτήν, ἀλλ᾽ εἰς ἐννόημα καὶ ἰδιότητα ἀπολήγουσαν, οὔτε χρόνῳ οὔτε ἰσχύι εἰδοποιουμένην, ἀλλὰ τῇ ἐξ αὐτῆς τοιουτότητι, καθ᾽ ἣν ποιοῦ ὑφίσταται γένεσις.

53   Cf. Long and Sedley 1987, i.172; Irwin 1996, 469.

relevant sense. Such things are ποιόν only in a less specific sense (Simplicius, *In Cat.* 212.12–213.1 = LS 28 N).

Thus, if the statement "Socrates is running" is true, Socrates may be said to be qualified (in some sense). However, while the predicate "running" holds of Socrates, there is presumably no quality (or qualified thing)—no corporeal item—*running* which needs to be posited in him (Simplicius, *In Cat.* 213.24–37 = LS 28 M4–5; Seneca, *Epistles* 117.7–8; compare Menn 1999, 220–1). Something similar would seem to apply to various other predicates; thus, for instance, when "large" is veridically predicated of Ajax there is presumably no quality of largeness—no portion of πνεῦμα suitably informing the relevant matter—in him. Equally, when a hand is arranged into a fist there is no need to posit a corporeal item expressed by "fist" within the hand which makes it so; a fist just is the hand disposed or arranged in a certain way (compare Galen, *Qual. Incorp.* 19. 466.17–467.13, 471.16–472.6, 480.6–481.3 = SVF 2.382–4).[54] Insofar as a peculiar quality qualifies a peculiarly qualified individual in the more specific sense of "qualified," there is reason to think that the peculiar quality is (a portion of) πνεῦμα which plays the relevant unifying, grounding, and individuating role. That, for so-called "orthodox" Stoics, peculiar qualities should be understood as qualities in the more specific sense is highly likely but is something I shall return to below.

IV The Nature of Peculiar Qualities

A *The Account of Dexippus*

Having seen the roles the Stoics seem to have expected peculiar qualities to fulfil, what then did the Stoics think might serve as an example of a peculiar quality? Direct evidence on this issue is extremely scarce. Dexippus in his commentary on Aristotle's *Categories* offers us the following:

> But if form is that which is predicated in the category of essence of a plurality of numerically different, in what does single individual differ from single individual, seeing that each is numerically single? Those who solve this difficulty on the basis of the peculiarly qualified (κατὰ τὸ ἰδίως ποιόν)—that one individual is distinguished, say, by hookedness of the nose, by blondness, or by some other combination of qualities (συνδρομή

---

[54] It is usually thought that it is for this reason that the Stoics were motivated to develop the third category (πως ἔχον, "somehow disposed") and fourth category (πρός τί πως ἔχον, "somehow disposed relative to something"). For detailed discussion, see Menn 1999.

ποιοτήτων), another by snubness, baldness, or greyness of the eyes, and again another by other qualities—do not seem to me to solve it well. (Dexippus, *In Cat.* 30.21–6 = LS 28 J)[55]

Due to the presence of the idiosyncratic term "peculiarly qualified," it used to be thought that the "they" in question are the Stoics and that Dexippus gives us the most explicit account of what the Stoics thought might serve as an example of a peculiar quality. According to Dexippus, a peculiar quality is a certain combination of qualities (συνδρομή ποιοτήτων). For instance, a particular human individual's peculiar quality will be his having-a-hooked-nose-and-blondness-and-so-on. This suggests that a human individual's peculiar quality will be some complex, epistemically accessible, physiological attribute unique to that individual. Dexippus's report is not without echoes in other sources (compare Porphyry, *In Aristotelis Categorias* 129.8–10 = FDS 848).[56]

The account described by Dexippus finds some (perhaps loose) parallels in medical literature (compare Sextus Empiricus, *Pyrrhoneae Hypotyposes* 1.79–80),[57] and is probably ultimately traceable to Plato's *Theaetetus* (a text which

---

[55] Ἀλλ' εἰ εἶδός ἐστι τὸ κατὰ πλειόνων καὶ διαφερόντων τῷ ἀριθμῷ ἐν τῷ τί ἐστι κατηγορούμενον, τίνι διαφέρει ὁ ἄτομος καὶ εἷς τοῦ ἀτόμου καὶ ἑνός· ἓν γὰρ ἀριθμῷ ἐστι καὶ οὗτος κἀκεῖνος. Οἱ μὲν οὖν λύοντες τὴν ἀπορίαν ταύτην κατὰ τὸ ἰδίως ποιόν, τοῦτ' ἔστιν ὅτι ὁ μὲν φέρε γρυπότητι ἢ ξανθότητι ἢ ἄλλῃ συνδρομῇ ποιοτήτων ἀφώρισται, ἄλλος δὲ σιμότητι ἢ φαλακρότητι ἢ γλαυκότητι, καὶ πάλιν ἕτερος ἑτέραις, οὐ καλῶς μοι δοκοῦσι λύειν·

[56] "However, they [a tenor (ἕξις) and a condition (διάθεσις)] differ from each other numerically, just as—for instance—Socrates differs from Plato. For Socrates does not differ from Plato by means of specific differences, but through a peculiar nature of combined qualities (ἰδιότης συνδρομῆς ποιοτήτων), it is according to this specificity that Plato differs from Socrates" (Porphyry, *In Cat.* 129.8–10 = FDS 848). This account does not explicitly name the Stoics and I myself am doubtful about it, but it has sometimes been taken, albeit with reservations (e.g., Sedley 1982, 273n27), as further evidence for the Stoic view of peculiar qualities sketched in Dexippus. One *might* find some corroborating evidence in other sources (e.g., Simplicius, *In Cat.* 229.16–18 = FDS 848; cf. Alexander of Aphrodisias, *In Aristotelis Analyticorum Priorum Librum Primum Commentarium* 181.12–19).

[57] "There are two things from which humans are said to be composed, soul and body, and in both these we differ from one another. For example, in body we differ in our shapes and our individual peculiarities (κατ' ἄμφω ταῦτα διαφέρομεν ἀλλήλων, οἷον κατὰ σῶμα ταῖς τε μορφαῖς καὶ ταῖς ἰδιοσυγκρισίαις. Sextus Empiricus, *PH* 1.80). "What I omitted to say is that what is truly the art of medicine is to make an estimation of the nature of the patient. I believe many doctors call this 'an individual peculiarity' and all agree that it is incomprehensible" (ὅπερ δὲ λέγων ἀπέλιπον, ἡ ὄντως ἰατρικὴ τῆς τοῦ κάμνοντος ἐστόχασται φύσεως· ὀνομάζουσι δέ, οἶμαι, τοῦτο πολλοὶ τῶν ἰατρῶν ἰδιοσυγκρασίαν, καὶ πάντες ἀκατάληπτον ὁμολογοῦσιν ὑπάρχειν· Galen, *De Methodo Medendi* 10.209 K; cf. *MM* 10.169 K). Notice that

there is reason to think the Stoics engaged with). It relies upon the intuitive thought that while many individuals might instantiate the simpler attribute of possessing a snubbed nose, or that of possessing bulging eyes, far fewer will instantiate the more complex attribute of having-a-hooked-nose-and-having-bulging-eyes.[58] With a sufficiently large conjunction of sufficiently detailed predicates, we come closer to expressing a complex attribute which (conceivably) would be instantiated by only one individual.

However, the account described by Dexippus is exceedingly problematic. While this account seems to fulfil one of the purported requirements—(γ), that the peculiar quality should be of use in identifying an individual—quite well, the other requirements (that is to say, being (α) unique; (β) lifelong; and (δ) grounding the unity and identity of the peculiarly qualified individual) are met only rather poorly or not at all. *Even if* a sufficiently complex combination of physiological attributes of the sort Dexippus describes might be found so as to satisfy the uniqueness requirement (and *even if* this could be done, it would be a highly contingent fact), it seems silly to suppose that the same complex combination would be lifelong and even more absurd to suppose that it might serve to unify an individual and ground their identity. It is difficult to believe that such problems would not have been obvious to the Stoics—indeed it is possible that at least some Stoics were committed to *not* holding

---

the term συνδρομή (cf. *Tht.* 157b9) was used by empiric doctors to denote the combination of symptoms through which one might identify a disease (Galen *Meth. Med.* 10.100–101; cf. Sextus Empiricus, *M.* 7.179). (The term "συνδρομή" is repeated at *M.* 7.180, 182 but there Sextus is not discussing a combination of properties, but a combination of appearances). Cf. ἄθροισμα (Porphyry, *Isagoge* 7.19–8.3; Sextus Empiricus, *M.* 7.277).

58 In the *Theaetetus* it is proposed that in order to have a thought about *x*, one must think of *x* under some description which in fact applies only to *x*. The thinker, we are told, must have some *mark* (σημεῖον, *Tht.* 208c7) by which to distinguish the object of thought from everything else. What is required is some suitably informative predicate (e.g., "having such-and-such a nose *and* such-and-such eyes") which applies *only* to the individual being thought about (209c5–10). If the description attributes to *x* a feature which is not unique to *x*, but is instead a common feature or quality (κοινότης, *Tht.* 208d9 [cf. the Stoic κοινὴ ποιότης]), one will not (the thought goes) be able to distinguish *x* from everything else (and Plato thinks that this means that one's thought will not be about *x*). Philological parallels between the *Theaetetus* (particularly in regard to discussion of the wax tablet) and what we find in the Stoic account of appearances have been noticed by Ioppolo (1990) and Long (2002) and the term ποιότης, which is ubiquitous in our Stoic sources, was coined by an apologetic Plato in the *Theaetetus* (*Tht.* 182a8–9).

such account[59]—and the obvious inadequacy of the proposal in meeting the relevant requirements has led recent scholarship to doubt whether Dexippus's report is in fact at all faithful or otherwise useful in reconstructing the Stoic account of peculiar qualities (for instance, Lewis 1995, 93–7; Irwin 1996, 474–5, 480n33; Chiaradonna 2000).

B *Alternative Accounts of the Peculiar Quality*

As a result of the inadequacy of the account described in Dexippus, scholars have dismissed Dexippus's remarks and sought alternatives.[60] The leading proposal, offered independently by Eric Lewis 1995 and Terry Irwin 1996, is that the Stoics took an individual's peculiar quality to be persistence of soul or πνεῦμα. Lewis dismisses the evidence from Dexippus and proposes that an individual's peculiar quality is simply the individual's πνεῦμα in a certain state or disposed in a certain way. In inanimate things, πνεῦμα is a ἕξις ("tenor"); in animate but non-perceptive things, such as plants, it is φύσις ("physique"); and in animate perceptive things, it is ψυχή ("soul").[61] Accordingly, Lewis proposes that:

> Having a particular "kind" of H–P–P [*hexis, physis, psyche*] fixes the natural kind one is a member of…, while having the particular H–P–P one has fixes *which* individual one is … it is soul, or the persistence of an individual soul, which is responsible for, and *is*, the peculiar quality of ensouled beings, and in particular that it satisfies the … features peculiar qualities must have. (Lewis 1995, 99–100; compare Irwin 1996, 470)

---

59 In discussing eternal recurrence the Stoics explicitly recognized that a man "does not become another man if he previously had moles on his face but no longer has them" (Alexander of Aphrodisias, *In An. Pr.* 180.33–6, 181.25–31 = LS 52 F3). This is not decisive evidence (perhaps the person's peculiar quality was some complex physiological attribute which didn't include their moles), but it is suggestive.

60 David Sedley seems agnostic on what the Stoics themselves might have offered, but suggests that perhaps something akin to fingerprints or genetic code (which he takes fingerprints to be a manifestation of) might have fit the Stoic requirements (e.g., Sedley 1982, 266; cf. 1999, 404). However, even these friendly suggestions do not seem to entirely satisfy the requirements placed on peculiar qualities. Distinct individuals, such as clones, may have the same genetic code and if Socrates' genetic code is damaged by radiation, he may get ill but he still remains Socrates.

61 The difference between these states of πνεῦμα seems to reside in the amount of "tension" (τόνος) or "tensility" (εὐτονία). For discussion, see Plotinus, *Enneads* 4.7.4; Galen, *Introductory Treatises* 14.726.7–11 = LS 47 N; Philo of Alexandria, *Legum Allegoriae* 2.22–3 = LS 47 P; *Quod Deus Sit Immutabilis* 35–6 = LS 47 Q; Simplicius, *In Cat.* 237.25–238.20 = LS 47 S.

Lewis thus takes an individual's peculiar quality to be its πνεῦμα or πνεῦμα disposed in a certain way. This, he thinks, successfully meets the requirements the Stoics impose upon peculiar qualities (Lewis 1995, 93). While Lewis's account is promising, it seems problematic for several reasons.

First, it is troubling that Lewis disregards Dexippus's report on purely philosophical grounds (this applies also to Irwin 1996). Even if the position Dexippus describes is obviously flawed and it is not absolutely certain that the position is being attributed to the Stoics, unless the case can be made that it is an outright invention or the position described by Dexippus can be convincingly ascribed to some other thinkers, then any interpretation of the Stoic view of peculiar qualities needs to say something about this evidence.

Secondly, while such an account does allow the peculiar quality to fulfil its purported unifying role (as per (δ)), there seems to be something amiss with arguing that it is precisely because πνεῦμα fulfils role (δ) that one should think the Stoics took peculiar qualities to be πνεῦμα disposed in a certain way. As we have seen above, all qualities, when spoken of in the more specific sense, refer to πνεῦμα (compare Stobaeus, 1.49.33 = SVF 2.826) and this provides form, unity, and so forth to the matter in which it inheres. However, as far as I am aware there does not seem to be any independent evidence that peculiar qualities are meant to fulfil this role apart from the assumption that they are qualities in what the Stoics regarded as "the more specific sense." To say that peculiar qualities ought to fulfil the metaphysical role described because they are qualities in the more specific sense, and then to claim that peculiar qualities should be understood as πνεῦμα (that is to say, qualities in the more specific sense) precisely because they fulfil this role seems to present a slightly problematic circularity. While it seems to me likely that so-called "orthodox" Stoics took peculiar qualities to be qualities in the more specific sense, and that those who took peculiar qualities to be qualities in the more specific sense took peculiar qualities to perform a unifying function, it is not clear to me that there was an independent requirement that peculiar qualities needed to fulfil a unifying function.

Thirdly, it is not clear how taking an individual's peculiar quality to be πνεῦμα disposed in a certain way satisfies the purported epistemic requirement regarding the identifying of individuals (as per (γ)). Lewis argues that for the Stoics πνεῦμα is perceivable (1995, 91n7) and in support he cites evidence from Philo (*Quaestiones Et Solutiones In Genesim* 2.4 = SVF 2.802 [= LS 47 R3]);[62]

---

62 "Now our body, which is composed of many parts, is united externally and internally, and it holds firm by its own tenor. And the higher tenor of these parts is the soul: being at the centre, it moves everywhere, right to the surface and from the surface it returns to the

Simplicius (*In Cat.* 237.25–238.20 = LS 47 S);[63] and Seneca (*Ep.* 120.3).[64] However, these reports do not, I think, suggest that πνεῦμα can fulfil the epistemic role in the manner that Lewis hopes.

Philo's report speaks of the unifying function of πνεῦμα and says that the soul moves everywhere "right to the surface and from the surface it returns to the centre."[65] However, even though πνεῦμα is corporeal (see above), there is nothing here to suggest that the soul is directly perceivable by agents such as ourselves (let alone that it is regularly perceived). Equally, Lewis says: "Tenors, we know from Simplicius (*In Cat.* 237.25 and following) are perceptible, since

---

centre. The result is that a single animate nature is enveloped by a double bond, thus being fitted to a stronger tenor and union" (*Corpus autem nostrum, ex multis compositum, extrinsecus et intrinsecus unitum est atque propria habitudine constat; superior autem habitudo conexionis istorum anima est, quae in medio consistens ubique permeat usque ad superficiem deque superficie in medium vertitur, ut unica natura spiritualis duplici convolvatur ligamine in firmiorem soliditatem unionemque coaptata*; Philo, *Quaest et Sol. In Gen.* 2.4 = SVF 2.802 = LS 47 R3 [Aucher's Latin translation of the Armenian, printed in SVF]).

63 "There is a further question of whether perhaps state (σχέσις), for the Stoics, is the same as condition (διάθεσις) is for Aristotle, differing from tenor (ἕξις) by reference to ease or difficulty of its destruction. But they do not agree on this either. Aristotle says that unreliable health is a condition (διάθεσις); but the Stoics do not admit that health of any kind is a state (σχέσις). In their view it has the peculiarity of a tenor (φέρειν γὰρ τὸ τῆς ἕξεως ἰδίωμα). For they take states to be characterized by acquired conditions, tenors by their intrinsic activities (τὰς μὲν γὰρ σχέσεις ταῖς ἐπικτήτοις καταστάσεσιν χαρακτηρίζεσθαι, τὰς δὲ ἕξεις ταῖς ἐξ ἑαυτῶν ἐνεργείαις). So tenors (ἕξεις), for them, are not specified by their duration or strength, but by a certain peculiar nature (ἰδιότης) and particular feature (χαρακτήρ). Just as things with roots are rooted in different degrees but have the single common peculiarity (τὸ κοινὸν ἰδίωμα) of holding to the earth, so tenor has the same meaning in things which change with difficulty and in those which change easily. It is a general truth that many things which are qualified generically are defective in the peculiarity (ἰδίωμα) by which they are specified, such as sour wine, bitter almonds, Molossian and Maltese dogs. These all carry the particular feature (χαρακτήρ) of their genus, though to a slight and relaxed extent, and their tenor persists in a single settled way so far as its actual defining terms are concerned; but frequently it is easy to change for some other reason" (Simplicius, *In Cat.* 238.5–20 = LS 47 S4–5).

64 "Certain people say that we just happened on the concept (*notitia*); but it is implausible that anyone should have come upon the form of virtue by chance. We believe that it has been inferred by the observation and comparison of actions done repeatedly. Our school holds that the honourable and the good are understood by analogy" (Seneca, *Ep.* 120.4, trans. Inwood).

65 Other reports also speak of πνεῦμα extending to various parts of the body (e.g., Stobaeus, 1.49.33 = SVF 2.826; Seneca, *Ep.* 113.23 = SVF 2.836; Calcidius, *In Tim.* 220 = SVF 2.879) though it is not clear that in these particular cases πνεῦμα reaches the surface.

sour wine, and Maltese dogs all 'carry the mark' of their genus" (Lewis 1996, 92n7). However, the passage from Simplicius only claims that certain sub-par members of a species still carry the "peculiarity" (ἰδίωμα) (that is to say, a seemingly unique or distinctive attribute [see above]) of that species, even though this might be in attenuated form. The report is not explicitly discussing peculiar qualities and even though the "peculiarities" spoken of in the examples cited are indeed presumably perceptible, this does *not* indicate that the πνεῦμα itself is perceptible. For instance, I may be able to identify a Dalmatian from its spots, and the Dalmatian may indeed be the way it is (including having its spots) due to its πνεῦμα structuring the relevant agglomeration of matter. However, in seeing the spots, I am not thereby seeing the πνεῦμα, but merely something that has come about as a result of πνεῦμα's activity. The evidence adduced by Lewis from Seneca is problematic in much in the same way.[66]

This is not to say that for the Stoics πνεῦμα is *not* at all perceivable.[67] Indeed, given the corporeal nature of πνεῦμα we would expect it to be perceivable in some sense since all corporeal things, due to their capacity to enter into causal interactions with other bodies, are presumably such that they can potentially be perceived (whether directly or indirectly) (compare Pseudo-Plutarch, *Placita* 902f11–903a8).[68] That is to say, πνεῦμα can enter into contact, impose pressure, and so forth (Hierocles, 3.56–4.3, 4.38–49 = LS 53 B5–7). However, the

---

[66] The evidence from Seneca does not claim, for instance, that things like virtues may be directly perceived. Instead, Seneca says that it is "through analogy" (per analogian, Seneca, *Ep.* 120.4) that we grasp things we cannot perceive, such as a person's character or goodness. That is to say, we reflect upon our perceptual experience and *infer* (rather than perceive) the nature of the relevant feature. Lewis seems to recognise this ("One can perceive the soul through its effects" 1995, 92n7) but does not, as far as I can tell, recognise the manner in which it curtails the prospect of positing πνεῦμα as fulfilling the relevant epistemic functions.

[67] There is other evidence (not cited by Lewis) that virtues and vices are perceivable. Thus, for instance, in *De Natura Deorum*, Balbus, the Stoic spokesman, defends the value of the senses and says of the eyes "you see, they also recognize virtues and vices, the angry and the well-disposed, the joyful and the sad, the brave and the cowardly, the bold and the timid" (*nam et virtutes et vitia cognoscunt, iratum propitium, laetantem dolentem, fortem ignavum, audacem timidumque*; Cicero, *Nat. Deo*, 2.145–6). However, it is not clear that even this securely indicates direct perceivability. Other evidence speaks of goods and evils being perceivable (SVF 3.85) but the same points apply.

[68] By "perceived indirectly," I have in mind situations such as the following. The naked human eye cannot typically perceive the pores on one's skin or the rings of Saturn but the pores and rings are, nonetheless, perceivable in some sense insofar as with sufficiently good eyesight (as another animal species might have) or technical aid (such as a telescope), they may be perceived.

problem is that much depends upon how one construes "perceivable" and—as would befit its nature of being a compound of fire and air—if πνεῦμα is perceivable, then it seems to be perceivable in much the same way that something like the wind is. That is to say, it may be felt, and its effects may be perceived, but it is not typically seen or tasted and it is usually not *directly* perceivable by our more acute senses.

If one proposes instead that πνεῦμα is detectable through its effects then there is a problem insofar as it is not clear how—on the accounts proposed by Lewis and Irwin—πνεῦμα *or its effects* could manifest themselves in a recognizable, unique way *or* be perceived sufficiently precisely so as to be used to identify individuals. Even if one adverts to some form of πνεῦμα which would be especially prone to manifesting itself in action, such as an individual person's virtue (compare Irwin 1996, 471), it seems very difficult to make a case for being able to distinguish Plato from Socrates on the basis of—for instance— their different, unique ways of being virtuous.[69] As a result of these worries, it is hard to see how—according to Lewis and Irwin—peculiar qualities (construed as πνεῦμα) might be deemed to satisfy their purported epistemic function (as per (γ)). *If* peculiar qualities are indeed meant to serve an epistemic function, significantly more would have to be said on the matter (see below).

---

69 "If Socrates' individual soul is distinguished from others by its virtuous characteristics, then these characteristics belong to the peculiar quality that is the source of Socrates' difference from other human beings at a time and of his persistence as the same human being through time" (Irwin 1996, 471). It has been put to me that I dismiss this notion too quickly. Just as someone experienced on matters of handwriting can distinguish individuals on the basis of their handwriting (i.e. their ways of forming letters), so too—the thought goes—someone experienced on matters concerning virtue *could* distinguish individuals on the basis of their way(s) of being virtuous. Here I can only note the following points which would seem to me to merit further discussion. First, the Stoics thought that there were few if any virtuous human individuals in history (Alexander of Aphrodisias, *De Fato* 199.14–22 = LS 61 N; cf. Seneca, *Ep.* 42.1; Sextus Empiricus, *M.* 9.133 = LS 54 D). Secondly, presumably only sages can identify individuals by their virtue and this means that, among other things, there are few people who would know enough about virtue (or vice) to perform the relevant identifications—a bit like attempting to identify people by their handwriting in an illiterate society. Thirdly, if virtue is an individual's peculiar quality, then becoming virtuous would not be a change (the sources seem to describe it as a change but it must be admitted that the evidence on this matter is rather difficult to understand; cf. Plutarch, *De Profectibus In Virtute* 75c = LS 61 S; Clement, *Stromateis* 4.6.28.1 = SVF 3.221; Brouwer 2007), but seemingly an instance of generation (of a new, virtuous individual) and destruction (of an old, non-virtuous individual).

Fourthly, there are also significant additional problems when it comes to considering whether πνεῦμα or πνεῦμα disposed in a certain way could fulfil the uniqueness and permanence requirements (that is to say, (α) and (β)). Lewis proposes, on behalf of the Stoics, that the uniqueness requirement would be satisfied because of the complexity of our mental lives. Supposing mental content to be highly fine-grained, Lewis argues that for two persons to have *precisely* the same beliefs, desires, and so forth, they would have to have been in exactly the same place (for instance, someone else would have to be in the *precise* location where my own body is located) at all points in time. However, this is impossible (Lewis 1995, 107–8).[70]

The problem with this line of thought is that it simply seems like a dressed up, psychological (or pneumatological) version of what Dexippus offers and suffers from the same flaws. Even if a fine-grained specification of an individual's peculiar pneumatological profile or disposition could fulfil the uniqueness requirement, this will almost certainly guarantee that it will not be true of an individual throughout its existence. Just as it is silly to suppose that Theaetetus need always instantiate a certain fine-grained physiological profile, it seems equally silly to suppose that he should always instantiate a certain fine-grained psychological profile and so it is hard to see how an individual's peculiar quality, thus construed, could remain *the same* throughout its existence (compare Simplicius, *In De An.* 217.36–218.2 = LS 28 I; Plutarch, *Comm. not.* 1083e3–6 = LS 28 A5; cited above).

This is especially apparent when one keeps in mind that the Stoics, from very early on,[71] took πνεῦμα to be highly dynamic. Parts of the soul, such as those involved in bodily perception, are described as flowing (for instance, *manare*, Calcidius, *In Platonis Timaeum* 220 = SVF 2.879) and πνεῦμα seems to be constantly changing in tension. Thus, for instance, in the very act of receiving appearances, the configuration of the soul is altered (for instance, Aetius,

---

70 "If two putatively distinct souls were to be indistinguishable, they would each have to [have] indistinguishable beliefs, desires, memories, concepts, etc.... Although two people may assent to what seems to be the same *lekton* when they both view a sunset, their appearances will necessarily include how the sunset appears from their necessarily distinct spatial perspectives ... no other individual can occupy the same place as I do, and so have my perspective on things" (Lewis 1995, 107–8).

71 The influence of the study of Heraclitus (Diogenes Laertius, 7.174 = SVF 1.481), including the well-known rivers fragment(s) (DK 22 B12), upon the early Stoic conceptions of πνεῦμα seems to have been pronounced (Eusebius, *Praep. Evang.* 15.20.2 = SVF 1.141, 519 = LS 53 W) and manifested itself in Stoic conceptions of the fiery and dynamic (i.e. ever-changing) nature of πνεῦμα (SVF 1.134, 135). For later discussions, cf. Seneca, *Ep.* 58.22–3.

4.12.1–5 = LS 39B),[72] and it seems that within a short period of time even deep-seated psychological attributes, such as our moral character, may undergo profound changes (compare Plutarch, *De sera numinis vindicta* 559b–c). Furthermore, given the relevant causal interactions and that the πνεῦμα identified as a human's soul is in or coextensive with the matter of the body, it seems that changes in the body would correspond with changes in the tension and other attributes of the soul (Hierocles, 1.5–33, 4.38–53 = LS 53 B5–9).[73] That is to say, when the conditions of the body vary, the conditions of πνεῦμα vary and vice versa (Hierocles, 4.11–13; Tertullian, *De Anim.* 5; Nemesius, *De Natura Homini* 2, 32 = SVF 1.518) and when the physiological attributes of an individual change, so does the individual's pneumatological attributes. Accordingly, it does not seem that pneumatological attributes are significantly more stable than physiological attributes and even if certain pneumatological or psychological attributes were to remain stable across a typical individual's life, they will certainly not be those with respect to which the individual is unique. Furthermore, *even if* πνεῦμα could somehow be accurately perceived, it is unclear how it could be used to identify and re-identify individuals.

Finally, I should mention that Irwin's proposal (1996) concerning the peculiar quality is similar to that of Lewis but, in contrast to Lewis, Irwin recognises that it is hard to see how, on such an account, peculiar qualities could be taken to be lifelong (as per (β)) (for instance, Irwin 1996, 471–2). He suggests that a peculiar quality which included "historical or developmental characteristics" might do the job of satisfying both the uniqueness and permanence requirements (as per (α) and (β)).[74] Thus, "Socrates, for instance, will be the one who

---

[72] Cleanthes (Sextus Empiricus, *M.* 7.228, 372; 8.400; *PH* 2.70 = SVF 1.484) and Chrysippus (Diogenes Laertius, 7.45 = SVF 2.53, 50 = SVF 2.55; Sextus Empiricus, *M.* 7.228–232) disagreed on the nature of these alterations in the soul, but both thought the configuration of the soul was changed.

[73] "For by stretching out and relaxing, the soul makes an impression on all the body's parts, since it is blended with them all, and in making an impression it receives an impression in response. For the body, just like the soul, reacts to pressure; and the outcome is a state of their joint pressure upon, and resistance to, each other" (Hierocles, 1.5–33, 4.38–53 = LS 53 B5–9).

[74] "If Socrates has his own peculiar quality … his peculiar quality must be some more specific determination of his humanity … Socrates' individual soul distinguishes him from all other human beings, because it includes the traits and characteristics that are distinctive of him and his way of life, but not because it includes any of the purely spatio-temporal properties of Socrates" (Irwin 1996, 470–1). Cf. "The soul of an individual persists for the life of the individual (as composite), and individuates the individual. It is the peculiar quality of the individual whose soul it is. Persistence of soul is both necessary and sufficient for persistence of the individual" (Lewis 1995, 104).

develops his bravery and self-knowledge in this specific way" (Irwin 1996, 472).[75] Precisely how to construe this is, Irwin recognises, problematic.[76] But even if, in attempting to develop the accounts of Lewis and Irwin, we propose that for the Stoics a peculiar quality was a certain sort of pattern of πνεῦμα (not a static snapshot of its attributes, but rather some pattern of change it exhibited over time) it seems that the same criticisms as before apply and, again, even if such developmental characteristics were posited, it is not easy to see how they might meet the epistemic requirements seemingly imposed upon peculiar qualities.

C A Modest Proposal

The Stoics, we have seen, are thought to impose what I regarded as four sorts of requirements upon peculiar qualities. Peculiar qualities were to be: (α) unique; (β) lifelong; (γ) of use in identifying individuals; and (δ) something which

---

[75] "If Socrates has his own peculiar quality, he does not differ from other human beings simply in so far as he has a different date of birth and is composed of a different piece of matter … His peculiar quality must be some more specific determination of his humanity … Socrates' individual soul distinguishes him from all other human beings, because it includes the traits and characteristics that are distinctive of him and his way of life, but not because it includes any of the purely spatio-temporal properties of Socrates" (Irwin 1996, 470–1).

[76] "We might try to meet this objection by understanding 'Socrates' character' broadly enough to allow for the sorts of changes that would allow Socrates to persist while he gets wiser and more temperate … In that case, however, our conception of an individual's character may well appear too broad to constitute anything peculiar to Socrates" (Irwin 1996, 472). Such difficulties are incidental because Irwin takes a passage from Simplicius, (*In. Cat.* 222.32–3 = LS 28 H) to rule out any appeal to temporal or developmental characteristics of such a sort because qualities (in, one must add, the specific sense) do not have such temporal or developmental aspects. According to the report in Simplicius, the Stoics think that the quality which differentiates matter is "not specified by its duration or strength but by the intrinsic 'suchness'" (οὔτε χρόνῳ οὔτε ἰσχύι εἰδοποιουμένην, ἀλλὰ τῇ ἐξ αὐτῆς τοιουτότητι, Simplicius, *In. Cat.* 222.32–3 = LS 28 H). Irwin takes this to stipulate that the relevant (peculiar) quality must distinguish its bearers from other beings "in non-material and non spatio-temporal terms" (Irwin 1996, 473). However, a passage from slightly later on in Simplicius's commentary offers similar phrasing and may provide a better clue as to what is meant. In speaking of the difference between a tenor (ἕξις), state (σχέσις), and condition (διάθεσις), Simplicius says: "For they take states to be characterized by acquired conditions, tenors by their intrinsic activities. So tenors, for them, are not specified by their duration or strength, but by a certain peculiar nature (ἰδιότης) and particular feature (χαρακτήρ)" (τὰς μὲν γὰρ σχέσεις ταῖς ἐπικτήτοις καταστάσεσιν χαρακτηρίζεσθαι, τὰς δὲ ἕξεις ταῖς ἐξ ἑαυτῶν ἐνεργείαις. ὅθεν οὐδὲ χρόνου μήκει ἢ ἰσχύι εἰδοποιοῦνται αἱ ἕξεις κατ' αὐτούς, ἰδιότητι δέ τινι καὶ χαρακτῆρι; LS 238.10–14 = LS 47 S4–5).

grounded an individual's unity and identity. It is difficult to see how any quality of a thing could meet requirements (γ) and (δ) as these seem to pull in different directions. (γ) encourages a view of peculiar qualities as easily detectable attributes, while (δ) encourages a view of peculiar qualities as deep, recondite attributes which do significant work at a fundamental physical (and perhaps metaphysical) level. These are significant difficulties, but it is especially disappointing that the accounts so far examined struggle to meet even the requirements of being unique and lifelong—(α) and (β)—in a satisfying manner, let alone of simultaneously fulfilling all the purported requirements mentioned.

Where then does this leave us? Putting aside the dispiriting possibility that Stoic thought concerning peculiar qualities was simply incoherent and the Stoics never addressed this fact, it seems likely that the standard scholarly account concerning the requirements imposed upon peculiar qualities requires some modification or the account of the nature of peculiar qualities requires some modification. While a number of reasonable suggestions might here be made, my own proposal—which is both modest and speculative—is twofold. Simply put, it seems to me possible to discern between at least two plausible views concerning peculiar qualities which I will label as follows:

> (ORTHODOX) a peculiar quality qualifies something in the more specific sense, in which case the Stoics took a peculiar quality to be a portion of πνεῦμα and seemingly privileged the unifying and individuating role of peculiar qualities.

> (LATER) a peculiar quality qualifies something qualified in the less specific sense, in which case the relevant thinkers seemingly privileged the requirements of being unique and life-long and may have not made the relevant epistemic or metaphysical demands of peculiar qualities.

With regard to (ORTHODOX)—which seems likely have been an earlier and so-called "Orthodox" Stoic view (associated especially with Chrysippus)—we have seen that there are problems in taking an individual to have a pneumatological attribute (or combination thereof) which is (α) unique, (β) lifelong, and (γ) of use in identifying individuals. If we construe the peculiar quality as a pneumatological quality, then we should—I think—adapt the account proposed by Lewis in such a way as to: recognise more emphatically the corporeal nature of peculiar qualities and what this implies for questions concerning qualitative and numerical identity; either discard the requirement concerning identification or else avoid relying upon the thought that πνεῦμα is directly perceivable; incorporate the evidence from Dexippus; and (this marks a significant departure from Lewis) recognise the shortcomings of such an account.

In this vein, we should begin by emphatically recognising the corporeal nature of πνεῦμα. In an earlier work, Chrysippus seems to have maintained that the virtues (and perhaps other attributes that we would be inclined to regard as qualities) are ποιά (Diogenes Laertius, 7.202 = SVF 2.17), construed as discrete bodies.[77] This allows more easily for talk of the peculiar quality persisting throughout the individual's existence (for instance, Plutarch, *Comm. not.* 1083e3–6 = LS 28 A5 [cited and discussed above]) insofar as the relevant portions of πνεῦμα do not always remain the same qualitatively (that is to say, they undergo real change) but do remain the same *numerically*.[78] Thus, for instance, a person's prudence or knowledge—a corporeal entity within the relevant human—would persist even in the face of qualitative change (for instance, as the person develops their prudence) in a manner similar to that in which a blank book which is written in, and even has pages added or removed (or its binding changed) might remain the same book. The same could be said for πνεῦμα more generally.

As regards the purported epistemic requirement, discarding or disregarding it would free the Stoics from the objections that it is not clear how the relevant πνεῦμα, being somewhat recondite, is not easily or especially accurately perceivable *and* that a quality which changed would not serve as a good basis for identification (for instance, if I am meant to identify Socrates on the basis of his height but his height frequently and unpredictably changes, this reduces the feasibility of my identifying him). Insofar as the evidence in favour of

---

[77] If we follow Menn 1999, Chrysippus initially thought that the virtues were ποιά (Diogenes Laertius, 7.202 = SVF 2.17) but then abandoned this view and saw virtues as being the ἡγεμονικόν disposed in a certain way (Sextus Empiricus, *M.* 11.22–6 = LS 60 G). For spirited resistance to this developmental account, see Collette-Dučić 2009.

[78] Sometimes it seems that Lewis should be understood in this way and that he thinks an individual maintains identity with itself by means of maintaining *numerically* the same peculiar quality (e.g., 1995, 97; cf. 94n15, 104; cited below). However, several of Lewis's remarks also tell against this (e.g., "one would be clearly begging the question concerning identity, for one would be attempting to ground the identity of an individual; in the persistence of a quality whose very identity is itself grounded in being the quality *of* the very individual whose identity it grounds," Lewis 1995, 95–6), as does his argument concerning qualitative distinctness of subjects (1995, 107–8; cited above). On balance, it seems that Lewis is proposing that an individual maintains identity with itself by means of maintaining *qualitatively* the same peculiar quality, which is πνεῦμα disposed in a certain way (e.g., "they ground the identity of individuals in the persistence of qualities (in the case of ensouled entities, the persistence of soul as quality)" 1995, 90; cf. 1995, 107–8; partially cited below).

identification is not certain, this is a possible interpretation of the orthodox Stoic account.

On the other hand, *if* peculiar qualities are indeed meant to fulfil an epistemic function (the Stoic interest in identification gives some—but only some—support to such a view), then the account proposed by Lewis should be adapted in a number of ways. First, even if an individual's peculiar quality is πνεῦμα somehow disposed, we should not suppose that the πνεῦμα is directly used in identifying an individual (for the reasons given above).

Secondly, given the co-variance between pneumatological and physiological attributes (Hierocles, 4.11–13; Tertullian, *De Anim.* 5; Nemesius, *De Natura Homini* 2, 32 = SVF 1.518), it should be recognised that the account of Dexippus (which is usually dismissed by scholars as not faithfully reporting a Stoic view) may in fact be fairly reliable insofar as it describes how one identifies an individual by perceiving the *effects* of a peculiar quality (rather than perceiving the peculiar quality directly). That is to say, in perceiving an individual's physiological attributes, one perceives the effects of an individual's peculiar quality.

Thirdly, that an individual's peculiar quality, a portion of πνεῦμα, might be perceived through a person's physiological attributes is supported by Stoic interest in physiognomy—which was significant from early on (Diogenes Laertius, 7.173; SVF 3.84–5) and yet seems to have been largely neglected in the relevant literature on peculiar qualities. Despite the ignominy of the pseudo-discipline, one would have to hold one's nose and further investigate Stoic views of physiognomy in order to tell precisely how the Stoics thought physiological attributes might correlate with pneumatological or psychological attributes (for instance, certain kinds of beauty seem to have been regarded as indicating a virtuous inclination, Diogenes Laertius, 7.129).[79]

Finally, and crucially, the orthodox account still faces significant objections (which modern commentators such as Lewis seem to have neglected) in that the shortcomings that have been noticed with regard to the account Dexippus describes seem to recur *and* in that questions concerning how it is that individuals might persist in the face of change recur once again with regard to the bodily item—the relevant πνεῦμα—in question. This is especially apparent given that an individual's πνεῦμα is added to (and probably subtracted from)—receiving influx from blood and air—in much the same manner as an individual's body is sustained by food (Galen, *In Hippocratis Epidemiarum Libri* 270.26–8 = LS 53 E). That is to say, on the pneumatological view of peculiar qualities, the problems raised by the Growing Argument thus seem to remain unresolved and such an account seems little different (and also little better)

---

79 For a useful discussion of Stoic views of physiognomy, see Boys-Stones 2007, 78–93.

than saying a person's body (by "body" here I mean the observable item with a head, limbs, and so forth) serves as the person's peculiar quality. Saying that Socrates remains the same (numerically identical) across time in virtue of instantiating the same (numerically identical) soul (or virtue, or knowledge, etc.) across time is little better than saying Socrates remains the same (numerically identical) across time in virtue of instantiating the same (numerically identical) body across time. In both cases, we have merely introduced an additional explanandum—how it is that a body (or one's soul) can remain the same (numerically identical) across time while (qualitatively) changing—and it is not clear that we have done much in the way of explaining. Furthermore, we do not seem to have a good basis for qualitatively distinguishing numerically distinct individuals and we may well have introduced further bothersome questions as well as certain recursive worries about qualities having qualities.

That at least some Stoics, most notably Chrysippus (at *some* stage in his thought), opted for an account of this nature seems very likely and criticisms in the vicinity of those I raised—especially concerning the perceivability of πνεῦμα and various worries concerning regresses (for instance, about qualities having qualities, or about πνεῦμα, which is a body grounding the unity of another body, itself needing some grounds of unity)—were seemingly made by opponents of the Stoics (Nemesius, 70.6–71.4 = LS 47 J; Alexander of Aphrodisias, *Mantissa* 113.29–114.4, 24–26, 36–115.1; Galen, *CC* 6.1–7.3; Seneca, *Ep.* 113.3; Simplicius, *In Cat.* 276.30–33).[80] It is crucial, I think, to appreciate (in a manner that the existing literature has not) that the proposal that a peculiar quality is some portion of πνεῦμα (or πνεῦμα somehow disposed) does not felicitously fulfil the functions the Stoics desired. That is to say, such an account should *not* be judged as being successful.[81]

---

80 Some worried that if all corporeal entities required some external cause to grant them cohesion and πνεῦμα was itself corporeal, this would lead to an objectionable regress (Nemesius, 70.6–71.4 = LS 47 J). Other worries in this vicinity were also raised. E.g., "He objects: 'If virtue is an animal, then virtue itself has virtue.' Why shouldn't it have itself? Just as the wise person does everything through his virtue, so virtue does everything through itself..." (*'Si animal est' inquit 'virtus, habet ipsa virtutem.' Quidni habeat se ipsam? quomodo sapiens omnia per virtutem gerit, sic virtus per se.* Seneca, *Ep.* 113.3; cf. Alexander of Aphrodisias, *Mant.* 114.4–6). There is also evidence in Plutarch (*De Virtute Morali* 440e–441d = LS 61 B) which talks of the virtues, construed there as ποιά (qualified items), having peculiar qualities. For discussion of Alexander's criticisms of the Stoic view that qualities are bodies, see Kupreeva 2003, 311–325.

81 In addition, pace Sedley (1982, 266; 1999, 404), it should not be thought that the Stoic account requires only a little tinkering in order to be successful in its aims.

The second option described above—(LATER)—proposes that peculiar qualities do not qualify something in the more specific sense. It seems to me unlikely that so-called "orthodox" Stoics would have taken this option, but I would suggest that some later Stoics (that is to say, Stoics after Chrysippus and probably after Panaetius) or thinkers heavily influenced by the Stoics appealed to impure properties to fulfil at least some of the functions attributed to peculiar qualities.

Impure properties are or include relations to particulars individuals. For instance, "being the student of Aristotle" expresses an impure relational property of Alexander. These would have been regarded as qualities in the less specific sense. The suggestion that a relational property of any kind might serve as peculiar quality faces some objections. In particular, David Sedley considers but dismisses such a possibility for two reasons (1982, 262–3; compare Long and Sedley 1987, i.174). First, he takes such relational properties to belong to the fourth category (πρός τί πως ἔχον) and thinks that these are not eligible to be peculiar qualities. Secondly, he thinks that relational properties are not in fact permanent and thus unsatisfactory peculiar qualities (and moreover, they are often vulnerable to so-called "mere Cambridge change," compare Irwin 1996, 467). For instance, being-the-husband-of-Xanthippe cannot be a peculiar quality of Socrates as it is not possessed by Socrates throughout his existence.

With regard to the first objection, this seems to be based on the assumption that something peculiarly qualified must be qualified in the most specific sense of "qualified." However, we have seen that the Stoics recognised that things could be "qualified" in a looser sense, so as to denote something within the third category (πως ἔχον, "somehow disposed") which did *not* require positing a distinct corporeal item within the relevant subject as the referent and it is not clear to me (as I signalled above) that peculiar qualities *have* to be qualities in the more specific sense or that there should be an independent reason for claiming that relational properties cannot serve as peculiar qualities.[82] With regard to the second objection, even if this were grounds for denying that relational properties could serve as peculiar qualities (and we have already seen the difficulties presented in finding unique, lifelong peculiar qualities when qualities are spoken of in the more specific sense), it should be noticed

---

[82] The Stoics regarded entities having certain relational properties or entities being somehow directed at other things as being among "the things relative" or "relatives" (τὰ πρός τι). Note however that relatives were not exclusively within the fourth category (πρός τί πως ἔχον). For instance, knowledge and sense-perception were taken to be relatives and thought to fall either into the second category (ποιόν, "qualified") or the third (πως ἔχον, "somehow disposed") (Simplicius, *In Cat.* 166.15–19 = LS 29 C).

that not all relational or impure properties are of this nature. Thus, while Socrates may cease to be the husband of Xanthippe, it seems that there are other impure properties, such as being-the-first-born-son-of-Sophroniscus (compare Plato *Laches* 180e8–181a1), which he will never lose. One need, then, only find the right impure properties.

There is, I think, some limited textual evidence which suggests that some later Stoics or thinkers heavily influenced by the Stoics may indeed have taken peculiar qualities *not* to be qualities in the more specific sense but rather relational properties of a particular sort (more concretely, impure relational properties) or else hoped that qualities in the less specific sense could perform some of the functions expected of peculiar qualities. In particular, some Christian thinkers who borrow heavily from the Stoics describe an account along such lines. Thus, Basil of Caesarea, like some other Christian thinkers (for instance, Origen, *De Oratione* 24.2.1–7),[83] draws heavily upon Stoic thought concerning peculiar qualities (associated in our evidence with the post-Chrysippean Stoic Diogenes of Babylon; compare Diogenes Laertius, 7.58) when discussing the meaning and reference of proper names. In a discussion of peculiar natures and peculiarities (which does not explicitly name peculiar qualities, though the account of Origen, which is similar, does name them), Basil draws upon explicitly and distinctively Stoic notions (such as their usage of the term οὐσία) and offers the following remarks:

> For this reason [that we are all men] in most respects we are the same as one another, but each of us differs from the others solely by virtue of a peculiarities which are observed concerning each individual (τοῖς δὲ ἰδιώμασι μόνοις τοῖς περὶ ἕκαστον θεωρουμένοις ἕτερος ἑτέρου διενηνόχαμεν). Hence the names are not signifiers of substances, but of the peculiar natures (ἰδιότητες) which characterise the individual. So when we hear "Peter," we do not from the name think of his substance (οὐσία)—by "substance" I mean now the material substrate (τὸ ὑλικὸν ὑποκείμενον), which the name in no way signifies—but we are imprinted with the notion of the peculiarities (ἰδιώματα) which are observed concerning him. For

---

[83] "A [proper] name is a summarising appellative that displays the peculiar qualities of what is named. For instance, there is a peculiar quality (ἰδία ποιότης) of the Apostle Paul—one for his soul, by which it is the way it is; one for his intellect, by which it is contemplative of its object, one for his body, by which it is the way it is. The peculiar characteristic (ἴδιον) which is incompatible relative to another—for there is no one else in existence indistinguishable (ἀπαράλλακτος) from Paul—is indicated (δηλοῦν) by the naming of Paul" (Origen, *De Oratione* 24.2.1–7). Cf. Diogenes Laertius, 7.58 (cited above). I largely follow the translation offered by Sorabji 2005, 227.

immediately from the utterance we think of the son of Jonah, the man from Bethsaida, the brother of Andrew, the man called forth from the fishermen into the service of the Apostolate, the man pre-eminent through faith who received upon himself the edifice of the Church. (Basil of Caesarea, *Adversus Eunomium* 29.577.35–580.4)[84]

If this is not an innovation of Basil's and does indeed reflect some later, unnamed Stoics' thinking on the topic (or the thinking of so-called "Stoics"),[85] it supplements the report concerning Diogenes of Babylon (cited above in full, see section III), which claims that a proper name "is a part of language which indicates a peculiar quality" (δηλοῦν ἰδίαν ποιότητα, Diogenes Laertius, 7.58 = LS 33 M), and offers a loose parallel to Dexippus's report in that it proposes that what satisfies (at least some of) the functions expected of peculiar qualities is in fact a *combination* of attributes or a complex attribute. However, unlike the account of Dexippus (which adverted to a complex physiological attribute of combination of physiological attributes), the account here described appeals to certain impure properties—which concern an individual's relation to other individuals (being-the-son-of-Jonah, being-from-Bethsaida, being-the-brother-of-Andrew, etc.)—of the relevant individual.

The combination described by Basil is such that it is (at least ideally and in theory) possessed only by one individual (in this case the Apostle Peter). The relevant combination of attributes is a much stronger (and arguably successful) candidate for being unique *and* a number of these attributes are such that they are plausibly lifelong (such as being-the-son-of-Jonah, being-from-

---

84 Διόπερ ἐν τοῖς πλείστοις οἱ αὐτοὶ ἀλλήλοις ἐσμέν· τοῖς δὲ ἰδιώμασι μόνοις τοῖς περὶ ἕκαστον θεωρουμένοις ἕτερος ἑτέρου διενηνόχαμεν. Ὅθεν καὶ αἱ προσηγορίαι οὐχὶ τῶν οὐσιῶν εἰσι σημαντικαί, ἀλλὰ τῶν ἰδιοτήτων, αἳ τὸν καθ' ἕνα χαρακτηρίζουσιν. Ὅταν οὖν ἀκούωμεν Πέτρον, οὐ τὴν οὐσίαν αὐτοῦ νοοῦμεν ἐκ τοῦ ὀνόματος (οὐσίαν δὲ λέγω νῦν τὸ ὑλικὸν ὑποκείμενον, ὅπερ οὐδαμῶς σημαίνει τοὔνομα), ἀλλὰ τῶν ἰδιωμάτων ἃ περὶ αὐτὸν θεωρεῖται τὴν ἔννοιαν ἐντυπούμεθα. Εὐθὺς γὰρ ἐκ τῆς φωνῆς ταύτης νοοῦμεν τὸν τοῦ Ἰωνᾶ, τὸν ἐκ τῆς Βηθσαϊδᾶ, τὸν ἀδελφὸν Ἀνδρέου, τὸν ἀπὸ ἁλιέων εἰς τὴν διακονίαν τῆς ἀποστολῆς προσκληθέντα, τὸν διὰ πίστεως ὑπεροχὴν ἐφ' ἑαυτὸν τὴν οἰκοδομὴν τῆς Ἐκκλησίας δεξάμενον. As with Origen, I largely follow the translation offered by Sorabji (2005, 227).

85 I say so-called Stoics because of the state of the textual evidence, the decline of the traditional Athenian schools of philosophy from the first-century BC onwards, and the advent of (what is nowadays typically regarded as) eclecticism. As regards this last, there was a certain seemingly self-described eclectic school, associated with Potamo of Alexandria (Diogenes Laertius, 1.21), but I use the term "eclecticism" in the slightly more old-fashioned "mix-and-match" sense (though it is not intended to be derogatory).

Bethsaida).[86] Such attributes are, of course, not intrinsic to the individual and will not serve a metaphysical role in unifying the individual or grounding its identity but—as noted above—this is not a problem so long as we do not take peculiar qualities to be predicated in the more specific sense. Equally, this particular combination of impure properties is not directly perceivable, but that need not be a problem if the purported epistemic requirement is disregarded (we have seen the evidence in its favour is not certain) *or* if the Stoics should have dropped the requirement (more on this possibility in section V). Even later Stoics would presumably not have discussed the case of the Apostle Peter, but Basil's remarks may advert to the fact that some later Stoics or thinkers heavily influenced by the Stoics (perhaps Basil himself) were attracted to an account of the sort just described and that they adapted the earlier Stoic account of peculiar qualities in the manner described or else thought that some other attributes (such as those just mentioned) might better fulfil some of the functions ascribed to peculiar qualities. If that is right, then it suggests that at least some later Stoics or thinkers heavily influenced by the Stoics were sensitive to the problematic nature of the orthodox Stoic account of peculiar qualities and attempted to revise the account accordingly.

V   An Academic Indiscernibility Argument

A   *An Academic Argument*

In the discussion above, I have suggested that, for orthodox Stoics, either the purported epistemic function of peculiar qualities in identifying individuals should be discarded or that it should be recognised that a peculiar quality was not directly perceived but detected through examining its effects, that is to say

---

86   Supposing that the properties are not temporal, then not all the individual attributes mentioned by Basil hold of Peter throughout his existence (I thank Albert Joosse for this objection). For instance, there exists a time such that Andrew was not always pre-eminent in his faith at that time. If that is right, then it may be admitted that Basil's example—which is surely his own—is infelicitous in that respect while it should also be recognised that at least some of the attributes *are* such that they hold of Peter throughout his existence (e.g., being from Bethsaida, being the son of Jonah). Equally (though this strikes me as less likely), it might be the case that Basil (*perhaps* like Mnesarchus, for whom see above) aims to advert to some form of temporal attributes. If that is right, then the relevant attributes could hold of Peter throughout his existence. That is to say, Peter would not, at t_1, gain the property (which he did not have before) of being pre-eminent in his faith. Instead, Peter always has the property of being-pre-eminent-in-his-faith-at-t_1. Leibniz, as I read him, proposes something similar (e.g., *Discours de Métaphysique* §8).

by examining an individual's physiological attributes. I shall conclude by indicating some difficulties in supposing that a peculiar quality might fulfil an epistemic role. I shall do so by reconstructing a simple but potent Academic argument against the notion that in order to identify an individual securely, one needs to discern a (perceivable) attribute or combination thereof which is unique to that individual. The argument is best illustrated by targeting an account akin to that described by Dexippus (which appeals to an individual's physiological attributes) but will function similarly for other relevant sorts of account (notably, pneumatological accounts). This argument would, I think, have given the Stoics good reason to revise the notion that peculiar qualities served an epistemic purpose in identifying individuals (if indeed this was ever a requirement of peculiar qualities).

The argument in question takes the form of an Academic exploitation of "indiscernibilities" (ἀπαραλλαξίας, Plutarch, *Comm. not.* 1077c6–7). As usually understood, the Academics invoked the indiscernibility of true and false appearances to argue that there were no kataleptic appearances (for instance, Sedley 1982, 263; Perin 2005). For instance, the (supposed) phenomenological indiscernibility of dreaming and waking appearances was meant to show that there was no mark or peculiarity exclusive to kataleptic appearances and to impugn the reliability of perceptual appearances by showing that for any true perceptual-type appearance, there is or could be a *false* perceptual-type appearance, experienced while the agent is asleep or otherwise cognitively impaired, such that the epistemic agent may not tell them apart (for instance, Cicero, *Acad.* 2.52; compare Sextus Empiricus, *M.* 7.252).

However, I am here suggesting that the Academics also had available to them (and indeed seemingly employed) a second, different kind of indiscernibility argument (which, as far as I can tell, has received little in the way of attention).[87] The argument concerns *not* our distinguishing between veridical and non-veridical *appearances* (as the dreaming argument does), but our distinguishing the *objects* of our appearances on the basis of our (presumably veridical) appearances of them:

> Are you saying that Lysippus couldn't have made a hundred Alexanders just like one another, if he used the same bronze, the same process, the same tool, etc.? Tell me what marking (*notio*) you would have used to differentiate (*discernere*) them! How about if I stamp a hundred seals into wax of the same type with this ring? Are you really going to be able to find

---

[87] Striker 1990, 153–4 seems to also notice this form of the argument but does not discuss it in any detail. As far I am aware, it has not received detailed discussion elsewhere either.

a means of distinguishing them? Or will you need to find a ring-maker like that Delian chicken-farmer you found who could recognize eggs? (Cicero, *Acad.* 2.85–6)[88]

The same sort of Academic complaint against the Stoics is reported (albeit not terribly clearly) by Sextus:

> For example, if there are two eggs exactly alike, and I give them to the Stoic one after the other, will the wise person, after fastening upon them, have the capacity to say infallibly whether the egg he is being shown is a single one, or the one and then the other? ... When a snake has poked its head out, if we want to give our attention to the underlying object, we will fall into a great deal of impasse, and will not be able to say whether it is *the same snake* that poked its head out before or another one (ὁ αὐτός ἐστι δράκων τῷ πρότερον προκύψαντι ἢ ἕτερος), since many snakes are coiled up in the same hole. (Sextus Empiricus, *M.* 7.409–410)[89]

As I understand these accounts, the Academic complaint centres on our (in)ability to distinguish between highly similar objects on the basis of our appearances of them *even if our appearances are veridical* (and thus it differs from more familiar form of the indiscernibility argument). The problems may be put quite simply and are as follows.

First, *even if* we suppose that individuals do have unique attributes, and *even if* we suppose that the relevant content of our appearances is true, nonetheless our appearances may not enable us to grasp the difference between similar individuals. Thus, suppose that we grant that there are some numerically distinct individuals and that, as per (DISC) (which claims that for any two numerically distinct individuals there is an attribute one of them has which the other lacks), some individual *a* instantiates some attribute that its apparent duplicate (which is nonetheless a numerically distinct individual) *b* does

---

[88] Dic mihi, Lysippus eodem aere, eadem temperatione, eodem caelo atque ceteris omnibus centum Alexandros eiusdem modi facere non posset? qua igitur notione discerneres? Quid si in eiusdem modi cera centum sigilla hoc anulo impressero, ecquae poterit in agnoscendo esse distinctio? an tibi erit quaerendus anularius aliqui, quoniam gallinarium invenisti Deliacum illum qui ova cognosceret?

[89] οἷον δυεῖν ᾠῶν ἄκρως ἀλλήλοις ὁμοίων ἐναλλὰξ τῷ Στωικῷ δίδωμι πρὸς διάκρισιν, εἰ ἐπιβαλὼν ὁ σοφὸς ἰσχύσει λέγειν ἀδιαπτώτως, πότερον ἕν ἐστι τὸ δεικνύμενον ᾠὸν ἢ ἄλλο καὶ ἄλλο.... ἐὰν γὰρ προκύψαντος δράκοντος θέλωμεν τῷ ὑποκειμένῳ ἐπιστῆναι, εἰς πολλὴν ἀπορίαν ἐμπεσούμεθα, καὶ οὐχ ἕξομεν λέγειν, πότερον ὁ αὐτός ἐστι δράκων τῷ πρότερον προκύψαντι ἢ ἕτερος, πολλῶν ἐνεσπειραμένων τῷ αὐτῷ φωλεῷ δρακόντων.

not. This does *not* mean that an accurate appearance of *a* cannot represent its object in exactly the same way that an accurate appearance of *b* represents its object. For instance, Tweedledee and Tweedledum might be (intrinsically) the same but for one minor difference. Tweedledee has seven moles on his back; Tweedledum does not. Even though Tweedledee and Tweedledum do differ in their intrinsic attributes, perfectly accurate photographs of them taken from the front (in the same light, position, etc.), or of them wearing their clothes, etc. will not differ in their representational content because typical photographs of typical objects—like appearances—do not capture all the attributes of their object.

If such an argument was indeed employed by the Academics against the Stoics, what then would the Stoics say in reply? In light of their response to the Sorites and other cases, it seems the Stoics would respond by saying that in such cases one should not assent to something like "this is Tweedledee" but hold off until one can distinguish between *a* and *b* (compare Cicero, *Acad.* 2.92; Sextus Empiricus, *M.* 7.416; *PH* 2.253). If, for instance, you cannot distinguish between Tweedledee and Tweedledum from the front, then you should get closer and get a good look at them from the back and sides (compare Cicero, *Acad.* 2.19, 57; Sextus Empiricus, *M.* 7.258). When one sees that Tweedledee has seven moles and that Tweedledum does not, *then* one may assent to identity claims regarding the two individuals. Thus, for one to distinguish Tweedledee from Tweedledum, one need have some rough account of their general appearances and be aware that one (Tweedledee) has seven moles on his back while the other (Tweedledum) does not.

This seems reasonable as far it goes, but it brings us to a second problem. While awareness or detection of some attribute which two duplicates do not share will help a subject distinguish one individual from the second, it will not suffice for detecting the attribute unique to each individual and so to appropriately identify (and re-identify) that individual in a range of situations, especially if there are (or there is a salient possibility of there being) many other highly similar individuals.

Thus, suppose that when confronted with apparent duplicates *a* and *b* one refrains from assenting to identity statements until one finds an attribute which *a* and *b* do not share and by which one distinguishes *a* and *b*. This attribute (which *a* has and *b* lacks or vice versa) will likely be of little help in discovering the unique attribute of *a* or of *b*. This is because the attribute which *a* and *b* do not share need not be the same attribute that *a* and *c* (another "duplicate") do not share. In fact, if there are sufficient "duplicates" and the "duplicates" are sufficiently similar (which is easily imaginable in the case of eggs which the Stoics hoped a Delian farmer might distinguish), then there will most likely be no single more-or-less simple attribute possessed by a such that it distinguishes a from the others ($b, c, \ldots$). More pressingly, there is no way—short of omniscience about the relevant individuals—of finding out what each individual's unique attribute is.

In this vein, imagine that we are confronted with a very large number of eggs (or chickens, or snakes, etc.). They all seem, to a non-expert, indistinguishable. However, close acquaintance and an expert eye allows one to distinguish between a and b on the basis of their diameter. a's diameter to six significant figures is 10.7014cm, whereas b's diameter to six significant figures is 10.7012cm. This might lead us to think that a's precise diameter, along with some rough characterisation of a's other attributes, can be used to identify them. However, this would be too hasty. While diameter may allow one to distinguish a and b, it will not enable one to distinguish a from another "duplicate," namely c, whose diameter to six significant figures is also 10.7014cm. Instead, in order to distinguish a from c, one will need to appeal to some other attribute, for instance weight. Yet while that might distinguish a from c (and, let us presume, b), it will not distinguish a from d. And so on. Given a sufficiently large number of sufficiently similar duplicates (or the possibility of there being such) the demand for greater precision and comprehensiveness is ever increasing and identifying a unique attribute of an object requires omniscience about that object and its duplicates! The problem is, of course, only exacerbated when one takes into account the fact that an individual's attributes change over time and the problem seems to remain the same regardless of which sorts of attributes (physiological, psychological, etc.) one appeals to.

B   *A Lesson from the Academic Argument?*

The Academic argument seems to raise significant obstacles for the hope that peculiar qualities or their manifestations might act as something akin to number plates and that humans might securely identify similar individuals by means of detecting some unique attribute(s) of the individuals in question. Even though the Stoics did not seem to be committed to the view that an ideal epistemic agent can identify an individual in any conceivable case, nonetheless if the Academics could make salient the possibility that for any given individual there are other highly similar individuals (even if one does not already know of·them), then it seems that the problem described extends beyond the case of the Delian farmer confronted with a large number of highly similar eggs. To make the possibility of highly similar but previously unknown duplicates less remote, the Academics could presumably appeal to historic (or semi-historic) cases, such as the trick that Persaeus apparently played upon Aristo of Chios wherein Persaeus arranged for one twin to leave a deposit of some money with Aristo and then for the other twin (whose existence Aristo presumably did not know of) to collect that deposit (Diogenes Laertius, 7.162 = SVF 1.347).[90] Given the Stoic interest in identification and hopes for infallibility (such that the sage, even if he were merely an ideal figure, could attain the infallibility in question), the Academic argument described seems to strike a significant blow. Even the sage who was well acquainted with a particular individual would be impelled to refrain from assenting to identity statements about that individual if such statements require discovering an individual's unique attribute. Accordingly, the sage should, it seems, refrain from putting too much trust in the abilities of Delian farmers and either not attempt to infallibly identify individuals (if they wish to remain secure) or else perhaps adopt an approach which does not require detecting a unique attribute of an individual in order to identify that individual.

Supposing the argument I have described here was indeed employed by the Academics, then it seems that if the Stoics ever thought the peculiar quality (or some unique attribute) should play an epistemic role in identifying individuals, then the Academic argument would have revealed a number of difficulties with such a view. Accordingly, if the Stoics did think that peculiar qualities might play an epistemic role, they would have been given good reason to abandon the notion and perhaps sought some other means by which to identify individuals. As regards this last, the Stoics would have done well to follow an approach which Sextus describes and attributes to the Academy. The approach in question is more modest in neither seeking to vindicate the pretensions of Delian farmers nor aiming at infallibility. Crucially, it is also more holistic in not seeming to require the detection of some more or less permanent unique, intrinsic attribute(s) of the individual but instead appeals to some combination of context-sensitive features and relational attributes:

> For example, someone who catches an appearance of a human being necessarily also grasps an appearance of features that attach to him and of external features: features that attach to him, such as colour, size, shape, movement, talk, clothing, footwear, and external features, such as atmosphere, light, day, sky, earth, friends, and all the rest. Whenever none

---

90 "Diocles of Magnesia says that, after meeting Polemo, while Zeno was suffering from a protracted illness, Aristo recanted his views. The Stoic doctrine to which he attached most importance was the wise man's refusal to hold mere opinions. And against this doctrine Persaeus was contending when he induced one of a pair of twins to deposit a certain sum with Ariston and afterwards got the other to reclaim it. Ariston being thus reduced to perplexity was refuted" (Diogenes Laertius, 7.162 = SVF 1.347, trans. Hicks).

of these appearances distracts us by appearing false, but all of them in unison appear true, our trust is great. For we trust that this is Socrates from the fact that he has all his usual features too: colour, size, shape, opinion, ragged cloak, and his being in a place where there is no one indistinguishable from him. (Sextus Empiricus, *M.* 7.176–8)[91]

91 οἷον ὁ ἀνθρώπου σπῶν φαντασίαν ἐξ ἀνάγκης καὶ τῶν περὶ αὐτὸν λαμβάνει φαντασίαν καὶ τῶν ἐκτός, τῶν μὲν περὶ αὐτὸν <ὡς> χρόας μεγέθους σχήματος κινήσεως λαλιᾶς ἐσθῆτος ὑποδέσεως, τῶν δὲ ἐκτὸς ὡς ἀέρος φωτὸς ἡμέρας οὐρανοῦ γῆς φίλων, τῶν ἄλλων ἁπάντων. ὅταν οὖν μηδεμία τούτων τῶν φαντασιῶν περιέλκῃ ἡμᾶς τῷ φαίνεσθαι ψευδής, ἀλλὰ πᾶσαι συμφώνως φαίνωνται ἀληθεῖς, μᾶλλον πιστεύομεν. ὅτι γὰρ οὗτός ἐστι Σωκράτης, πιστεύομεν ἐκ τοῦ πάντα αὐτῷ προσεῖναι τὰ εἰωθότα, χρῶμα μέγεθος σχῆμα διάληψιν τρίβωνα, τὸ ἐνθάδε εἶναι ὅπου οὐθείς ἐστιν αὐτῷ ἀπαράλλακτος.

COLLOQUIUM 4

Commentary on Nawar

Sarah Byers
Boston College

Abstract

I offer an interpretation of the Stoic "peculiar qualification" (ἰδία ποιότης) which provides for the identity of individuals over time and the distinguishability of discrete individuals. This interpretation is similar to but not the same as one of the strands in Lewis's interpretation as presented by Nawar. I suggest that the "peculiar qualification"—what makes the individual be the individual—is *the particular* ἕξις *or* φύσις *or* ψυχή that is in an individual. That is, the peculiar quality is not the *kind* of πνεῦμα an entity has, nor some *further qualification or disposition* of the kind of πνεῦμα that it has, such as acquired characteristics of the tenor or nature or soul in its particular lived history, but simply the discrete soul or nature or tenor, *extended in its own particular spatial location*. The so-called peculiar quality is that portion of πνεῦμα that is proper to that individual.

Keywords

Stoic metaphysics – cataleptic impression – distinguishability – identity – breath (*pneuma*)

Nawar ably discusses two related riddles present in Stoic metaphysics and epistemology, as these have come down to us. The metaphysical problem is that of the identity of individuals over time, while the epistemological problem is the distinguishability of discrete individuals.

The problem of identity is that of how the same individual can exist over time in the Stoic schema, given that the Stoics are strict materialists about "what exists." If each individual is merely an agglomeration of matter, and if matter is by definition in constant flux, then each individual's constitutive matter is continuously changing. The "Growing Argument" pertains to cases of

---

* These comments were offered to the initial version of the paper. Subsequently the paper was changed significantly by Nawar.

quantitative change, and draws the conclusion that there is no growth or diminution properly speaking, because there can be no enduring subject of quantitative change in the Stoic schema. The item in question is having matter added and subtracted to it through erosion or accretion in the case of inanimate things, or metabolism in the case of living things. So, how can there be a referent that remains the same through these changes? The same basic philosophical point could be made regarding any other type of material change, as Plutarch notes (Nawar pp. 116–117). Material objects have internal parts that are subject to local change, and their constitutive matter may undergo alteration, a change in condition. A single item may be changing in all of the above ways at once. So, how can there be a referent that remains the same through these changes?

The epistemological problem is: How can the Stoics claim that particular individuals are distinguishable or identifiable, rather than merely recognizing them as *kinds* of things (to know that this is Socrates, as opposed to knowing that this is a human being, for example), given that some individuals, such as twins, have similar or identical perceptible properties? This problem arises for the Stoics because they define knowledge as assent to the propositional content of a kataleptic impression. The kataleptic impression is defined in such a way as to suggest that it is an impression that correctly identifies the individual—a kataleptic impression is said to "arise from what is," to be "stamped and impressed exactly in accordance with what is," and to be "of such a kind as could not come from what is not." More to the point, however, the examples of kataleptic impressions given in our Stoic sources (notably Sextus Empiricus and Cicero) are cases of correct identification of individuals, such as "That is Helen," or "This is Quintus Servilius Geminus." The fact that some individuals seem to be so similar in their intrinsic properties that they cannot be told apart even by an expert poses a problem for the Stoic account of knowledge of individuals. Cases of minute objects would seem to be particularly problematic, as Nawar notes.

These two problems are related to one another insofar as the Stoics seem to have held that what makes the individual thing persist as the same individual over time, is also *unique* in each individual. Hence what makes the individual *persist* as an individual also makes it *knowable* as a unique individual. Individuals are individuals because they are "peculiarly qualified," and the "peculiar qualification" (ἰδία ποιότης) of a thing is unique, lifelong, and something that grounds the individual's unity. Given that what makes the individual persist as an individual is also what makes it be unique, *grasping that* an object is the particular individual that it is, is grasping it as peculiarly qualified. Thus the "peculiar qualification" was "of use in identifying the individual."

I shall here offer an interpretation that I take to be compatible with the essentials of the Stoic position as we have it. It is similar to but not the same as

Lewis's interpretation as presented by Nawar (for the differences, see e.g., Nawar pp. 140–141 and 143).

It seems plausible to say that what makes the individual be the individual is *the particular* ἕξις[1] or φύσις[2] or ψυχή[3] that is in an individual. That is, the peculiar quality is not the *kind* of πνεῦμα an entity has, nor some *further qualification or disposition* of the kind of πνεῦμα that it has, such as acquired characteristics of the tenor or nature or soul in its particular lived history,[4] but simply the discrete soul or nature or tenor, *extended in its own particular spatial location*. The so-called peculiar quality is that portion of πνεῦμα that is *proper* to that individual. It is that πνεῦμα that is the exclusive property of that individual. Note that the particular portion of breath that constitutes the individual ἕξις or φύσις or ψυχή arguably has all the metaphysical characteristics that the peculiar qualification is supposed to have. It is arguably unique, lifelong, and something that grounds the individual's unity and identity.

It is obvious how the discrete portion of "breath" that is in this particular entity is *unique*: this breath is located in this entity and is not located elsewhere; it is proper to this thing. With regard to the particular qualification's ability to ground the unity of the thing, as Nawar notes, the Stoics thought that πνεῦμα—whether as ἕξις, φύσις, or ψυχή—structured matter. It also seems reasonable to suppose that Stoics held that each individual thing's ἕξις or φύσις or ψυχή was lifelong, given that they thought that this was what made the thing be the kind of thing that it was.[5]

Despite the differences in Stoic and Aristotelian ontology,[6] it seems to me that we are helped to understand that this is plausibly what the Stoic concept of the "peculiar quality" is, via a comparison with Aristotle's account of form and matter, and by his sometime usage of the term "quality." Whether or not

---

1 Possessed by inanimate things.
2 Possessed by plants.
3 Possessed by animals.
4 The position held in Lewis 1995 and Irwin 1996, per Nawar pp. 143–145.
5 This would mean that the ἕξις /φύσις /ψυχή is not subject to quantitative change for so long as the entity endures (otherwise the ἕξις /φύσις /ψυχή would itself be subject to the Growing Argument). See Stobeaus in note 11 below. Change of quantity of the ἕξις /φύσις /ψυχή would be the destruction of the individual in which it was.
6 Unlike Aristotle, the Stoics are committed to saying that what makes a thing be the kind of thing that it is (its ἕξις, φύσις, or ψυχή), is corporeal. For Aristotle, in contrast, form and matter are two distinct kinds of principles. The Stoics do, however, want to say that the corporeal structuring breath is active rather than passive, and is ontologically superior to the matter that it structures. Again, "substance" (οὐσία) for the Stoics names matter, rather than the individual entity itself (primary substance) or its structuring form (secondary substance), as it does in Aristotle.

the Stoics actually articulated their account in conversation with Aristotelian texts, or with self-described disciples of Aristotle, is a historical question that does not really concern me here. My point is simply that the conceptual schemata themselves can be put into conversation with one another, and that it is not implausible to imagine that fourth- and third-century Greek-speaking philosophers (Zeno and his followers) might see the metaphysical problem in this way.

If we consider the way that Aristotle accounts for change and stability in individual items, we can see a problem about the identity of individuals which the Stoic model seems able to address. Aristotle accounted for *identity over time* by means of *form*, and the *individuality* of a thing by means of its *matter*. This raises the question: If all of the *matter* in a thing can be changed out over the course of its lifetime, with only the form remaining the same, but the form is only the *kind* of thing something is, and not its individuating principle, then how does a thing remain the same *individual thing*, rather than becoming *a new individual thing of the same kind as the previous thing*? The Stoic answer to this question would then be that each structuring principle is a corporeal thing, the ἕξις /φύσις /ψυχή, and that this thing's corporeal content remains numerically identical over the life of the entity. Since what perdures is a discrete parcel of corporeal stuff, what perdures is a corporeal individual, and not merely a natural kind.[7]

Again, I am not asserting here that the Stoic account was in fact historically elaborated as a response to Aristotle's ontology, merely that it is fruitful for us to know Aristotle's distinctions in order to think through what the Stoics might be doing. But it is notable that there are passages from the Aristotelian commentators which explain the Stoic ontology of individuals by comparison with Aristotle's account of form and of "subject" (ὑποκείμενον).[8] In particular, Simplicius says that the Stoics speak of "something peculiarly qualified" as having individual form (τὸ ἀτομωθὲν εἶδος).[9] Plutarch and Stobaeus tell us that the

---

7   Note that the Stoics would then be committed to saying that in each thing, an individual is structuring an individual (the "breath" is an individual and the entity of which the "breath" is a part is an individual). That this is the correct interpretation seems to be indicated by the sources' claim that the Stoics said that where there appeared to be one thing there was really two.

8   ὑποκείμενον has two referents: the underlying substrate (οὐσία, matter) of the peculiarly qualified thing, and the qualified thing. Each is "receptive," but of different things: the substrate is receptive of the peculiar quality, and the peculiarly qualified individual is receptive of predication and of changes which require a persisting subject. Stobaeus (LS 28D8), Porphyry (LS 28E).

9   Simplicius, *On Aristotle's On the Soul*, LS 28I.

peculiar qualification is a "part" of the individual and that it lasts as long as the individual lasts, and is distinct from the matter that is changing.[10]

With regard to the sense of "quality" intended in "peculiar quality," it seems to me that the Stoics are in these texts using the term "quality" or "qualification" in a sense of τὸ ποιόν that Aristotle happens to allude to in *Categories* 5. Aristotle says there that terms which name the species of a thing, such as "human being," indicate a certain quality. This is one of two senses of "quality," he explains; this is "quality in reference to [secondary] substance" (περὶ οὐσίαν τὸ ποιόν), which names the kind of thing something is, its essential property—it tells you what sort of individual something is. The second sense of "quality" is that which is "simply a quality," that is, an accidental condition, such as being white (3b19 and following). So the Stoic "peculiar quality" is the peculiar or proper form, the portion of πνεῦμα proper to that entity, which structures the (other) matter of that entity.

This interpretation that I am proposing—namely, that the Stoic "peculiar quality" is the individual tenor/nature/soul—also would allow the Stoics to explain how the peculiar quality is of use in identifying the individual, thereby solving the epistemological problem, despite the fact that it is not perceptible. The peculiar quality is expected to be useful in identification of individuals given its uniqueness in each individual, as I mentioned toward the beginning of my remarks.

How is the particular peculiar quality, that is, the ἕξις /φύσις /ψυχή both useful in identifying the individual and also not perceptible? The idea seems to be that it is incidentally or indirectly perceptible. When one is perceiving a given individual, one is *de facto* perceiving the breath of the ἕξις /φύσις /ψυχή, even though the ἕξις /φύσις /ψυχή itself is not sensible because it is too rarefied and thoroughly penetrating all of the entity, so that it cannot be discerned as such. To use a more modern example to illustrate the same epistemological point, if I am seeing this glass, there is a sense in which I am aware of the molecules that are in the glass, because they are present in what I see, even though the molecules themselves are below the threshold of perceptibility for me.

So, when I succeed in discerning one twin from another, or when I tell two eggs apart, I am in fact recognizing that there are two entities comprised of distinct particular souls or tenors, although I do not see the soul or the tenor itself. And the presence of numerically distinct souls or tenors in these two objects is what makes it possible for me to perceive two individuals at all.

---

10   Plutarch, *On Common Conceptions* 1083a–1084a (LS 28A5); Stobaeus (apparently reporting Posidonius), LS 28D7: "Therefore each individual's quality actually remains the same from its generation to its destruction."

You will notice that I have said here, "*When I succeed* in discerning one twin from the other," and this brings us back to the epistemological question as originally posed. That question was, "How can the Stoics claim that particular individuals are distinguishable or identifiable given that some individuals, such as twins, have similar or identical perceptible properties?" It is open to the Stoics here to say that the individuals are always *in principle* distinguishable because they are located at distinct places in space, given that the discrete soul or tenor is different. However, individuals may not be distinguishable *in fact*, even by the wise person, when the wise person cannot synchronically compare them. Snakes of the same species, size, and color when lying side-by-side are distinguishable as two individuals, but the same two snakes successively sticking their heads out of a hole would not be distinguishable; even the wise person would have no way of knowing whether she had seen one snake twice, or two snakes. In such a case the wise person would not assent to the sayable, "those were two distinct snakes." The definition of the kataleptic impression, and the examples of kataleptic impressions given by Sextus Empiricus and Cicero merely tell us that *when* there is a kataleptic impression, it correctly identifies an individual. They do not indicate that the Stoics taught that it is possible to have a kataleptic impression in every situation. Nonetheless, the Stoics seem to have held that when I correctly distinguish individuals of the same type and having other similar characteristics, it is owing to the fact that each has it own particular ἕξις /φύσις /ψυχή.

COLLOQUIUM 4

Nawar/Byers Bibliography

Annas, J. 1990. Stoic Epistemology. In *Epistemology: Cambridge Companions to Ancient Thought 1*, ed. S. Everson, 184–203. Cambridge: Cambridge University Press.

Ariew, R. and D. Garber, tr. 1989. *Leibniz, Philosophical Essays*. Indianapolis and Cambridge: Hackett.

von Arnim, H., ed. 1903–24. *Stoicorum Veterum Fragmenta*. 3 vols., Leipzig: Teubner.

Barnes, J. 1988. Bits and Pieces. In *Matter and Metaphysics*, eds. J. Barnes and M. Mignucci, 224–294. Napoli: Bibliopolis.

Bett, R., tr. 2005. *Sextus Empiricus, Against the Logicians*. Cambridge: Cambridge University Press.

Black, M. 1952. The Identity of Indiscernibles. *Mind* 61:153–164.

Bowin, J. 2003. Chrysippus' Puzzle about Identity. *Oxford Studies in Ancient Philosophy* 24:239–251.

Boys-Stones, G. 2007. Physiognomy and Ancient Psychological Theory. In *Seeing the Face, Seeing the Soul: Polemon's Physiognomy from Classical Antiquity to Medieval Islam*, ed. S. Swain, 19–124. Oxford: Oxford University Press.

Brittain, C., tr. 2006. *Cicero, On Academic Scepticism*. Indianapolis and Cambridge: Hackett.

Brouwer, R. 2007. The Early Stoic Doctrine of the Change to Wisdom. *Oxford Studies in Ancient Philosophy* 33:285–315.

Brunschwig, J. 1984. Remarques sur la théorie stoïcienne du nom propre. *Histoire Épistémologie Langage* 6:3–19.

Brunschwig, J. 2003. Stoic Metaphysics. In *The Cambridge Companion to the Stoics*, ed. B. Inwood, 206–232. Cambridge: Cambridge University Press.

Chiaradonna, R. 2000. La teoria dell'individuo in Porfirio e l'ἰδίως ποιόν stoico. *Elenchos* 31: 303–331.

Collette-Dučić, B. 2009. On the Chrysippean thesis that the virtues are "poia". *Proceedings of the Boston Area Colloquium in Ancient Philosophy* 25:193–223.

Frede, M. 1983. Stoics and Skeptics on Clear and Distinct Impressions. In *The Skeptical Tradition*, ed. M. Burnyeat, 65–93. Berkeley: University of California Press.

Frede, M. 1999. Stoic Epistemology. In *The Cambridge History of Hellenistic Philosophy*, eds. K. Algra, J. Barnes, J. Mansfeld, and M. Schofield, 771–797. Cambridge: Cambridge University Press.

Hicks, R.D. tr. 1979. *Diogenes Laertius, Lives of the Eminent Philosophers Books 6–10* Cambridge, MA: Harvard University Press.

Hülser, K.H., ed. 1987–8. *Die Fragmente zur Dialektik der Stoiker*, 4 vols. Stuttgart: Frommann-Holzboog.

Ioppolo, A.M. 1990. Presentation and assent: a physical and cognitive problem in Stoicism. *Classical Quarterly* 40:433–449.

Inwood, B. ed. 2007, *Seneca, Selected Philosophical Letters*. Oxford: Oxford University Press.

Irwin, T.H. 1996. Stoic Individuals. *Philosophical Perspectives* 10:459–480.

Kupreeva, I. 2003. Qualities and Bodies: Alexander against the Stoics. *Oxford Studies in Ancient Philosophy* 25:297–344.

Lewis, E. 1995. The Stoics on Identity and Individuation. *Phronesis* 40:89–108.

Long, A.A. and D.N. Sedley, eds. 1987. *The Hellenistic Philosophers*, 2 vols. Cambridge: Cambridge University Press.

Long, A.A. 2002. Zeno's epistemology and Plato's *Theaetetus*. In *Zeno of Citium and his Legacy: The Philosophy of Zeno*, eds. T. Scaltsas and A.S. Mason, 113–131. Larnaca: Municipality of Larnaca.

Menn, S. 1999. The Stoic Theory of Categories. *Oxford Studies in Ancient Philosophy* 17:215–247.

Nawar, T. 2014. The Stoic Account of Apprehension. *Philosophers' Imprint* 14:1–21.

Perin, C. 2005. Academic Arguments for the Indiscernibility Thesis. *Pacific Philosophical Quarterly* 86:493–517.

Rodriguez-Pereyra, G. 2014. *Leibniz's Principle of Identity of Indiscernibles*. Oxford: Oxford University Press.

Sedley, D. 1982. The Stoic Criterion of Identity. *Phronesis* 27:255–275.

Sedley, D. 1999. Stoic Physics and Metaphysics. In *The Cambridge History of Hellenistic Philosophy*, eds. K. Algra, J. Barnes, J. Mansfeld, and M. Schofield, 382–411. Cambridge: Cambridge University Press.

Sedley, D. 2002. Zeno's Definition of *Phantasia Kataleptike*. In *Zeno of Citium and his Legacy: The Philosophy of Zeno*, eds. T. Scaltsas and A.S. Mason, 133–154. Larnaca: Municipality of Larnaca.

Sorabji, R., ed. 2005. *The Philosophy of the Commentators, 200–600 AD: A Sourcebook*. Ithaca, New York: Cornell University Press.

Striker, G. 1990. The Problem of the Criterion. In *Epistemology: Cambridge Companions to Ancient Thought 1*, ed. S. Everson, 143–160. Cambridge: Cambridge University Press.

COLLOQUIUM 5

Plato's Philosophical Politics

V. Bradley Lewis
The Catholic University of America

Abstract

This paper suggests an alternative account of the political character of Plato's political philosophy. After pointing toward some problems of the common developmental paradigm, which emphasizes discontinuities between Plato's Socratic early writings, the mature utopianism of the *Republic*, and the late pessimism of the *Laws*, it proposes that Plato's two large constructive works, the *Republic* and *Laws*, are related to two actual historical events in which Plato played a role, the trial of Socrates and Plato's failed intervention in Sicilian politics. On this view, the *Republic* is to the *Apology of Socrates* as the *Laws* is to the *Seventh Letter*. The *Republic* is an imaginative reconstruction of the sort of defense of philosophy under more favorable conditions than obtained in the actual trial; the *Laws* is an imaginative reconstruction of the sort of political reform that Plato advocated under more favorable conditions than obtained in Syracuse under Dionysius II. The paper suggests this as the basis of a unified interpretation of Plato's political philosophy.

Keywords

Plato – political philosophy – *Republic* – *Seventh Letter* – *Laws*

I   Introduction

While Plato's thought has always stood at the head of the canon of Western political philosophy, its specifically political character has always posed sharp challenges. The most durable source of these challenges has been the place of honor assigned by countless surveys of the history of political thought to the *Republic*, interpreted as a radical utopia to which one is invited to respond, at best, with wonder at the new heaven and new earth revealed by Plato's metaphysics, or, at worst, with horror at Plato's anticipation (and advocacy) of a totalitarian politics that would only come to its full ghastly fruition in the twentieth century. At once less wonderful and (somewhat) less horrible is the equally durable fallback position that complicates the picture by constructing a chronological narrative according to which Plato's political thought becomes more realistic as he moves successively through a youthful period of "Socratic" individualism to his mature commitment to metaphysical foundationalism and philosophical dictatorship, which in turn gives way during his old age to a resigned settling for the rule of law.[1] The sense of resignation is increased when one sees that the more practical regime of the *Laws* is also, alas, an authoritarian theocracy. If one is concerned, as a political philosopher should be, with the truth about political things (and not just about books), it is difficult to see what Plato, on this common view, is other than a potent source of error and perhaps misery; Karl Popper was right and Plato has nothing to offer us save the negative example of just how wrong the mind can go even when guiding the pen of a supremely gifted writer.[2]

My purpose in this paper is to question this view and suggest an alternative framework for understanding Plato as a political thinker. This entails rejecting both of the points just noted as well as an ancillary point about Plato's infamous and ill-starred intervention in Sicily. Some parts of my proposal are less original than others, but fully assembled, I think they amount to a coherent and more fruitful perspective on Plato's political philosophy. First, I reject the interpretation of the *Republic* as a political work in the ordinary sense. Its proposal for rule by eugenically bred communist polygamous philosophers is, at best, bizarre, and no thoughtful student of Plato could see it as desirable or even plausible in any practical way.[3] Moreover, to link this with the second point, the usual view seems to privilege one period of Plato's "development," that is, the "mature" middle period characterized by metaphysical foundationalism. But why privilege that period? An alternative hypothesis might see the development in stages as one of assent, privileging the later work, or one of decline, privileging the earlier.[4] But this may be beside the point, since the whole chronological project is subject to serious doubt, given the evidence

---

1 This view has been common for a very long time. For representative recent examples see Josiah Ober's 1998 moderate version (156–247), and George Klosko's 2006 more extreme version.
2 Popper 1943 famously criticizes Plato as a proto-totalitarian. For similar accounts see Richard Crossman 1939; and more recently Havelock 1999.
3 And, of course, none that I know of do see it as desirable or plausible. Just that should cause more to ask how it is that Plato could have seen things otherwise.
4 These alternative possibilities have had their defenders: in the former case Bobonich 2002; in the latter case Gould 1955.

that Plato revised the dialogues during his life, and the dialogue form itself, which resists the hope of establishing a Platonic doctrine stable enough to underwrite the developmental narrative.[5] The ancillary point about Plato and Sicily concerns the slightly less common view that it was the spectacular failure of the Syracusan episode that caused Plato to lose faith in the idealism of the *Republic* and embrace the dreary realism of the *Laws*. This view finds little support in the text of the *Seventh Letter*, however, where Plato tells us that his intentions in Syracuse were to effect a reform of that city by subjecting it to the rule by law, even while repeating the basic principle stated in the *Republic* that a union of philosophy and power would be the solution to political problems.

My proposal is that we can best grasp the character of Plato's political philosophy by seeing the relationship between two pairs of works and the structural and substantive parallels they have with one another. The *Apology of Socrates* and the *Seventh Letter* are both works that refer in detail to real historical events, indeed, the two preeminent political events of Plato's life: the trial and death sentence of Socrates and the Sicilian affair. Both really happened; both involved Plato personally in some way; and both ended in failure. Nevertheless, these two events led Plato to write his two largest works, the two peaks of the Platonic corpus: The *Republic* was the fruit of his reflection on the death of Socrates and the *Laws* was the fruit of Plato's reflection on the failure of his own Sicilian expedition. The substance of this reflection was not a revised view of politics, a repudiation of philosophical rule as a kind of standard, but concerned the conditions and possibilities of political reform. The two large works, therefore, constitute imaginative reconstructions of two failures in ways that suggest what forms success might have taken. In the *Republic* we have a kind of reconstructed *Apology of Socrates* made under ideal conditions[6] and in the *Laws* we have a reconstruction of the reform effort in Syracuse under similarly idealized circumstances. There is no need to posit a change in Plato's views about politics; the aims of the two great works are different but the fundamental political principles are consistent. Among the merits of this view is its treatment of Socrates and Plato as different persons with what would seem to be somewhat different attitudes towards politics.[7] In the *Apology* and *Republic* we are presented with what I characterize as a Socratic anti-politics; in the *Seventh Letter* and *Laws* we are presented with what I characterize as a

---

5 For surveys of the developmental project see Taylor 2002, and Kahn 2002, as well as the briefer surveys in Prior 2012, Nails 2012. For criticisms of the chronological project see especially Howland 1991, and Griswold 2002.

6 Allan Bloom 1991 referred to the *Republic* as "the true *Apology* of Socrates" (307).

7 Ober's 1998, 184–89, discussion of this difference is illuminating.

Platonic philosophical politics. "Anti-politics" is a way of indicating Socrates' simultaneous concern for the real common good of the city and his practical repudiation of conventional political activity in his practice of questioning individuals about their understanding of and commitment to the virtues. "Philosophical politics" is meant to indicate Plato's simultaneous concern with precisely the reform of laws and political institutions in accord with the truth about the virtues and realization of the limits of such accord, especially in light of Socrates' fate. My account does not necessarily entail that Plato's thought underwent no development at all, but it supports a unitarian reading of at least his political thought.[8]

II   The Anti-Politics of Socrates

Plato, who seems to have been present at the trial (*Apology* 34a, 38b), has Socrates describe the charges against him as "Socrates does injustice by corrupting the young, and by not believing in the gods in whom the city believes, but in other daimonia that are new"(*Ap.* 24b8–c1).[9] The legally precise version of the charges attributed by Diogenes Laertius to Favorinus, who claimed to have seen the documents, has Socrates prosecuted for "not believing in the gods in whom the city believes, but in other new/strange daimonia" and also "corrupting the young" (Diogenes Laertius, 2.40). Xenophon's version is nearly the same.[10] The principal difference between Plato's version of the charges and those of Favorinus and Xenophon is the order of the two offenses. While it may be, as Burnet argued, that this reflects a slight flagging in Socrates' memory during a speech delivered *ex tempore*, we may doubt such an *ad hoc* solution when we consider the importance of accurate memory for ancient philosophers and Plato's studied lack of historical scrupulosity in other contexts.[11] It seems more likely that Plato's version of the indictment reflected his own (and perhaps Socrates') sense of the importance of the charges as reflected in Socrates' distinction between his earlier accusers and his actual prosecution by Anytus, Meletus, and Lycon. While there is evidence that "corruption of the

---

[8]   There are of course other unitarian readings, e.g., Shorey 1914; Morrow 1960, 573–590; Laks 1990; Shiell 1991; Pradeau 2002; Brisson 2005; Zuckert 2009; and, in a certain way, Schofield 2006. I have previously defended a unitarian reading on rather different grounds in Lewis 1998a.

[9]   Plato is cited throughout by reference to Burnet 1900–1907 by Stephanus page and line numbers where more precision is wanted.

[10]   Xenophon, *Memorabilia* 1.1.1.

[11]   Burnet 1924, 102–105.

young" was at some point in Athenian history an actual offense, attested prosecutions are hard to find; impiety, on the other hand, was clearly an offense, one that had been levelled at philosophers before.[12] Plato may give priority to the corruption charge to indicate that it was the main cause of Socrates' prosecution even if it was legally ancillary to the more common charge of impiety, a charge that was, as Socrates says, always available against philosophers.[13]

Socrates certainly takes the charge of corruption to be the most serious charge and he spends the most time discussing it. Since the charge is intimately related to his philosophical life, it is that life that must be defended and so the *Apology of Socrates* is an apology for philosophy. There are two particularly striking and related features of the defense that Plato has Socrates make. First, and most important, Socrates indicates twice that he expected it to fail. After describing the calumnies that he attributes to his first accusers to the effect that he was a sophist who investigated the things in the heavens and under the earth and made the weaker argument stronger, Socrates says that it is that charge and not the actual legal charges that he "supposes" (οἶμαι) will convict him (28a2–b1). Later, upon hearing the court's verdict, Socrates says that it was "not unexpected" (οὐκ ἀνέλπιστόν, 36a2). This is perhaps a function of the second striking feature of Socrates' defense: while aiming to refute many details of his accusers' case, he seems to concede much of the substance behind their charges. He denies studying things in the heavens and below the earth and he denies taking fees from students; nevertheless, he admits that young men like listening to him undermine the claims to knowledge made by their elders, and from the perspective of respectable men like Anytus, who Plato describes undergoing this very trial in the *Meno*, Socrates' effect doubtless looked very like corruption. Moreover, Socrates' deft muddying of the waters in his cross-examination of the hapless Meletus notwithstanding, the substance of the most important allegation is not refuted. Nor is what would seem to be the most legally important charge, that Socrates did not believe in the gods in whom the city believed. Socrates distracts Meletus from the question of orthodoxy by drawing him into an unwinnable dispute over whether he is an atheist

---

12   For Anaxagoras, see Diogenes Laertius, 2.12–14; for Protagoras of Abdera, see Diogenes Laertius, 9.51–52; and for Diagoras of Melos, see Diodorus of Sicily 13.6.7. There are grounds for skepticism in all of these cases. On impiety laws, see MacDowell 1978, 197–202, and Todd 1996, 307–15. On corruption of the young as possibly a real offense, see Burnet 1924, 103–104.

13   It seems significant in this respect that Plato also has Socrates emphasize the corruption charge at the start of the *Euthyphro* (2c).

and ends his speech by telling (or should we say confessing to?) the jury that he believes "as none of my accusers does" (35d6–7).[14]

While Socrates' actual practices and beliefs and his unwillingness either to lie or play on the emotions of the jurors may have led him to expect conviction, he indicates another important reason for this. Three separate times Socrates refers to the time limit on his defense speech. Such speeches were allotted specific time periods as measured by a water clock in the courtroom.[15] Socrates first observes that he must remove the slander of his first accusers "in this little time" (ἐν οὕτως ὀλίγῳ χρόνῳ; 19a2), later observing that it would be a wonder if he could take away the slander of his first accusers "in this little time" (24a3). Finally, after learning the verdict, he attributes his failure to persuade the jurors to the "little time" he has conversed with them (24a3) and notes that in other cities capital cases require a trial of more than one day, under which procedure he might have succeeded, but concludes that the answer to the slanders is not easy "in a little time" (37b2). Socrates thus alludes in his defense of philosophy to his philosophical method; indeed, a large chunk of the speech is an attempt to explain that method, which is introduced with an account of his attempt to refute the Delphic Oracle's judgment that no man was wiser than Socrates. This leads Socrates to converse with individuals and to persuade them to care for the virtues that are the goods of the soul. Such conversations take time and they occur in private. Socrates repeatedly emphasizes how he takes each interlocutor aside individually in order to have a lengthy conversation (30a–b, e, 31b4, c4, 32a2–3, 36bc).

This treatment of individuals as such is described at more than one point by contrast to the role of the laws of the city, which cannot converse dialectically. Socrates and philosophy aim to persuade and teach, while law proceeds by punishment (26a, 35c). It is important that Socrates does not condemn or reject law as such; rather, he compares it unfavorably to the kind of engagement that can occur between living intellects. When Meletus replies to Socrates' question about who in Athens improves the young (Socrates having been accused of corrupting them), he replies that the laws do so. Socrates does not deny this; rather he says, "But I am not asking this, best of men, but rather what human being is it who knows first of all this very thing, the laws?" (24e1–2). Socrates does not reject laws; they simply are not his concern. His "politics" is personal rather than legal or institutional, which is why I have called it anti-

---

14   At the same time Socrates' views have been seen as entailing a dangerous critique of conventional Athenian religious practice: see McPherran 1996, and Lännström 2011.
15   MacDowell 1978, 248–50; Todd 1996, 130–32.

politics. It was Plato, reflecting on the fate of Socrates, who tried to fully understand its political implications in the *Republic*.

The greatness of the *Republic* is integrally related to the many levels on which it can be read; I am here concerned with three. At an initial doctrinal level the *Republic* is the proposal of a political utopia that is part of the stock of doctrinal proposals that make up the conventional history of western political thought. Of course, the doctrinal content of the *Republic* also contains theses about the character of justice, a moral psychology of the virtues (or rather, moral psychologies, for there are at least three),[16] education, and aesthetics. Readings of the *Republic* at this level have, of course, yielded important philosophical reflection. But with respect to politics they have also led to the view that Plato was at best a utopian dreamer and at worst a proto-totalitarian.[17] The popularity of the simply doctrinal reading of the *Republic* has declined in proportion with the increasing focus of scholars on the dialogue form of the work. While earlier readers tended to treat the dialogue form as a kind of sugar coating meant to ease the path of Plato's bitter rational medicine and concentrate on the abstraction and criticism of individual theses and arguments, interpreters increasingly see a more organic relationship between form and content.[18]

A second level of interpretation begins, as it were, with the literal sense of the dialogue, but takes the form very seriously. So the *Republic* is, on this view, first and foremost the presentation of a lengthy conversation between Socrates and a group of friends and acquaintances. The conversation takes various twists and turns, but its intelligibility is clear: a discussion of justice suggests that conventional understandings of the term are inadequate and that a serious inquiry into the question requires an inquiry into the nature of the city itself. The search for a perfectly just city leads to the hypothesis that such a city would be completely unified and operate on the basis of reason, like a fully just individual. But the city emerges through several concrete proposals of astonishing audacity or silliness. The analogy between city and soul clearly breaks

---

16 I refer to the three successive accounts of the virtues proposed by Socrates: 386a–392c (a conventional account set at odds with the poetry Socrates criticizes), 428a–433c (the moral psychology of the auxiliaries), and 484d–487a (the moral psychology of the philosophers).

17 See above, n2.

18 For a recent indicative survey see McCabe 2011. One should note also an important related distinction between reading Plato as making very concrete political proposals and Plato as exploring the foundations of political principles, institutions, and practices in a way distinct from any concrete political positions, a distinction articulated well in Waldron 1995.

down and leads to wild paradoxes: the perfectly just city must be one based on a lie about people's souls containing precious metals, in which the family is abolished, and in which philosophers rule. When asked how such a city could be established, Socrates suggests alternately that philosophers might agree to rule and that people might agree to be ruled by philosophers, but also that a more likely event would be the same effect brought about through divine intervention (499b–c). Later, when asked how the transformation of the city might be accomplished, Socrates recommends the removal of all the children from an actual city, so as to start afresh (540e–541a). If any final evidence of the practical impossibility of the city is needed, Socrates supplies it by telling Glaukon that he should found this city in his own soul (592b), reminding us that the soul rather than the city was always the main object of interest.

But why should such a problematic political regime serve as the basis for a moral psychology? Because at the heart of the *Republic* is a picture of the philosophical life as sublime as the politics is ridiculous. The central books of the *Republic* intend to convince Glaukon that, contrary to the usual view, philosophy does not have to be either evil or useless. Philosophy does represent a peak of human possibility and a boon to any community in which it exists. Part of what Glaukon and Adeimantos are to take away from the discussion is a willingness and ability to refute the slanders against philosophy that are commonplaces in Athens (499d10–500a2). One of the most important benefits of philosophy is its influence on education. Philosophers pursue and encourage others to pursue the good of knowledge, which is genuinely common. To the extent that this becomes a widespread interest, the damaging factional strife that was the most serious threat to stable politics in the classical city can be mitigated (520e–521b). Philosophy can aid in the construction and deployment of a moral education grounded in the beautiful and noble aimed at replacing the now inadequate Homeric poems, an example of which Socrates provides in the Myth of Er that ends the *Republic*. So, rather than a wildly implausible political utopia, what Plato has given us is an argument against both cynical political realism and immoderate political idealism. The *Republic* aims at a kind of middle way between these twin threats to order through an encounter with two young men on the threshold of what may be civic prominence in which he both encourages their moral seriousness and tempers their enthusiasm for idealistic politics (an idealism that, as we will see, Plato himself may have once shared). In Leo Strauss's now classic formulation, he shows them and us the "limits of politics,"[19] but at both ends, between extremes of cynicism and idealism. What we have in the *Republic*, then, is a lengthy defense

---

19 See Strauss 1964, 138.

of the philosophical life against a variety of criticisms. It is a defense that, unlike the one mounted by Socrates before the Athenian jury, can unfold at its own pace before a small audience of friendly if often skeptical interlocutors (and at an even more deliberate pace in the hands of readers).

A further indication of this may be that passage in the ninth book in which Socrates tells Glaukon to see Kallipolis as a "pattern" (παράδειγμα) in the heavens on the basis of which he should order his own soul, living in his own earthly city as if he were in the heavenly one (592b2). In the *Apology*, Socrates concludes the story of his own mission, inspired by the Oracle, by suggesting that the god has used him to make a pattern (παράδειγμα) showing the wise man as the man who knows he is not wise (23b1). We should see both Kallipolis and Socrates as παραδείγματα of the philosophical life, albeit from different perspectives: in the case of the *Apology* from Socrates' own perspective; in the case of the *Republic* from Plato's perspective on Socrates.

There is yet a third level at which one can read the *Republic*, at once more illuminating and more disturbing. For the argument in favor of genuine moral seriousness and against utopianism suggests a tension in the character of human life itself. The city exists for the benefit of human life and well-being, but is in tension with the very peak of human excellence. The best life is that of philosophical contemplation, but such a life is available only to a few. Moreover, that life is in tension with the city, itself necessary for human fulfillment.[20] Man is just as much a political animal for Plato as for Aristotle, but the height of human excellence transcends the city. At its deepest level this might be taken to indicate a kind of contradiction or incoherence in nature.

At all three of these levels, the *Republic* is related to the drama played out in the *Apology of Socrates* and, through it, to the other characteristic forms of moral discourse in classical Greek life. Plato's Socrates does there what cannot be done in the Athenian courtroom. All of this suggests that while the *Republic* carries a great deal of meaning for political thought, it cannot be read as a text in the history of political theory in the rather straightforward way that one would read, say, Locke's *Second Treatise*. To do so is to distort it into the caricature denounced by Popper, Crossman, and Havelock, among others. It is a sweeping dramatization of the central paradox in human affairs, symbolized for Plato by the tension between Socrates and the city of Athens, a tension between the need for political order and the object of human longing for a good beyond the political, indeed beyond the simply human. The specifically political dimension of this paradox remained an object of interest to Plato, but

---

20   See Hyland 1995, 59–86; Howland 1998.

became unavoidably immediate when he experienced it first hand, but in a rather different way, in Syracuse.

III   Plato's Philosophical Politics

The *Seventh Letter* purports to be Plato's reply to a request for advice from the friends and followers of Plato's friend, Dion.[21] While it may be just this, readers have long suspected that what we have is—revised or not—also intended as a kind of open letter in which Plato explains and defends his role in a series of political events in Syracuse, the most consequential of the Western Greek cities.[22] Plato probably visited Syracuse for the first time between 390 and 387 BC, during which trip he met and befriended Dion, brother-in-law of the city's ruler, Dionysius I (circa 430–367 BC). After the tyrant's death Dion invited Plato to return with an eye to their educating Dionysius I's heir, Dionysius II (circa 397–343), and reforming the city's government, and Plato did return in 367. Court intrigue, however, seems to have turned Dionysius against both Dion and Plato, leading to the exile of the former and the temporary house arrest of the latter. Eventually, Plato was allowed to leave, only to be invited back six years later by Dionysius, who claimed to have made great progress in philosophy and who threatened that Plato's refusal might have grave consequences for Dion. In 363 Plato made his third visit, which went no better than the second. After leaving he related what had happened to the still-exiled Dion, who then resolved on a course of coercive regime change: he assembled an expeditionary force that included some of Plato's students from the Academy and succeeded in overthrowing Dionysius II. However, the new regime itself fell into stasis and Dion again found himself an exile. Eventually Dionysius II mounted a counter-attack, which Dion returned to successfully beat back, regaining power in the city only to be assassinated in 353. His followers went to Leontini and solicited Plato's advice on what they should do next.

I am arguing for a large account of Plato's most important political works in which the *Seventh Letter* is to the *Laws* as the *Apology* is to the *Republic*, but there are also important correlations between the two works related to Socrates and the two works related to Plato. Three are of particular moment. First, where Plato has Socrates present us with a kind of (highly selective) autobiographical statement in the *Apology*, Plato provides his own such account in the

---

21   I have discussed the letter in more detail in Lewis 2000a and 2000b.
22   For the history summarized in this paragraph see especially Morrow 1962, 145–80, and Brunt 1993, 314–30.

Seventh Letter; indeed, the letter as a whole has the character of an apology. Second, not only was the effort in which Plato took part a failure, but the letter suggests that Plato never had high hopes for its success. What convinced him to undertake the second journey was a personal loyalty towards Dion and a more abstract concern for the reputation of philosophy itself (328c–329b, 347e; compare 326b). If he turned down a clear opportunity to realize the political principles he had advocated then he would betray those very principles. In this respect too the letter is, like the *Apology*, a defense of philosophy. Third, there are the principles themselves, and here it is crucial that they are closely connected both to Plato's autobiographical remarks and to his understanding of the character of philosophy itself. How so?

While Plato's family history and connections made possible for him a political career, Plato's experiences as a young man led him away from politics. The Spartan-backed government of the Thirty Tyrants seemed initially to be a welcome change from the chaotic democracy saddled with responsibility for the loss of the Peloponnesian War, but the conduct of the new regime massively failed to meet Plato's expectations, not least in its attempt to co-opt Socrates into acts of injustice. However, it was the restored democracy that, after a course of score-settling against old enemies, actually tried and executed Socrates.[23] The story told in the *Apology* is, then, strategically placed within Plato's apology for himself. The result of all this was Plato's decisive withdrawal from political affairs. He concluded that all cities were badly governed and that the condition of their laws was hopeless without the intervention of "something amazing following fortune" (θαυμαστῆς τινος μετὰ τύχης, 326a5). Only from the perspective of true philosophy could one see the nature of justice either in the city or in the individual, and, he concluded, "the ills of the human race would never end until either those who are sincerely and truly philosophers come into political power, or the rulers of cities, through some divine chance, learn true philosophy" (326a7–4).[24]

We can recognize this principle from the *Republic* and there is no doubt that Plato's aim, at least as far as the letter goes, was to implement it in Syracuse: If

---

23 See Ober 1998, 162–65. While I agree with Ober's emphasis on the fate of Socrates in Plato's thinking, his more general stress on Plato's opposition to democracy seems to me overstated inasmuch as Plato seems to be just as critical of all the other contemporary political regimes.

24 Plato's Academy has, of course, often been seen as a kind of training ground for political action and there are reports of students and even Plato himself having been asked to help legislate for cities. The most substantial examinations of the evidence here counsel skepticism about the extent of the Academy's political mission and involvement. See especially Brunt 1993, 282–342; Baltes 1993; and Schofield 2005.

Dionysius was serious about his zeal for philosophy and if others at his court could be persuaded to change their lives accordingly, then Dion certainly thought it possible there to effect "that union, in the same persons, of philosophers and rulers of great cities" (328a6–b1; and see 335d). The statement of the principle and of Plato's plan to implement it in Syracuse does make it seem as if Plato was hoping to achieve something like Kallipolis there. But that is not the case. The question here concerns just what Plato hoped to accomplish by converting Dionysius: did he hope to make the tyrant a philosopher-king like those in the *Republic*? I think not. First, the guardians of the *Republic* form a class, one of three classes that, rigidly established and maintained, make up the imaginary city. Plato never even hints at anything like this in the *Seventh Letter*. Second, and more important, when Plato does give more precise indications of the sort of regime he hoped to see established in Sicily, he repeatedly characterizes it as a city to be ruled by laws. Plato writes that Dion's aims were always to reconcile the city's factions, safeguard its freedom relative to the surrounding powers, and establish the best laws (324b2, 332e4, 336a4–5, 351c1–d1). Plato also says this was his own consistent advice (332e4, and 334c6–7, where he refers to this as "my argument," ἐμὸς λόγος; and compare 332b, 336d). Most importantly, speaking abstractly of his and Dion's views, he notes the evils caused by civil strife and the need for a victorious party to renounce vengeance, exercise self-control, and enact laws aimed at the common good and not factional interests. The point about the need for laws that aim at the common good of the whole city is made twice (337a2, c4–6).

Plato's goal in Syracuse, therefore, was not the establishment of Kallipolis. It was the establishment of a city in which various factions were reconciled to living together by a law code ordered to the common good and not to the good of a tyrant or tyrannical faction. The relatively scant details about the plan suggest a real resemblance to what Plato recommends for the imaginary Magnesian city of the *Laws*. But the Syracusan enterprise was a failure. The reforms Plato imagined suffered shipwreck of the worst sort due to the character of Dionysius, the disordered Syracusan court, and perhaps also errors on the part of his friend, Dion. The reform effort, like Socrates' attempted defense of philosophy, failed, but one need not think the failure caused Plato to rethink his political philosophy in any decisive respect. Since he never intended to found Kallipolis in Syracuse, there was no reason to reject Kallipolis in the *Laws*. Rather, the *Laws*, like the *Republic*, is an imaginative reconstruction undertaken in response to the historical failure that preceded it. In the *Laws* Plato imagines what a successful political reform might look like under more propitious conditions than obtained at the Court of Dionysius II. To see this we need first to attend to the stated goals of the Magnesian city and then to Plato's account of what conditions would make such a reform possible. First I need to briefly discuss the character of the *Laws* more generally.

While I have expressed skepticism about the pursuit of a chronology of the Platonic corpus, it seems clear enough that the *Laws* was a very late work.[25] We have credible testimony that the manuscript was found at Plato's death and at least to some degree polished by his assistant, Phillip of Opus (who probably wrote the *Epinomis* outright).[26] There have been scholars (mainly in the nineteenth century) who doubted the authenticity of the *Laws*, but almost no one now does. Moreover, despite what clearly seem to be rough edges to the text, we seem to have a whole work.[27] The dialogue describes a long conversation between three elderly men, a Spartan named Megillos, a Kretan named Kleinias, and a nameless Athenian, walking from Knossos to the cave and temple of Zeus on Mount Ida. So the action is a kind of pilgrimage—Mount Ida is where, according to legend, King Minos was instructed by his father Zeus, leading to the promulgation of the oldest law code among the Greeks. The pilgrimage is therefore to the birthplace of law in the very cradle of Hellenic civilization. The work is made up of twelve books, and there is one obvious fact about its organization: at the end of the third book the Kretan, Kleinias, announces that he is a member of a commission charged by the Knossians with promulgating a law code for a prospective colony. He asks his companions to discuss such a law code with him during their walk and for the remaining nine books that is what they do. The first three books of the *Laws* are a largely theoretical account of the purpose of law, which falls into three sections corresponding to the three books: the end(s) of the city, the character of education, and the city's constitution or regime. The next four books are a work of construction following generally the plan of the introduction although not in the same order; that is, it contains more specific legislation concerning the end of the Magnesian city, the city's regime, and the education that will be provided to citizens. Books eight through ten treat what one might call sources of psychological resistance to such a regime, first *eros*, next *thumos*, and finally *logos*. The twelfth book discusses in more detail the institution of the νυκτερινός σύλλογος, often misleadingly translated as the "nocturnal council," but which I prefer to call simply the "nightly meeting," which is the Athenian's way of

---

25   Aristotle, *Politics* 1264b26.
26   Diogenes Laertius, 3.37; and see Tarán, 1975, 128–39.
27   Against this view, Nails and Thesleff 2003 offer a challenging argument for multiple authorship of the *Laws* over time.

institutionalizing and protecting the practice of philosophy in the city. It is Plato's best attempt at a solution of the Socratic problem.[28]

One other general aspect of the *Laws* is significant for my argument, namely, the absence of Socrates. The main speaker is a nameless Athenian stranger. Sometimes the absence of Socrates is explained by the fact that the historical Socrates never visited Crete, but I've already referred to Plato's insouciance about historical details.[29] Some identify him as a stand-in for Plato himself,[30] which seems plausible, but unnecessary. Catherine Zuckert has argued in her monumental study of Plato that we should see the Athenian as a pre-Socratic philosopher, especially because of his concern with the philosophy of nature in the tenth book and the lack of allusions to fifth and fourth-century historical events.[31] As I will discuss more below, I think the Athenian's concern with the philosophy of nature is directly related to the fate of Socrates. While there are almost no direct historical allusions, the characterization of Athenian democracy given by the stranger is very much in line with other negative characterizations of the democracy in the fourth century (see especially 698b–701b). Finally, the Athenian stranger more than once evinces his acceptance of the Socratic thesis that no one does injustice knowingly (731c, 734b, 860de). This does not make him Socrates, but I think it is warrant for seeing him as (like Plato) a Socratic philosopher.

The end and character of the Magnesian city are most clearly revealed in the first and fourth books, which I suggested earlier treat the question of the ends of the city first as a matter of abstract theory and then with specific respect to the city Kleinias will be involved in founding. The dialogue begins with the Athenian asking Kleinias and Megillos who is credited with legislating for their cities. They both answer that it is a God, Zeus in the case of the Kretans, and Apollo in the case of the Spartans. The Athenian then proposes that they spend their long walk discussing the regime and laws, to which they happily agree. He asks them what end their legislators had in mind and both reply that it was victory in war. The Athenian perplexes Kleinias by reducing the conflict all the way down into the soul of the individual person and asking how it is possible that the individual, parts of whose soul are at war with one another, can be considered stronger or weaker than himself. He then asks him to imagine a single family with many brothers. Most likely more would be unjust than just, so who, the Athenian asks, would be an appropriate judge? Would it be one

---

28   See Lewis 1998.
29   A point made in Strauss 1975, 2.
30   E.g., Halverson 1997.
31   Zuckert 2009, 51–62.

who destroyed the wicked brothers and had the just ones set up to rule themselves? Would it be the judge who has the just rule over the unjust? Or would it be a judge that reconciled the just and unjust with one another by laying down laws that secured their friendship? Kleinias chooses the third, even though there are senses in which the first and second options are superior (627e–628a). Indeed, one might identify the second option with Kallipolis. That Kleinias chooses the third is significant and I think the reason for his choice is likely that the first two options may well weaken the city in the face of potential enemies. The Athenian's conclusion is that laws are made in this case not for the sake of war, but for the sake of peace, to which Kleinias voices agreement, which may seem odd given what I just suggested about Kleinias's motivations. Laws aimed at reconciliation and peace (among other things) in the city also make the city stronger against possible foes. The Athenian stranger himself later suggests just this (641c). Recall also that this aim of reconciliation through the rule of law was one that Plato stressed in his advice to Dion's followers in the *Seventh Letter*. This initial compromise is emblematic and definitive of the more practical political character of the *Laws*.

The fourth book of the *Laws* takes up this theme in a more concrete way, with a view to the circumstances of the city Kleinias is charged with founding and so considers its geographical features and the natures of the prospective settlers. This leads the Athenian to make a series of reflections on the difficulties of founding cities and the importance of fortune. Just before raising initially the question of the Magnesian city's regime the Athenian makes his most expansive comment: "when prudence and moderation coincide in a human being with the greatest power, there the best regime comes to be naturally and laws as well, but otherwise it will never come to be" (711e7–712a3). In response to the Athenian's posing of the regime question, however, neither Kleinias nor Megillos can muster an adequate answer: both the Spartan and Kretan regimes elude the conventional categories and seem to encompass features of more than one regime. The Athenian says this is because their regimes really are regimes, where the conventional regimes are really just rule by factions, and the names of the conventional regimes reflect this.[32] If one is to name a good city this way, the Athenian says, it should be named for the God "who truly rules as master over those who possess intellect" (712e9–713a4). The Athenian explains himself by recounting the myth of Kronos, who is said to have ruled over human beings in a previous age in a manner that provided "peace and awe and good laws and justice aplenty" (713e1–2). He concludes

---

32 This is, I think, the background to Aristotle's notion of the generic regime in his *Politics*: see Lewis 2013, 79–82.

that this situation should be approximated by regimes now and that "there can be no rest from evils and toils for those cities in which some mortal rules rather than a god" (713e3–5).

These two passages show how the main principle of Plato's political thought leads to the rule of law as defended in both the *Seventh Letter* and the constructive parts of the *Laws*. It also builds on the teaching of the *Republic*. Socrates himself admits that getting philosophers to rule is as difficult to bring off practically as getting others to accept rule by philosophers. This is because philosophers do not want to rule, and only in the most just city, the city that exists nowhere but as a paradigm in the soul of the just man, the philosopher, is he compelled to rule. As a practical matter, the closest one can get to philosophical rule is the rule of law because it is grounded in intelligence and limits the rule of men, that is, it constrains the ambitions and desires of those who do want to rule (874e–875d). In this way the rule of wisdom and that of law are not opposed to one another: the first is a standard and the second represents the best possible approximation of the standard.[33] Both are stated in the *Seventh Letter*; they are intimated in the *Laws*, which differs with the Letter in a number of practical details. Why this is so brings us to the second point, which concerns the conditions under which the Magnesia city is conceived.

My argument is that the *Laws* is an imaginative reconstruction of the failed reform effort in Syracuse.[34] We should be able to see in it then both continuities and systematic deviations from the situation that faced Plato at the court of Dionysius II. The main continuities are the goal of a regime put under the rule of law, which I have already discussed, and the account of how reform can best take place. One reason that Plato tells us he undertook the Syracusan mission was his conclusion that "if anyone ever was to attempt to realize these principles of law and government, now was the time to try, since it was only necessary to win over a single man and I should have accomplished all the good I dreamed of" (328b8–c3). In the fourth book of the *Laws* the Athenian stranger shocks his companions arguing that the optimal city from the perspective of fundamental reform would be one ruled by a tyrant because the example and efforts of the tyrant would most quickly and easily spread through

---

33   Thus Laks's 2005 suggestion that it is difficult to determine whether we should call the Magnesian regime a "nomocracy" or a "noocracy" (271). The issue is discussed in more detail in Laks 2005, 33–43.

34   I should say that I do not think my view entails that the *Laws* was written in its entirety after Plato's final return from Syracuse. It seems to me entirely possible that Plato was already working on a dialogue presenting a far more realistic and practical approach to politics, but that the Syracuse affair had a decisive influence on the *Laws* as we have it.

the population and change the character of the city. But the tyrant must be of a certain type: he must be young, have a good memory, learn easily, he must be courageous, magnificent, and have a naturally moderate nature (709e6–710b2). These characteristics fall short of those Socrates attributes to the philosophic nature in the *Republic*, most notably in leaving out love of learning and truth (485a1–487a5); at the same time, they clearly seem to go beyond those exhibited by Dionysius II. Did Plato think this before his intervention or only come to it as a conclusion in light of its failure?[35] We cannot know, but by the time he wrote the *Laws*, he clearly understood it. In any case, what was required was still the union of wisdom and power that he had first described in the *Republic* and he still understood such a union to be the result of chance (702bc, 709a–c, 710c, 711d; compare 968e–969a), and the chance could occur in another way, the one actually described in the *Laws*. There the reform effort does not take place with respect to an existing city, but in the colonization of a new one. The nameless Athenian philosopher advises, even teaches, Kleinias about legislation. In one respect the situation of the *Laws* is already described in the Letter. In advising Dion's friends about the evils of factional politics in which the victors disenfranchise and persecute the vanquished, he recommends selecting eminent men from other Greek cities to come and assist in reform efforts aimed at the common good of the whole city (337b3–c6). At the beginning of the sixth book of the *Laws* the Athenian recommends that the first election of magistrates in the new city be assisted by a group of trustworthy men from the mother city in order to establish appropriate traditions and smooth over initial difficulties (752e–753a).

In an important paper, Malcolm Schofield considered and rejected something very close to the view I have argued for.[36] He reads the passage from the fourth book about the moderate young tyrant as an ironic reference to the *Republic*, indeed, as part of a repudiation of the ideal of the philosopher king from the *Republic*. It is a repudiation of the idea that the best city can come about via the union of political power and philosophy, a point made by the obviously paradoxical notion of a moderate tyrant. Schofield thinks the passage refers to the *Republic* partly because it seems incongruous with the general dramatic frame of the *Laws*, which is related to Kleinias's colonial enterprise. To see it as related to the Sicilian affair one must, as the Letter envisions, see Plato's effort as that of converting Dionysius to philosophy in order to establish something like Kallipolis. As stated above, however, I do not think the Letter does this. Schofield cites the passage at 328a where it is stated as an argument

---

35   Stalley 1983, 92 writes that the passage "reeks of the Syracusan affair," but nothing more.
36   Schofield 1998.

in favor of Plato's involvement with Dionysius that "now, if ever, was the time when we might hope to realize the coming together in the same person the philosopher and the ruler of a great city."[37] Consider, however, two things about this passage: first, it is Plato's report of Dion's argument to him and not a report of Plato's own views; second, it does not strictly speaking imagine Kallipolis in any detail. Since elsewhere in the Letter Plato describes his goal in Syracuse as a city under the rule of laws aimed at the common good, it makes sense to interpret this passage in that light as well. Plato goes on in the Letter to refer (in his own voice) to the challenge in Syracuse as the winning over of one man (328bc), just the thing contemplated in the *Laws* 4 passage. And that is the important fact about the passage: the Athenian considers there the problem of political reform simply in terms of speed and ease, envisioning not the conversion of the tyrant from tyranny to benevolent despotism, but out of the business of *ruling*. The situation contemplated here must be of a kind of reform followed by resignation or perhaps conversion into a kind of constitutional monarch, so, *pace* Schofield, nothing in the passage implies a contradiction with the many negative things the Athenian says about tyranny. I do not deny that such a thing seems massively improbable and would have to Plato—just this seems to account for the many reservations he had about becoming involved with Dionysius in the first place. The passage considers a theoretical possibility distinct from Kleinias's colonization project, a risky possibility to be sure, and, on my view, one revealing precisely why reform through colonization should be preferred, as Plato saw first-hand in Sicily.

There is one remaining detail of the *Laws* I want to discuss, which takes us back to the *Apology of Socrates* itself and the relationship of the *Laws* to the *Republic*. Socrates' defense before the Athenian jury against the charge of impiety was a failure he himself anticipated largely because he thought it impossible to erase long-standing slanders in the short time allowed for a defense speech by Athenian law. Moreover, Socrates' characteristic method of teaching could not work on a jury of five hundred people. His defense of philosophy is carried out in the *Republic* over an entire night and in the company of a small group of friendly interlocutors. Interpreters of the *Laws* have often harshly criticized the official religion that the Athenian stranger proposes there, complete with a prescribed orthodoxy, which would have been rather unusual in any Greek city. Some, like the great George Grote, have seen it as kind of posthumous betrayal of Socrates.[38] This view is mistaken for at least two reasons. First, the theses established as orthodoxy in the Magnesian city are quite general and

---

37   Schofield 1998, 237.
38   Grote 1875, 409–12; cf. Gould 1955, 109; Klosko 2006, 233.

open-ended. Second, the punishment prescribed for those convicted of impiety is rather different from that in fourth-century Athens: those convicted of impiety out of an honest disagreement with the religious views of the city are confined to a facility called the σωφρονιστήριον or "moderatorium," where they remain for five years and are permitted only to speak with the members of the Nightly Meeting.[39] Had Socrates lived in the Magnesian city it seems unlikely that he would ever have been prosecuted, much less convicted, but if he had, he would be even more unlikely to have been put to death.[40] It is noteworthy in this respect that Plato's Socrates himself seems to have predicted the sort of challenge to the Magnesian city that the impiety law is aimed to counter. At the start of the tenth book the Athenian conjures up for his interlocutors the image of arrogant young men under the influence of "new and wise men" (or perhaps merely using them as a pretext) who deny the existence of the gods and thereby threaten the very foundations of social order. In his final remarks to the jury Socrates had said that he himself was a check on some kinds of dangerous thought and that without him "there will be more who will refute you." He characterizes them as "harsher, insofar as they are younger" and predicts that the citizens' response will be "more indignant" (39d). The elimination of philosophy will not eliminate the dangers of the city that might be unleashed by reason; indeed, Socrates' suggestion seems to be that the encouragement of honest philosophical inquiry is the best check on the dangers of aggressive sophistry.

The peculiar institution of the Nightly Meeting, then, is important beyond its role in the prosecution of heretics. It is explicitly mentioned first in the tenth book and then described in more detail in the twelfth.[41] There we learn that it does considerably more than convert heretics. It is composed of many of the highest officials of the city, each of whom is permitted to bring as an aide a young man. The group meets not at night really, but just before dawn, so very early in the morning before the day's tasks begin. The Athenian stranger says the group will meet foreign envoys and those who return from trips abroad. They will also engage in wide-ranging discussions among themselves concerned with the unity of the virtues and the soul (965cd), the noble and the good (966a), and proofs of the existence of the gods (966c). The members will thus discuss philosophy. This does not entail that all the members are philoso-

---

39   See Lewis 2010.
40   This point was suggested in Strauss, 1975, 2.
41   Although it is presaged already in the discussion of drinking parties in the second book (evidence against those like Klosko 2006, 252–58, who see it as an ill-fitted—indeed contradictory—add-on to the *Laws*): see Strauss 1975, 31–34; Lewis 1998, 16; and Larivée 2003.

phers; perhaps some few will be, but surely not all or even most.[42] But those who do not attain philosophy will have been imbued with a deep respect for it. It will have a permanent protected place in the city and a kind of influence over the city's affairs. Nowhere does the Athenian say that the body itself is a governing institution; however, it includes many of the chief magistrates of the city who will be formed or influenced by philosophical discussion. The tension between Socrates and the city cannot simply be resolved, but the Nightly Meeting in the Magnesian city represents Plato's suggestion for how it might be managed in such a way as to do as much justice to both as possible. That such an institution should be conceived is not as radical as the idea that philosophers should simply rule, but it is radical enough, and there is ample evidence that Plato thought the odds against even this made it risky and unlikely to come to be (968e–969a). But this is true of all political reform and represents another continuity in Plato's thinking. As he has the Athenian stranger say, "lawgiving and the founding of cities really is the most complete virtue of men" (708d6–7; compare 752b, 769a).

IV   Conclusion

This picture of Plato's political thought is in many respects incomplete: there are important political aspects of many other dialogues that I do not discuss here. Let me note just three possible objections to my account. Many (but not most) scholars reject the authenticity of the *Seventh Letter*, most recently and notably Michael Frede and Myles Burnyeat.[43] If the *Seventh Letter* is pseudonymous, it does pose a problem for my account as an account of Plato's thinking, but not necessarily the substance of my interpretations of the *Republic* and *Laws*. It would remove an important buttress from my construction of the larger question of the coherence of the two works, but the foundation would remain. Frede and Burnyeat's arguments deserve more discussion than I can undertake here.[44] However, I think they can be contested. Frede's account, for example, relies heavily on inferences drawn from a characterization of the

---

42   Laks 2005, 283 describes the Nightly Meeting as "quasi-philosophical." It seems to me possible that the Nightly Meeting is also intended to evoke the fact that the conversation in the *Republic* takes place at night and to contrast both to the *Apology*.

43   Burnyeat and Frede 2015.

44   For what it is worth, relatively recent stylometric analysis has offered support for the authenticity of the *Seventh Letter*. Ledger 1989, 148–50, concludes that the *Seventh Letter* was written by the author of the *Laws*.

ancient tradition of pseudonomous epistolary literature, which do not seem to me decisive. This is supplemented by an account of the philosophical differences between the *Republic* and *Laws* that is itself contestable (and I have contested it above).

Secondly, of course, there are the other dialogues. I think the other Platonic dialogues that touch on political questions can be fitted into the framework I have set out, for example, the *Gorgias*, in which Socrates seems to acknowledge both the "antipolitics" that I associate with him above and Plato's "philosophical politics" as exemplified by the *Laws*.[45] But of course, there is also the *Statesman*, which has often been seen as something of a transitional dialogue between the *Republic* and *Laws* by those scholars who accept the developmental paradigm. How can any plausible rival theory fail to offer an alternative account of the *Statesman*? One inadequate response would point to the *Statesman*'s place in the trilogy that is occupied, mainly with questions of epistemology. More important is the growing body of literature on the *Statesman* that, taking the dialogue form seriously, distinguishes the perspective of the Eleatic stranger from those of both Socrates and the Athenian stranger.[46] That there is a third perspective on politics considered by Plato does, therefore, indicate a sense in which my account remains incomplete.

Finally, it could be objected that I have simply ignored or radically truncated the sense in which even the *Laws* is a kind of utopia. In the fifth book it is true that the Magnesian city is referred to as "second best" in comparison with one in which everything is held in common, suggesting something like Kallipolis (739a–c; compare 807b, 875d). The Athenian describes this strikingly as a city in which things that are "naturally private" become common, like the pains, pleasures, and other sense experiences of the citizens, but goes on to say that such a thing would only be possible in a city inhabited by gods or children of gods (739c–e). This passage seems to evoke Socrates' description of the best city in the *Republic* as that "most like a single human being," in which the citizens share one another's pleasures and pains (462cd). This ideal thus seems to inform the *Laws* as well. But what kind of ideal is it? It is an ideal of the best city as a kind of entity, a city that would be more fully and perfectly a unity of its parts than any other, one that would never suffer in the slightest bit from the sort of factional strife that leads to the degeneration of cities into tyranny or their total collapse internally and/or at the hands of external enemies. It is the

---

45 See, e.g., *Gorgias* 464a–465d, where Socrates contrasts the pseudo-art of sophistry with the true art of νομοθετική, legislation. If there is such an art then it indeed points to what the Athenian stranger has to say in the *Laws*.

46 See Kochin 1999; Schofield 2006, 136–93; Zuckert, 2009, 680–735; and Cherry 2012.

idealized version of a certain kind of human community and there is a sense in which it really would be best and so really is an ideal: we might call this the genuinely utopian moment in Plato's political thinking,[47] but in both the passages from the *Republic* and *Laws* mentioned, the moment seems to pass. Indeed, the passages seem to undermine themselves, since the degree of idealized unity imagined in them plainly cannot be realized. The pleasures and pains of individual persons cannot become common. Nothing can be as common as knowledge and a city maximally ordered by and to this end cannot be realized so long as it is composed of human beings. Nevertheless knowledge is an informing goal of the city and to that extent the city approximates perfection. Moreover, the many facets of the approximation and the many ways in which reality falls short of the ideal (only a few of which I have discussed above) illuminate the limits of idealism and the permanent limitations of any specifically political solution to the deepest problems of human life.

What I have sketched out in this paper retains in many respects the character of a research program; however, on the whole, I think this reading of the *Apology*, *Republic*, *Seventh Letter*, and *Laws* makes better sense of the texts than the usual developmental view and makes Plato a more compelling political thinker whose works continue to merit our study and reflection.[48]

---

[47] Schofield 2006, 194–249 is a very illuminating discussion of community and the unity of the city in Plato's thought.

[48] I am grateful to my commentator at the lecture, Joseph Lawrence, as well as to my audience at Assumption College, especially Patrick Corrigan and Daniel Maher, all of whose questions and criticisms helped me to improve my paper.

COLLOQUIUM 5

Commentary on Lewis

Joseph P. Lawrence
College of the Holy Cross

Abstract

If Lewis prefers the political Plato to the apolitical Socrates, I take my stand with Socrates. I also regard Plato as having been more profoundly invested in establishing a philosophical religion than in establishing a philosophical politics. Cultivating trust in the Good is ultimately of more importance than arming a state against potential enemies. Courage is a virtue greater than prudence. Plato's *Laws*, on my reading, is less concerned with maintaining the order of the state than with civilizing its inhabitants. In light of this contention, I understand Plato as being more Socratic—more open to question and thus more flexible—than Lewis's reading seems to allow. This is why I think Plato provides more attention to his extended preambles to the laws than to the laws themselves. As seriously as Plato took the quest for true law, he realized that any positive code of law (or any constitution) has to be subject to constant revision.

Keywords

religion – courage – prudence – Dionysus – education

Having elsewhere gone on record as favoring Socrates over Plato,[1] I feel a bit out of my element responding to a Plato talk that places such strong emphasis on the *Laws*. As the one indisputably Platonic dialogue where Socrates makes no personal appearance, it is also the one dialogue I know least. That said, I do have a perspective on the work that might at least suffice to throw Professor Lewis's excellent paper into relief.

Perhaps because of my lack of expertise, I found it easy to agree with almost all of Lewis's principal contentions, in particular the marvelous way he parallels the relationship between the *Apology* and the *Republic* with the relationship

---

[1] Lawrence 2015.

between the *Seventh Letter* and the *Laws*. And I certainly agree emphatically with his emphasis on the continuity of Plato's thought. The Kallipolis of the *Republic* is surely not to be read as a formula for how to establish utopia but rather as a way of suggesting that an ideal city would have been able to tolerate Socrates and even to let itself be guided by him. I still find myself, however, on the opposite side of the good neighborly fence Lewis has put in place, the one that separates Socrates (a fundamentally apolitical thinker) from Plato (a fundamentally political thinker). I call it a fence, for the separation is a real one, as real as the distance separating wise old Socrates, the man who relentlessly discards ideological and idolatrous fantasies, from Plato, the consummate man of knowledge who anchors his insights in reason and carefully records them for the sake of posterity. I call the fence good neighborly, for these two men loved one another and lived for the sake of a conversation so essential that Plato imaginatively kept it alive for long decades after Socrates' death. Still, one can't help but to take sides. I take my stand with Socrates. Lewis, it seems, has taken his with Plato, as if Plato could tell us just how much philosophy can—and cannot—offer to those in political power. As such, his Plato speaks directly to humanity's political concerns, even when prudence has led him to follow Socrates' retreat from an actively political life. And when, in Syracuse, he engaged actively in political struggle, he did so with a realistic understanding of how little he was likely to accomplish. A "philosophical" politics knows both sides of the coin, both the intractability of man and the ideal way they should be governed. The title of Lewis's paper, "Plato's Philosophical Politics," calls this tension to mind, not only as a tension within politics, but also as the always looming possibility that a Socrates will break from politics altogether.

Lewis's paper raises the important question of how to read the *Laws* in the light of such tensions. What he points to (and it is certainly there in the text) is a specifically Platonic concern with determining the shape a political state must take once one understands that philosophers are necessarily few and far between. What I notice, in contrast, is more the Socratic residue, a vision that is less political than cultural. As in the *Republic*, Plato's highest wish for the state is that it foster philosophical community by binding itself to a religious conception cleansed of idolatry and superstition. Laws are concerned less with preserving the order of the state than with civilizing its inhabitants. Their primary content has less to do with matters of war and money than with the proper rites of worship. As such, they are *experienced* less as rational decrees than as poetic responses to the beautiful order of the cosmos. Viewed in this way, the laws themselves are less important than the "preambles" attached to them (719e–720d; 722d–e), which, in order to educate citizens as to why the laws are necessary, reproduce the thinking of those who strive to formulate them. Products themselves of inspiration, their purpose is less to inform than to inspire.

But with such a large and complex text, it is surely appropriate to emphasize what one will. Lewis's more specifically political reading of the text is certainly sound—and anchored in good scholarship. On my view, it has the sole defect of drawing attention away from the religious context and, more specifically, the way that Dionysus, rather than Zeus or Apollo, has been chosen as the foundational deity of the new city that Plato envisions.[2] It is the god, according to Plato, who must animate law if it be true law and not (as our skeptics like to put it) a device for "rigging the system" by protecting the perceived interests of one faction over another. It is the god, in other words, who stands for human interest as such, as the sphere that nurtures the possibility of happiness. It is by no accident that so much of the opening two books of the *Laws* is dedicated to drinking parties, music and dance, all related to festivals that celebrate the god Dionysus (671a–672a). Where it is all headed is made clear in Book Three of the *Laws*. The course of history returns us to the beginning, but under the new condition that human beings will now have to discover within themselves the guiding spirits long ago sent by Cronos. Those spirits within (714a) I would liken to the one Socrates referred to as his δαιμόνιον: the voice that, like a good law, tells us not what we are supposed to do, but what we are supposed to avoid doing. As for what *to do*, we still have to follow the way of desire, which is why desire itself must be educated (and why the god of the emerging epoch can be understood as the god of Mystery Religion). If the legal systems of Sparta and Crete seek to achieve order by minimizing pleasure and frustrating desire, the Athenian stranger seeks not to dull or to eliminate desire, but to educate and refine it. It is a god, after all, who has equipped us, and with a higher purpose in mind, with both pleasures and pains.

"God," Plato explicitly says, "is for us the measure of all things, of a truth, more truly so than, as they say, man" (716c). On Lewis's account, religion itself is politically constituted and plays a political function. This I infer from the way he refers to the "impiety law" as simply a legalistic proposal by the Athenian Stranger who has political reasons for wanting to "establish" a religion. On my understanding of the *Laws*, in contrast, Plato's point is that religion makes itself manifest in the history of mythology; it is not something we establish for ourselves. It is mythology, not human deliberation, that determines when Zeus assumes the throne of Cronos—and when Dionysus is destined to take over from Zeus. The laws of a city have validity to the degree that they have a divine

---

2 Voegelin 1966, 239–241.

and not a human origin. It is for this reason that the dialogue begins with the Athenian elder asking his Cretan and Spartan associates: "To whom is the merit of instituting your laws ascribed, gentlemen? To a god, or to some man?" (624a). The question is crucial, for only from the perspective of a god, and a god, moreover, eager for sacrifice, can one resolve that central dilemma that Lewis infers from the execution of Socrates. As he puts it, "the city exists for the benefit of human life and well-being, but is in tension with the very peak of human excellence."[3]

I very much agree with Lewis on this central point, which raises the question of whether the philosopher is to stay true to God, and true to the task of disclosing the truth of God, or whether he is to devote himself to the clearly unrealistic (yet just as clearly understandable) goal of political realism, seeking to "secure" the life of mortal man. If Lewis is right and the latter is the real crux of Plato's project, then Heidegger was surely right to discern in Plato the original architect of Hegelian reason, complete with the confidence (whether one call it neoconservative or neoliberal) that rationality itself constitutes the end of history, that is, the end of all Socratic bickering about the meaning of life. As for myself, I believe that such a temptation to dogmatism (fixing forever, for example, the number of citizens and wives, of children and slaves) was something that Plato weathered and withstood, saved in the end by the need to maintain a relationship with the ever-dialogical Socrates. As "fixed" as the good statesman makes law *seem* to be, the genuine task of governance is in the hands of a Nocturnal Council, whose early morning meetings ritualized the way that daytime clarity is incubated in the darkness of night.

By gesturing in this way towards a wisdom that knows more than wisdom, I do not want to paint a picture of a God who, towering above politics, is indifferent to the well-being of people. No, the Athenian stranger makes it clear that any god who deserves the name must genuinely care about the plight of man (899d–900b). Even so, his wisdom is never exhausted by a set of laws. As the Stranger in the *Statesman* put the matter to the young Socrates, "it is impossible for something invariable and unqualified to deal satisfactorily with what is never uniform and constant" (294c). Laws have their limit. This does not simply mean, as Lewis seems to indicate, that, consonant with the infelicities of human nature, it is wise to deny the possibility of utopia. Instead, we have to acknowledge that even a modified code of law might have to change as history changes, for, as we also find in the *Statesman*, "the differences of human personality, the variety of men's activities, and the inevitable unsettlement attending all human experience make it impossible for any art whatsoever to

---

[3] See p. 177.

issue unqualified rules holding good on all questions at all times" (294b). The extensive foray into universal history that is the subject of Book Three of the *Laws* really matters. It is here, amidst all those astonishing twists and turns, all the way down to a cataclysmic Deluge, that we are to discern the mythical sequence of deities that only in the fullness of time deliver over to those capable of commanding themselves the license to rule others. Nor are we to forget the lesson of the divinely willed Deluge: God's loving concern for man does not mean that God wills what politics wills, which is stability and security for man. Above the prudent concern with law, which so aptly goes under the name of jurisprudence, is the image that can be found in Books One, Seven, and Ten of the dialogue, whereby God plays the game of order through history, with man as his puppet (644d–647a). The myth of the metals, which Lewis, reflecting the peculiarly modern sense that human beings cannot be thought of as "belonging" to the earth, cites (176) in order to underscore the deliberately unrealistic nature of the political proposals found in the *Republic*, has actually been reconstituted here at the heart of the supposedly much more "realistic" *Laws*. The string of gold (soft and malleable) that ties us to law is stronger in some than in others. Most of us are more vulnerable to the taut iron wire that pulls us toward pleasures and jerks us away from pain. Rare are the golden souls that follow easily in the footsteps of the Lord. To grow such a soul, moreover, one must not simply be regimented to live a certain form of life: God plays with his puppets, to be sure, but he plays with them not (like the all-too-human puppet players in Book VII of the *Republic*) in a sadistic display of his own superior power, but in an attempt to communicate to them the spirit of play. This is what Plato calls *education* (803c–804b). It leaves a person free to "search, for some thoughts, thine own suggesting mind," while trusting that "others, dictated by heavenly power, / shall rise spontaneous in the needful hour."[4] That Plato has in this way provided room for both trust and spontaneity is what I personally find attractive in the *Laws*. The more political reading, of course, will lay emphasis on obedience, something I tend to be wary of unless and until it is brought into union with persuasion.

    I want now to relate what I am saying a bit more concretely to Lewis's paper. I fully agree with his very central contention that Plato had no need to revise his political philosophy after his failure in Syracuse to found Kallipolis, the ideal state of the *Republic*, and this for the very simple reason that Plato had not tried to found Kallipolis. Instead, he was trying to make use of what he hoped was a friendly and moderate tyrant to establish a system of laws that would shield Syracuse from the excesses of immoderate tyranny. His failure to

---

4 This passage, from Homer's *Odyssey* 3.26, is quoted at 7.804a of the *Laws*.

accomplish this goal served as a reminder of what presumably Plato already knew: founding a state requires more than a vision. It requires a divine hand to establish the right condition. Such a "right condition" is imagined at the end of Book Three of the *Laws* when Kleinias discloses that Crete was preparing to establish a new colony and that he himself had been commissioned, with others, even to consult with foreigners in coming up with new laws adequate to the needs of a new city. Lewis rightly emphasizes that already in the *Republic*, Plato understood the need for such a fortuitous union of wisdom and power. But instead of accounting for that union, as I do, by referring to the hand of God, he is satisfied simply to call it "chance" (185). There may or may not be a real difference of opinion here. Whether one refers to fortune or to providence, it is in any case clear that the vagaries of history transcend human understanding.

But to evoke, as I have done, even the possibility that God might have a hand in the matter is to stay true to the spirit of Kallipolis. It is here, I think, that I might have a real and substantial disagreement with Lewis. I do, for instance, fully agree that the various waves of paradox in the *Republic* serve as reminders that Plato did not regard the *Republic* as a concrete proposal for how to found a state. As Lewis says, true Kallipolis was to be established in the soul of Glaukon. But this does not mean that the philosopher must, like Socrates, always find himself on the outside, standing alone. Indeed, Socrates himself was blessed with many friends—and he did not have to establish an Academy to enjoy that benefit. It was Plato, of course, who established an Academy. That he did so is one of the reasons that I started my response by saying that I do accept the political reading of Plato, even though I recognize that the fate of Socrates led him to curb his own political ambitions. The Academy was a little polis. Kallipolis, dedicated as it is to the education of desire, can at least be envisioned in the form of a university or college. The pursuit of utopia does represent a dangerous excess of politics, unless, that is, it is wedded to a genuine community. Anchored in a living culture, elements of Kallipolis can even be achieved in the nation as a whole. A simple example of this is that the regime described in the *Laws*, one that among other things institutionalized slavery, has in time given way to regimes more like that described in the *Republic*, which has no room for slavery. The ideal, in other words, is not just a fantasy land for philosophers. While it does not translate into a program or a set of rules to be enacted, its spirit is very much alive and capable of transforming the way we live. Whereas I agree with Lewis that cautions were built into the *Republic* that render it consistent with the *Laws*, I find it even more important to recognize the way the latter work continues to pay tribute to the highest ideals of the *Republic*, even as a matter for political reform. What better example could there be of using laws to rig the system than by establishing into perpetuity a system where slaves serve their masters? Given that this is so obviously the case, we cannot but conclude that the laws described by Plato were not yet true laws.

But it is here, where I see the possibility of Kallipolis as representing something *more* than the right ordering of an individual soul, that I recall just why I side more with Socrates than with Plato. Although I recognize the virtue of politically uniting people in a shared understanding or in a common cause, I do not believe that politics as such can ever constitute true community. At a much *deeper* level, community is constituted by a sense of shared fragility.

Let me be explicit about this. The part of me that stands in need of friendship is the part of me that is insecure, both in that I am unsure of who I am and what I believe, and in the still deeper sense that I am aware of my mortality. Life is not such that it can be secured, not, at least, in any ultimate sense. Here is where Socratic ignorance shows itself as something far more valuable than mere skepticism. Plato often artfully constructed his dialogues to present the illusion of the master philosopher who sees all the way through to the character of a man, speaking one way to one person and another way to another person, but always with the same goal of producing insight. But over against this easily enough generated illusion of the philosopher in complete control (Lewis seems to fall for it: his Socrates could not possibly have endured a lapse of memory) was the reality of a Socrates unable to defend himself adequately against the scorn of his neighbors. For this reason, I do not accept Lewis's argument that the failure of Socrates' defense had to do with the fact that he had not been given enough time to explain himself fully. This is something, after all, that he had already had whole long decades to accomplish. I think it is important to acknowledge the philosopher's limitations instead of using the fiction of the master philosopher in complete control as a device for securing that other great fiction, the one that tells us that "right government" is possible once we find the sweet spot that resides somewhere between idealism and cynicism. Those who wish to govern others, confident in their superior knowledge, should be subjected to a regular dose of elenchus. Not to do so is to run the danger that tyrants can emerge even among those dedicated above all else to the fight against tyranny.

If Plato may have been guilty on occasion of posturing as a god, Socrates was a human being and well aware of his limits. It helps to recall that, while successful in educating Plato to replace him and keep his spirit alive, Socrates failed completely when it came to the education of Alcibiades. One consequence of the way the good transcends knowledge is that we are left unable to teach excellence, unable to enact even the "second best" (690e) option of a truly just code of laws. But this intrinsic limit to politics is not the end of the story. Socratic ignorance is the honest avowal of a fragility that both needs love and can give love. Philosophy is discourse among friends and is always to be carried out in the spirit of searching for something more than we have. By recognizing a core of neediness in the self, alive in Socrates to the degree that he was always actively searching, one can clearly enough see why he might have been regarded as corrupting the young. We work hard at giving our young people good answers, only to have Socrates come along and throw everything into question. But Lewis seems not to take this altogether seriously (173). Noting that Socrates highlighted the corruption charge over the charge of impiety, he suggests that this was Socrates' artful way of drawing attention away from the more serious charge, the one, moreover, that ultimately led to his confession that, believer though he was, he did not in fact believe as his fellow Athenians believed.

But, here we must ask, how did Socrates believe? To answer this question, it helps to return to the *Apology* and recognize that, in addition to the formal charges brought against him, *and* in addition to "the calumnies that he attributes to his first accusers," there was a third more nefarious charge that was so deeply seated, and so generally assumed, that it would have escaped notice if Socrates himself had not brought it into the open. "Someone might say," he says, 'are you not ashamed, Socrates, to have followed the kind of occupation that has led to your being now in danger of death?'" (28b). The real charge, in other words, was that Socrates was imprudent, that he did not sufficiently fear death. And to this charge, Socrates had a clear yet profoundly paradoxical answer: "I do not think it is permitted that a better man be harmed by a worse; certainly he might kill me, or perhaps banish or disenfranchise me, which he and others think to be great harm, but I do not think it is so" (30e). That a good man cannot be harmed, even in death, is Socrates' deepest conviction. It is what makes Socrates into Socrates.

It is also a thought that undoes the assumption that Socrates' "anti-politics" was itself fundamentally a matter of prudence. I know of course that Socrates said clearly enough that "a man who really fights for justice must lead a private, not a public life if he is to survive for even a short time" (32a). He was indeed capable of prudence. The essential point, though, is that he was not bound to it.

The same, I suspect, was true of Plato, whose decision to return to Syracuse a third time was clearly a reckless one. Lewis points out something similar when he quotes the Athenian stranger as saying that "lawgiving and the founding of cities is the most perfect of all tests of manly virtue" (708d6–7). Even so, he seems to me still to accord the highest place of honor to security. From a political point of view, this might simply be the right thing to do. As Lewis says

(183), "Laws aimed at reconciliation and peace (among other things) in the city also make the city stronger against possible foes. The Athenian stranger himself later suggests just this" (at 641c). Here he was referring to the Athenian's pointed statement that "education brings victory in her train." What bothered me somewhat is that Lewis seemed not to ignore the warning implicit in the rest of the sentence, "though victory sometimes leads to loss of education, since victorious warfare often enough leads men to pride, and through pride they take the taint of other vices innumerable." There may, in other words, be a shadow side to victory, one that can lead whole nations to lose their collective soul. What this suggests is that the elevation of courage above prudence is not only important for manly individuals, but for the city as a whole—and, yes, even for entire nations. Given the contemporary war on terror, the issue is clearly one of great importance.

It raises the very interesting question of how entire nations might conceivably be educated towards a virtue like courage. It is precisely here that I personally discern the real importance of Plato's *Laws*. I agree with Lewis when he interprets Strauss's understanding of the "limits of politics" as a warning not only against excesses of idealism, but also as a warning against excesses of cynicism. But to avoid the latter, courage is required, not only in those who lead but in those who follow. When wondering how to cultivate it, I am reminded that Plato's *Laws* is far more than a treatise about law and politics. Book Ten is dedicated to a vision of philosophical religion (which features a god impervious to manipulation by prayer and sacrifice [905d]) that is deep enough to keep alive hope in the ultimate goodness of reality, even when the slaughter bench of history continues to push us in the direction of cynicism. But what I above all see in the *Laws* is a recognition that politics serves the needs of religion and culture, not the other way around. Laws are not simply to be legislated. They require long and capacious preambles. We must be persuaded that the laws in place are in fact genuine laws and not strategies for rigging the system.

But here is where Lewis and I surely agree. Philosophy knows the importance of politics. Our role, however, is to remind politics of the importance of philosophy. Socratic elenchus is a necessity for anyone called to rule over others.

COLLOQUIUM 5

Lewis/Lawrence Bibliography

Baltes, M. 1993. Plato's School, The Academy. *Hermanthena* 155: 5-26.

Bloom, A., tr. 1991. *The Republic of Plato*. 2d ed. New York: Basic Books.

Bobonich, C. 2002. *Plato's Utopia Recast: His Later Ethics and Politics*. Oxford: Clarendon Press.

Brisson, L. 2005. Ethics and Politics in Plato's *Laws*. *Oxford Studies in Ancient Philosophy* 28: 93-121.

Brunt, P.A. 1993. Plato's Academy and Politics. In *Studies in Greek History and Thought*. 282-342. Oxford: Clarendon Press.

Burnet, J., ed. 1900-1907. *Platonis Opera*. 5 vols. Oxford: Clarendon Press.

Burnet, J., ed. 1924. *Plato's Euthyphro, Apology of Socrates, and Crito*. Oxford: Clarendon Press.

Burnyeat, M., and M. Frede. 2015. *The Pseudo-Platonic Seventh Letter*, ed. Dominic Scott. Oxford: Oxford University Press.

Cherry, K.M. 2012. *Plato, Aristotle, and the Purpose of Politics*. Cambridge: Cambridge University Press.

Crossman, R. 1939. *Plato Today*. New York: Oxford University Press.

Gould, J. 1955. *The Development of Plato's Ethics*. Cambridge: Cambridge University Press.

Grote, G. 1875. *Plato and the Other Companions of Sokrates*, 3d ed. Vol. 3. London: John Murray.

Halverson, J. 1997. Plato, the Athenian Stranger. *Arethusa* 30.1: 75-102.

Havelock, E. 1999. Plato's Politics and the American Constitution. *Harvard Studies in Classical Philology* 93: 1-24.

Howland, J. 1991. Re-Reading Plato: The Problem of Platonic Chronology. *Phoenix* 45.3: 189-214.

Howland, J. 1998. The Republic's Third Wave and the Paradox of Political Philosophy. *The Review of Metaphysics* 51.3: 633-57.

Hyland, D.H. 1995. *Finitude and Transcendence in the Platonic Dialogues*. Albany: State University of New York Press.

Kahn, C. 2002. On Platonic Chronology. In *New Perspectives on Plato, Ancient and Modern*, eds. J. Annas and C. Rowe, 93-127. Washington, DC: Center for Hellenic Studies.

Klosko, G. 2006. *The Development of Plato's Political Theory*. 2d ed. Oxford: Oxford University Press.

Kochin, M.S. 1999. Plato's Eleatic and Athenian Sciences of Politics. *Review of Politics* 61.1: 57-84.

Laks, A. 1990. Legislation and Demiurgy: On the Relationship between Plato's *Republic* and *Laws*, *Classical Antiquity* 9.2: 209-29.

Laks, A. 2005. The *Laws*. In *The Cambridge History of Greek and Roman Political Thought*, eds. C. Rowe and M. Schofield, 258-92. Cambridge: Cambridge University Press.

Laks, A. 2005. *Médiation et coercition: Pour une lecture des "Lois" de Platon*. Villeneuve d'Ascq: Presses Universitaires du Septentrion.

Lännström, A. 2011. A Religious Revolution? How Socrates's Theology Undermined the Practice of Sacrifice. *Ancient Philosophy* 31.2: 261-74.

Larivée, A. 2003. Du vin pour le Collège de veille? Mise en lumière d'un lien occulté entre le Choeur de Dionysos et le *nukterinos sullogos* dans les *Lois* de Platon. *Phronesis* 48.1: 29-53

Lawrence, J.P. 2015. *Socrates among Strangers*. Chicago: Northwestern University Press.

Ledger, G.R. 1989. *Re-Counting Plato: A Computer Analysis of Plato's Style*. Oxford: Clarendon Press.

Lewis, V.B. 1998. The Nocturnal Council and Platonic Political Philosophy. *History of Political Thought* 19.1: 1-20.

Lewis, V.B. 1998a. *Politeia kai Nomoi*: On the Coherence of Plato's Political Philosophy. *Polity* 31.2: 331-49.

Lewis, V.B. 2000. The Seventh Letter and the Unity of Plato's Political Philosophy. *Southern Journal of Philosophy* 38.2: 231-50.

Lewis, V.B. 2000a. The Rhetoric of Philosophical Politics in Plato's *Seventh Letter*. *Philosophy and Rhetoric* 33.1: 23-38.

Lewis, V.B. 2010. Gods for the City and Beyond: Civil Religion in Plato's *Laws*. In *Civil Religion in Political Thought*, ed. J. von Heyking and R. Weed, 19-46. Washington, DC: The Catholic University of America Press.

Lewis, V.B. 2013. Aristotle, the Common Good, and Us. *Proceedings of the American Catholic Philosophical Association* 87: 69-88.

McCabe, M.M. 2011. Plato's Way of Writing. In *The Oxford Handbook of Plato*, ed. G. Fine, 88-113. Oxford: Oxford University Press.

MacDowell, D. 1978. *The Law in Classical Athens*. Ithaca: Cornell University Press.

McPherran, M.L. 1996. *The Religion of Socrates*. University Park: Pennsylvania State University Press.

Morrow, G.R. 1960. *Plato's Cretan City*. Princeton: Princeton University Press.

Morrow, G.R. 1962. *Plato's Epistles*. Indianapolis: Bobbs-Merrill.

Nails, D. 2012. Compositional Chronology. In *The Continuum Companion to Plato*, ed. G.A. Press, 289-92. New York: Continuum.

Nails, D. and H. Thesleff. 2003. Early Academic Editing: Plato's *Laws*. In *Plato's Laws: From Theory into Practice, Proceedings of the VI Symposium Platonicum Selected Papers*, eds. S. Scolnicov and L. Brisson, 14-29. Sankt Augustin: Academia Verlag.

Ober, J. 1998. *Political Dissent in Democratic Athens: Intellectual Critics of Popular Rule.* Princeton: Princeton University Press.

Popper, K.R. 1943. *The Open Society and Its Enemies,* Vol. 1, *The Spell of Plato.* Princeton: Princeton University Press.

Pradeau, J.F. 2002. *Plato and the City,* tr. Janet Lloyd. Exeter: University of Exeter Press.

Prior, W. 2012. Developmentalism. In *The Continuum Companion to Plato,* ed. G.A. Press, 288-89. New York: Continuum.

Schofield, M. 1999. The Disappearance of the Philosopher King. In *Proceedings of the Boston Area Colloquium in Ancient Philosophy, 1998,* Vol. 13, ed. J.J. Cleary and G.M. Gurtler, 213-41. Leiden: Brill.

Schofield, M. 2005. Plato and Practical Politics. In *The Cambridge History of Greek and Roman Political Thought,* eds. C. Rowe and M. Schofield, 293-302. Cambridge: Cambridge University Press.

Schofield, M. 2006. *Plato: Political Philosophy.* Oxford: Oxford University Press.

Shiell, T.C. 1991. The Unity of Plato's Political Thought. *History of Political Thought* 12.3: 377-90.

Shorey, P. 1914. Plato's *Laws* and the Unity of Plato's Thought I. *Classical Philology* 9.4: 329-69.

Stalley, R.F. 1983. *An Introduction to Plato's Laws.* Oxford: Blackwell.

Strauss, L. 1964. *The City and Man.* Charlottesville: University Press of Virginia.

Strauss, L. 1975. *The Argument and the Action of Plato's Laws.* Chicago: University of Chicago Press.

Tarán, L. 1975. *Academica: Plato, Phillip of Opus and the Pseudo-Platonic Epinomis.* Philadelphia: American Philosophical Society.

Taylor, A.E., tr. 1934. *The Laws of Plato.* London: J.M. Dent & Sons Ltd.

Taylor, C.C.W. 2002. The Origins of Our Present Paradigms. In *New Perspectives on Plato, Ancient and Modern,* eds. J. Annas and C. Rowe, 73-84. Washington, DC: Center for Hellenic Studies.

Todd, S.C. 1996. *The Shape of Athenian Law.* Oxford: Clarendon Press.

Voegelin, E. 1966. *Plato.* Baton Rouge: Louisiana State University Press.

Waldron, J. 1995. What Plato Would Allow. *Nomos,* Vol. 31, *Theory and Practice.* New York: New York University Press.

Zuckert, C.H. 2009. *Plato's Philosophers: The Coherence of the Dialogues.* Chicago: University of Chicago Press.

Index of Names

Alexander of Aphrodisias   7, 8, 10n17, 13, 14, 15, 16, 17, 18, 20, 21, 22, 23, 133, 134, 136n56, 142n69, 149, 150
Anaxagoras   7, 12, 20, 42, 173n12
Arafat, K.   43
Aristo of Chios   157, 158
Aristophanes   47, 51, 52, 55
Aristotle   1, 2, 10, 11, 12, 13, 14, 16, 17n32, 18n36, 19, 20, 24, 25, 26, 27n5, 29, 30, 31n12, 34, 35, 36, 37, 47, 48, 50, 55, 62, 100, 101, 106, 107, 108, 113, 115n3, 132n46, 134n50, 135, 140n63, 150, 162, 163, 164, 177, 181n25, 183n32
Augustine   128, 130n40

Basil of Caesarea   132n45, 151, 152, 153
Burnet, J.   172, 173n12
Burnyeat, M.   70n1, 73n4, 101, 188

Calcidius   12n25, 133-134n50, 140n65, 143
Cavell, S.   46
Chrysippus   3, 4, 5, 8, 13, 23, 44n5, 114, 115, 116, 125, 128n37, 133n49, 144n72, 146, 147, 149, 150
Cicero   121, 122, 123, 128, 129n38–39, 131n42, 133, 141n67, 154, 155, 156, 161, 165
Cleanthes   133n49, 144n72
Crossman, R.   170n2, 177

de Harven, V.   2n1
Dexippus   117, 135, 136, 137, 138, 139, 143, 147, 148, 152, 154
Diogenes Laertius   5, 11, 7, 44n5, 116n3, 125, 128n36, 129n39, 130n40, 132n46, 134n50, 143n71, 144n72, 147, 148, 151, 152, 158, 172, 173n12, 181n26
Diogenes of Babylon   125, 151, 152
Dion   124n27, 125n29, 126, 178, 179, 180
Dionysius II   169, 178, 180, 184, 185, 186

Empedocles   20
Epicharmus   115
Epicurus   132n46
Eusebius   133n48, 143n71

Favorinus   172
Frede, M.   131n42, 131n44, 188

Galen   11n20, 122, 133, 134, 135, 137n57, 138n61, 148, 149
Grote, G.   186

Harmodius   56
Havelock, E.   170n2, 177
Heidegger, M.   194
Heraclitus   143n71, 1, 20
Herodotus   28, 43, 51n19–20, 52, 55, 56
Hierocles   141, 144, 148
Hipparchus   56

Irwin, T.   138

Kant, I.   49

Leibniz, G.   121n18, 123, 153n86
Lewis, D.   6, 7
Lewis, E.   113, 114, 124n28, 128, 138, 139, 140, 141, 142, 143, 144, 145, 146, 147, 148, 160, 161, 162

Melissus   26, 27, 28, 29, 31n14, 32, 33, 37
Mnesarchus   119, 120, 153n86

Nemesius   133n48, 144, 148, 149
Nolan, D.   9, 10

Origen   151, 152n84

Panaetius   119, 150
Parmenides   20, 26, 27, 31, 32, 33, 34, 37
Penner, T.   107, 108n5–6
Phillip of Opus   181
Philo of Alexandria   125n29, 138n61, 139, 140n62
Philolaus   20
Pisistratus   55, 56
Plato   1, 2, 12, 14n28, 16, 17, 20, 24, 28, 41–65, 69–110, 118, 120n13, 132, 136, 137n58, 142, 151, 169–199
Plutarch   4, 115, 116, 117, 118, 121, 122, 123, 124, 125, 126, 127, 133, 134, 141, 142, 143, 144, 147, 149, 154, 163, 164
Popper, K.   170, 177

Porphyry   124n25, 136, 137n57, 163n9
Priander   44
Pythagoras   48

Schofield, M.   172n8, 179n24, 185, 186, 189n46, 190n47
Sedley, D.   15n30, 115n3, 116n4–5, 118n9, 119n11, 122n21, 124n26–28, 125n29, 128n35, 128n37, 134n53, 136n56, 138n60, 149n81, 150, 154
Seneca   133n48, 135, 140, 141, 142n69, 143n71, 149
Sextus Empiricus   3, 123, 124, 128, 129, 130, 131, 132, 133, 134, 136, 137, 142n69, 144n72, 147n77, 154, 155, 156, 158, 159, 161, 165
Simplicius   27, 29, 34n18, 117, 118n8, 123n23, 124n25, 126, 127, 131, 132, 133n48, 134, 135, 136n56, 138n61, 140, 141, 143, 145n76, 149, 150n82, 163

Stesichorus   44
Stobaeus   3, 4, 14, 119, 120, 126, 127, 133, 139, 140, 163, 164n11
Strauss, L.   176n19, 182n29, 187n40–41

Tertullian   133, 144, 148
Theophrastus   31n13, 34, 43n4
Thornton, B.   43
Thucydides   56

Varzi, A.   7
Vogt, K.   2n1, 10n19

Xenophon   46n7, 172

Zeno of Elea   26, 27, 29, 30, 34n18, 35, 131n42, 158n90, 163
Zuckert, C.   172n8, 182, 189n46

Printed in the United States
By Bookmasters